The Indian Grocery Store Demystified

The Indian Grocery Store Demystified

Linda Bladholm

RENAISSANCE BOOKS
Los Angeles

This book is for my sister, Sharon Bladholm

Library of Congress Catalog Card Number: 00-104906
ISBN: 1-58063-143-6

10 9 8 7 6 5 4 3 2 1

Production by Jesus Arellano, Geoff Bock, and Amanda Tan
Illustrations by Linda Bladholm

Published by Renaissance Books
Distributed by St. Martin's Press
Manufactured in the United States of America
First edition

Contents

Acknowledgments

The warm welcome that many Indian and Bangladeshi people gave me while I traveled in their countries contributed greatly to my understanding of a complex and fascinating land. Thanks for the experience and hospitality. Certain people who helped make this book possible deserve special mention: Leela and Dinu Patel of the Little Market in Ft. Lauderdale, Florida, who let me practically move into their grocery store as I worked on the book and for cheerfully answering my many questions. Joel Weltman for all his schlepping to and from the Little Market and for tasting my recipes (not to mention resolving computer crises). Shanon Duffey-Weltman for going along with it; and my ever-supportive parents, John and Ann Bladholm, and mother-in-law, Freda Weltman. A heartfelt thanks to both Thupten Rabgyla for his Hindi calligraphy, helpfulness, and prayers and to J. C. Harrison for his friendship.

More thanks go to all the patient Indian grocery-store wholesalers and owners in Chicago. They include Sam and Nirav Sanghavi of Nirav Foods; Sam, Javid, and Rakesh of Raja (Swad) Foods; Shawon Ahmed and Asif of the Fish Corner; Pradip Montu and Somabhai Patel of Jai Hind Grocery; T. V. Patel of Patel Brothers on Devon St.; Abid and Zahid of Indo Pak Foods; Kirti and Chef S. Thumma of Arya Bhavan Vegetarian Restaurant; and the beautiful Shilpa Mehta of

Kirana Bazaar. In New York I want to thank Spice Corner, Kalustyan's, Spice House, Pijush Chakraboty of the Bombay Bazaar; Arun and Anjani K. Sinha of Foods of India; and Abdul Patwary of Dowel Indian Grocery. In Jackson Heights, Queens, I'm grateful to Nazrul of Meghna Grocery; the lovely Balwinder of Apna Cash & Carry; Patel Brothers; Subzi Mandi of Indo Pak Grocery; and Madhur of the Diwan Express sweet-and-snack shop. In Miami I'd like to thank Mohammed Han of Dhaka Bazaar; Raju and Nisha Bombaywalah of the Bombay Super Bazaar in North Miami Beach; Farida Ladha and Mirza of the Indian Grocery on Douglas Road; and the charming Ishma of Continental Groceries.

Thanks to Dawn Reshen-Doty and Neil Reshen for continuing to believe in my talent and Editor Richard F. X. O'Connor for being right and thanks to the Renaissance Media staff, including Lisa Lenthall, Jesus Arellano, Amanda Tan, Geoff Bock, Ian Culver, Kimbria Hays, Miye Kim, Kathryn Mills, Arthur Morey, and publisher Bill Hartley. Special thanks to Neela Paniz; Marc and Eve Zimetbaum; Dema Shahavi at Veggie Times; Linda Gassenhiemer; Vijay Varky from Syracuse; Asako Severn; Vanita Kumar of Little India Publications; Chef Rimi Nahar of Nirvana; Ken Lee of Lotus Foods; Marc Novak; Barbara Ezell; Roberto Requena; Paul Wenzel; and Pear, Oz, Sonny, Mousie, Ed, Noko; the turtles; and most of all Frog, who I love with all my heart.

Foreword

When I came to the United States in 1968 I brought several spices and food items with me for my aunt. At that time there was only one market in Los Angeles that carried some Indian groceries, and it was a Middle Eastern market. In the past thirty odd years or so (as Linda Bladholm will tell you) that number has grown to over 9,000 markets throughout the country.

As a restaurateur, cookbook author (*The Bombay Cafe Cookbook,* Ten Speed Press), and, most importantly, a home cook, one of my favorite pastimes is to browse through different ethnic markets. With the growth of Indian markets and my lack of knowledge about many of the items sold therein, I now find myself taking many trips to Little India in Artesia, a suburb of Los Angeles. I conduct tours in conjunction with my cooking classes to help the participants recognize and avail themselves of the groceries needed to prepare an Indian meal. We explore the grocery stores with their large stock of lentils, flours, rice, spices, and even the fresh vegetables grown specifically for the Indian consumer. We stop at beauty salons for a little henna painting, play dress-up at sari boutiques and jewelry stores, sample the culture at music and video shops, and last but not least, indulge in some great street snacks.

In the past few years, India's culture and food have become very popular in the Western world. More and more people are frequenting

Indian restaurants. Its spices are being fused into other cuisines by master chefs; celebrities are buying pashmina shawls or donning traditional cosmetic enhancements such as bindis and mehndi, and fashion gurus are designing clothes in the Indian style. All these factors have helped contribute to the rise of neighborhood Indian grocery stores and boutiques. Today, Indian spices, basmati rice, and even some pre-mixed curry pastes and tandoori marinades are showing up in the aisles of large supermarkets, luring consumers to try them.

Shopping in ethnic stores can be both exciting and daunting when items are hard to identify. Often the storeowners themselves are unable to explain certain products in relation to the Western world. Let *The Indian Grocery Store Demystified* guide you through the shelves of the little neighborhood Indian market or entice you to visit the Little Indias in your city. Open your senses to the wonderful aromas of the spices and try the strange but alluring vegetables. Ask the boutique owner to drape you in one of the flowing saris and complement them with some of the ethnic jewels and glass bangles, or even paste a bindi onto your forehead. Listen to Indian classical and film music and, most importantly, try some of the freshly prepared snacks. You will feel as though you have just visited an exotic, faraway land.

—Neela Paniz, restaurateur
The Bombay Café
Los Angeles, California

Introduction

Indian cuisine is a rich mosaic of exotic spices, fragrant herbs, and earthy grains. It is unique in it's melding of both fiery-hot and delicately subtle flavors. The reason I wrote this book is to give anyone who wants to try their hand at Indian cooking an accessible guide to identifying and using a variety of these ingredients.

While the ingredients are readily available in over 9,000 Indian grocery stores in America, many potential cooks give up, neither knowing what to make of the mysterious items that crowd shelves nor understanding how to use them. If you are one of these people, I have designed this book to meet your needs by explaining what you will smell, see, and find. I will explain what it will look like, taste like, and be used for. I tasted the irresistible flavors of this food while traveling through India and Bangladesh, where I discovered there are as many cuisines to sample as there are regions to explore. I crunched bhel puri from newspaper cones sold by street vendors, savored onion fritters and spicy doughnuts in roadside restaurants called dhabas, and sipped tea with sweets bought from teawallahs at rail stations. I've eaten mounds of rice and vegetable curries with my fingers in South Indian banana-leaf curry shops and I've had multicourse, moghul-style meals in elegant Bombay restaurants. In Bangladesh I ate fish and drank moht, a fermented rice wine, in a mud hut in the hill-tribe village of Rangamati.

I tried spicy grilled pigeon at a Chittagong market stall. I learned to distinguish all the ingredients on countless trips to Indian groceries in America with the help of many patient store owners. This book is intended as a guide to understanding both the basic and unusual ingredients found in the typical Indian market. The purpose of this book is to help you, the reader, use your Indian cookbooks and recipes.

Indian grocery stores can seem intimidating with all those strange spices, unfamiliar vegetables, sacks of grains, and smells of sandalwood, spices, and incense. But you can learn to guide yourself by using this book.

Shopping in an Indian market is challenging, but with persistence and an open mind you will unearth a rich treasure trove of Indian ingredients. Also, keep in mind that you are in a food store, so you can assume that most everything is edible, if not recognizable. Experiment, explore, ask questions, taste, and try new things. Take your time. Talk to the store owners, who will be glad to assist you and gain a new customer.

Wherever there are Indian people living, you will find Indian markets. Older, well-established ones tend to be run by second-generation Indian-American families. Newer stores may be owned by Pakistanis or recent immigrants from Bangladesh. In some large cities such as New York, Chicago, Philadelphia, and San Francisco there are large Indian populations in "Little Indias." Several bustling blocks are lined with silk and saree shops,

valor beans

jewelry stores, luggage stores, electronic and video emporiums, and lots of food markets. Here you will find the most authentic and versatile

cauliflower

grocery stores, from brightly lit spice bazaars to megamarkets that glitter with stainless-steel cookware, rows of canned goods, jars of pickles, containers of chutneys and spice pastes, and glass cases filled with trays of fudgy, syrupy sweets. These huge complexes stock wares from all over India, Pakistan, and Bangladesh. Household goods, plaster Hindu deities, jars of ghee, sticks of incense, and clay dishes all have a place. Crates overflow with slender gourds, plump eggplants, finger-shaped okra, and snowy cauliflower heads. Musty bins are filled with root vegetables. Piles of blush-tinted mangoes tempt. Huge jute and burlap bags are piled near entrances, bulging with basmati rice, lentils, and split peas. Shelves are arranged in neat rows of small boxes of spice blends for everything from dal to chai. Some stores sell meals to go from deli counters, others offer savory deep-fried snacks, tandoori tikkas, and kebabs wrapped in hot naan. Smaller shops might sell walnuts, dried plums, and green tea from Kashmir, or they might stock ingredients to make South Indian specialties, depending on the owners place of origin or the predominant ethnic group in the local community. Hindus, Muslims, Jains, Parsis, and vegetarians all have specific needs that individual shops strive to meet.

basmati rice

Vast networks of suppliers provide locally grown and shipped-in produce, halal meats, dairy products, breads, frozen seafood, imported spices, dried goods, and teas. These are distributed to the grocery stores in "Little India" and to distant towns. The nearest city supplies different regions in every state. In midsized cities, Indian grocery stores are scattered across town, yet they are all connected by a village-type distribution system. One shop owner is the sweet supplier to all the other shops, while another owner supplies the halal meat or frozen fish. They both get their stock from national distributors. They supply one another, sending customers to one store for the prized hilsa fish and to another for the best selection of sweets. In your shopping excursions, you soon meet all the proprietors in the small community.

Large stores and those with branches in several cities buy many products such as rice, grains, dals, and spices wholesale in bulk quantities and have it bagged with their store's name on it. Smaller stores may bag wholesale items themselves. Of course, there are many nationally distributed brands to seek out. You will become familiar with all of these as you go through the book and see them in Indian grocery stores.

Wherever you live, you will find an Indian grocery store. Outside of large metropolitan areas, Indian grocery stores tend to be small. Some may only be two or three aisles in a little storefront cubbyhole, yet they manage to stock a broad range of goods—with the exception of fresh vegetables.

Once you locate the nearest Indian grocery store to you, make a list of what you want to buy. Orchestrate your purchases around a menu or specific recipe. First you will need to get the basics. The secret to good Indian cooking is to have a well-stocked pantry. Your stash of spices, herbs, grains and nuts can be mixed, matched, and interchanged to create a multitude of delicious meals.

To understand Indian ingredients is to glimpse the huge role that food plays in Indian culture. In India, more so than any other country, food is much more than sustenance. Foods, herbs, and spices have both culinary and medicinal properties. Food, mind, and spirit are all interconnected. This dietary approach to health was founded thousands of years ago in a system called the Ayurveda. Throughout this book I will mention the Ayurvedic healing properties of various ingredients and specific herbs.

Complex spice mixtures of complementary and contrasting seasonings are what define Indian cuisine. Dishes are composed of vibrant and diverse flavors: aromatic, sweet, bitter, nutty, pungent, sour, and astringent balanced with textures and colors. Creamy rich dishes are countered with lightly cooked greens. Fried foods are always served with rice, curry, and a crisp salad of sliced onions and fresh herbs for digestion. Smooth, milky sweets are subtly scented and flavored with sharp, peppery cardamom. Creative spice blends transform ingredients into extraordinary dishes bursting with flavors on several levels.

This may sound complicated, but once you start cooking with Indian ingredients the balancing of flavors and textures will become natural. To help you, Indian grocery stores are generally stocked in logical groups of food staples, spices, and seasonings. Lentils, cracked wheat, split peas, and dried beans are all in one place. Whole and ground spices are together in one row. Spice pastes, pickles, and chutneys are in another area.

First you will want to buy your main staples: rice and at least one type of bread. Rice and bread are the center of all meals as the starch that soaks up the hot, spicy, and tangy flavors.

A Walk Through the Rajas' Grocery Store

Imagine yourself in the bustling activity of a bazaar in Delhi, Dhaka, or Karachi, a kaleidoscope of dazzling colors and fragrances swirling about you—mounds of spices, piles of nuts, and wafting smells of ripe fruit, curry, and coconut oil. Not so far from this fantasy is the little Indian market where I shop. You pull open the door and a string of brass bells jangle, ushering you into another land. The heady aromas of cardamom, black pepper, perfumed incense, and rose-scented sweets fill the air. You are surrounded by exotic provisions with colorful wrappers and labels. The strains of a sitar resonate from a far corner. There is the rustle of a saree as the storeowner's wife emerges from an aisle to greet you. "Namaste! Welcome!"

Meet Mrs. Raja, who runs the grocery with her husband. The couple arrived more than twenty years ago from Surat, a city in Gujarat on the Arabian Sea just above Bombay. Gujaratis are a trader class, and many grocery stores are owned by people from this part of India. Since getting to know the Rajas and the contents of their store, they have become my friends and my Indian food gurus.

Mr. Raja, Sajavit, his wife, Aroona, and their two daughters, fifteen-year-old Meena and twelve-year-old Yasmin, form the nucleus of the grocery store. Everyone is involved, including extended family members who help out and offer advice to customers, dust shelves, and gossip over tea. The Rajas' store is the pulsing center of the small Indian community here. No festival, graduation, wedding, or dance

Ganesh statue

performance goes undiscussed or uncelebrated. Stacks of both the *India Post* and the *Pakistan Times* are near the front door, and posters announcing everything from astrologers' services and bridal mehndi to cooking classes and yoga lessons are tacked to a board above them.

Mr. Raja opens at 9:00 A.M. each morning, first sweeping the store with a straw broom, then lighting a stick of incense and invoking a prayer to Ganesh, the plump, pink, elephant-headed god. Made of plaster, his likeness is seated on a lotus blossom in a corner alcove of the store. Mr. Raja then has a cup of tea and begins unloading trays of sweets, crates of produce, and bags of grain from the suppliers' trucks out front. Mr. Raja is in his mid-40s, with a full head of thick, dark, wavy hair, an easy laugh, and sociable personality. He chairs the local Indian business association, and he caters weddings and dinner banquets with Mrs. Raja. He is always glad to answer questions, translate Hindi labels, and explain the rules of cricket, which he watches on a small television behind the front counter. His English is perfect with a slight British accent.

samosa

Mrs. Raja is tall and graceful, her henna-streaked, oiled hair coiled at the nape of her neck. The center part is smeared with red, signifying her married status. Her forehead dot matches the hue of her saree. She arrives an hour or so after Mr. Raja, bringing homemade samosas, steamed dhokla cakes, and aloovada, which are puffy, fried balls, stuffed with a spicy pea and potato mixture. In her lilting English she has shared many recipes and cooking tips, especially for Gujarati vegetarian dishes. She serves tea with boiled milk and sugar throughout the day, sipped Gujarati-style from saucers. Out front by the parking lot are a drumstick tree and an amla bush, planted by the Rajas when each of their daughters was born. The girls help out after school and on weekends.

As we take a quick tour of the store, don't concern yourself with the strange names and unfamiliar goods, all of which will be fully covered in the ensuing chapters. You might find it convenient to follow along by referring to the store layout on page 16.

chapati bread

Upon entering the grocery you face six aisles of ten shelves that run the width of the store, each shelf with a hand-lettered sign above it that states its contents—tea, spices, flours, and so on. Tiered shelves, like magazine racks, are at the front of shelves 1–6, filled with plastic bags of crispy snacks, mixed blends of puffed rice, roasted nuts, and chickpea flour noodles, and chips tossed with salt and spices. At the front of shelves 7 and 8, racks are filled with bags of fresh chapati, corn roti, and naan breads. A pineapple pyramid is piled at the end of shelves 9 and 10, with a box of watermelons on the floor.

puja offering

Huge rice bags, some a hefty 55 pounds, occupy the left side of the store's front window. At the far end in a little nook is both a large, plaster statue of Ganesh and a water-filled kumbha (container), covered with four fresh betel leaves for placing puja offerings. More rice is piled three and four bags high, down the central floor space from the front door to the refrigerator cases along the back wall. Smaller bags of rice and rice products are on shelf 7.

Rajas' Grocery Store Floor Plan

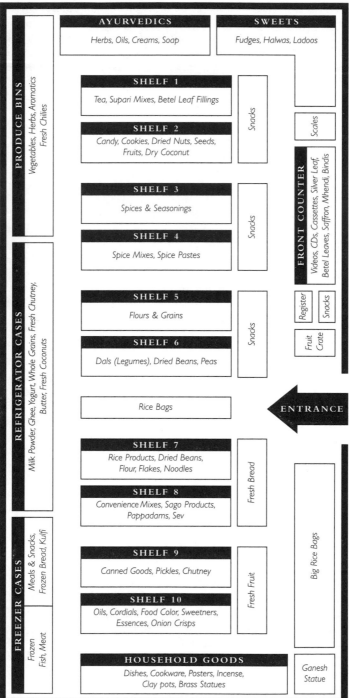

AYURVEDICS
Herbs, Oils, Creams, Soap

SWEETS
Fudges, Halwas, Ladoos

PRODUCE BINS
Vegetables, Herbs, Aromatics
Fresh Chilies

SHELF 1
Tea, Supari Mixes, Betel Leaf Fillings

SHELF 2
Candy, Cookies, Dried Nuts, Seeds,
Fruits, Dry Coconut

Snacks

Scales

SHELF 3
Spices & Seasonings

SHELF 4
Spice Mixes, Spice Pastes

Snacks

FRONT COUNTER
Videos, CDs, Cassettes, Silver Leaf,
Betel Leaves, Saffron, Mhendi, Bindis

REFRIGERATOR CASES
Milk Powder, Ghee, Yogurt, Whole Grains, Fresh Chutney,
Butter, Fresh Coconuts

SHELF 5
Flours & Grains

SHELF 6
Dals (Legumes), Dried Beans, Peas

Snacks

Register

Snacks

Fruit
Crate

Rice Bags

ENTRANCE

SHELF 7
Rice Products, Dried Beans,
Flour, Flakes, Noodles

SHELF 8
Convenience Mixes, Sago Products,
Pappadams, Sev

Fresh Bread

FREEZER CASES
Meals & Snacks,
Frozen Bread, Kulfi

SHELF 9
Canned Goods, Pickles, Chutney

SHELF 10
Oils, Cordials, Food Color, Sweetners,
Essences, Onion Crisps

Fresh Fruit

Big Rice Bags

Frozen
Fish, Meat

HOUSEHOLD GOODS
Dishes, Cookware, Posters, Incense,
Clay pots, Brass Statues

Ganesh
Statue

To the right of the front door is a glassed-in front counter where one of the Rajas is usually perched on a stool, ensconced behind a wall of videos—the latest Hindi Masala films from Bollywood, pop-star concerts, and technicolor Ramayana sagas. Rows of CDs and cassettes range

from Ravi Shankar and the Qawwali music of Nusrat Fateh Ali Khan to Hindi ballads and dance tunes. A video is often playing on the little television. You might catch a snippet of a steamy Shashi Kapoor romance or a drama featuring Krishna and his consorts. Other times you will be serenaded by a Punjabi crooner or a Pakistani diva as you shop. Near the register is a stack of fresh betel leaves for paan, boxes of Mrs. Raja's snacks, and a dish of fennel seeds and sugar balls, which

mehndi stencil

are a breath freshener. To the left of the register crates of fruit—mangoes, papaya, chickoo, and soursops—are nestled in straw or in cupped cardboard trays on the floor below the snacks. Under the glass-topped counter are shelves that display folded lengths of saree silk, packets of bindi, mehndi stencils, glass bangles, wood carvings inset with bits of mirror, sandalwood beads, and Hindu amulets. Tiny boxes of saffron and packets of silver leaf are stashed here too, along with tongue cleaners, black-eye khol, and henna hair powders.

The sweets counter is wedged against the back end of the front counter, wrapping around the corner of the right wall. The thick, glass, refrigerated cases display a dizzying array of creamy pastel balls, silver-leaf flecked diamonds, rainbow-layered bars, orange sugar pretzels, and perfumed globes oozing

sweet box (mixed)

rose syrup. As fantastic as Faberge eggs, these confections can be purchased by the piece or the pound. Ask Mr. or Mrs. Raja, who will pluck the sweets from their trays and pack them into clear plastic boxes.

After the end of the sweets counter a long shelf stretches the length of the store to the back wall. This is the Ayurvedic and herbal goods section of the grocery store. There are bags of whole dried roots, fruits, seeds, and bark. There are also packets of powder, jars of tablets, herb pastes, medicated oils, scented soaps, balms, and shampoos. Here is where you can pick up some neem toothpaste, turmeric face cream, Dushanda herbal tea, Parachute coconut hair oil, and Mysore sandalwood soap. Sinus cleaning tools, aromatherapy massage oils, tonics, toners, and cotton wicks for ghee lamps are also found here. All of these are used in the world's oldest system of alternative medicine.

A row of open produce bins begins where the herbs end and extends halfway down the back wall. The wood bins are divided into dozens of compartments, each one filled with vegetables, leafy greens, fresh herbs, and aromatics. Included are lavender eggplants, white radishes, gingerroot, long beans, green drumsticks, yams, ridged and wart-covered gourds, banana blossoms, and striped cucumbers. Plastic baskets hold bunches of fresh mint, fenugreek, coriander leaves, wispy dill, fragrant curry leaves, and red and green chilies.

Beyond the produce bins are several floor-to-ceiling, glass refrigerator cases fitted with metal shelves. Doors swing open from each paneled door, letting out an arctic blast. The racks are full with plastic bottles of flavored lassi, cans of mango juice, large cartons of plain yogurt, bags of milk powder, jars of buttery ghee, and bars of creamed coconut. There are also bottles of mint, tamarind, lemon, and coconut chutneys and garlic, ginger, and onion pastes. You will also find bags of whole-wheat kernels and buckwheat flour. Hairy, brown coconuts stare at you with little black eyes over in one section. Should your sweet tooth need more enticement, there are more sweets: sugar-spun noodles, almond and cashew milk fudge, sweet saffron yogurt, creamy cheese doughballs, and rice pudding.

Along the last stretch of the back wall next to the refrigerator cases are two large, white freezer cases with lift-top lids. Pull the first one open and peer down into the frosty vapors to discover a variety of breads: packages of plain or spiced naan, flat chapati, and stuffed paratha. In here you will find boxes of heat-and-eat vegetarian entrees, chicken curries, bean dishes, samosas, and fried cubes or blocks of paneer cheese. There are also jumbo bags of mixed, diced, frozen vegetables—peas, carrots, and corn—along with 1-pound packages of exotic vegetables like Punjabi tinda and spiny bittergourds, handy when fresh are not available. Tubs of kulfi tempt in flavors such as creamy saffron-pistachio, milky rose, cashew-raisin, or fig.

The other freezer case is packed with plastic-wrapped fish and blocks of tiny, sweet-water specimens from the rivers of Bengal. There are 3- to 4-foot long river cruisers, which resemble catfish, silvery pomfret, and the large herring-like hilsa. The other portion of the freezer is filled with carefully wrapped and labeled hunks of zabhina (blessed) halal meat, including minced mutton, lamb shanks, chicken parts, kebab cuts, and goat chops. Not for the squeamish are the brains, innards, and trotters.

A long shelf lines the left wall of the store, stretching toward the front window and ending at the Ganesh statue. It is packed with household merchandise: copper pots, cast-iron skillets, the wok-like kadhai, idli steamers, cake molds, teapots, breadboards, rolling pins, sieves, tongs, coconut scrapers, oil lamps, and unglazed clay dishes for setting yogurt. There are balls of cotton thread, seviya presses, deep-fryers, spice grinders, brass mortars and pestles, stainless-steel thali trays, small metal bowls, prayer rugs, candles, incense, posters of Hindu deities, puja kits, red gulal powder, tinsel garlands, door decorations with auspicious inscriptions, and brass statues of gods and goddesses.

Throughout the day fresh fruits, flower blossoms, and sweets are placed on the leaf-covered vessel in front of Ganesh, who is the remover of obstacles, granter of favors, and giver of success. No enterprise is undertaken without first invoking the blessings of Ganesh to ensure success. Each day the Rajas humbly ask for another successful day—both professionally and spiritually. Now let's tour shelves 1–10 and check out the contents of each.

Shelf 1 is opposite the Ayurvedic and herbal-ointment shelf. The teas are here. Tins, paper-wrapped blocks, bags of tea leaves, and boxes of tea bags abound. All the major Indian teas are represented: Assam blacks, Darjeelings, and well-balanced blends of whole-leaf, broken, and tippy teas. There are also Ceylon teas from Sri Lanka and green teas from the Middle East. Then there is a small section with jars of flavored teas, instant coffee, spiced coffee powder, tins of Milo and Ragimalt, and cans of sweetened condensed milk. Here too are small jars of tea-masala powder for flavoring chai. The end section of the shelf has supari blends: little packets of candy-coated fennel seeds, plastic boxes of colorful mixes containing toasted or mint-coated fennel seeds, silver candyballs, bits of dyed betel nut, and anise seeds. There are also jars of betel chew fillings, red acacia powder, whole betel nuts, curled chips, scented dates, rose-petal jam, and perfumed saffron jelly.

Turn the corner to stroll up the next aisle. On shelf 2 you will find dried nuts, seeds, fruits, crackers, cookies, and candy. Take your pick from almonds (whole, sliced, slivered, or powdered), cashews, peanuts, pistachios, pine nuts, raisins, apricots, dates, melon seeds, and several forms of coconut. There are bags of coconut shreds, chips, and powder. There is also copra, which are dried, halved coconuts in the shell. Puffed lotus seeds that resemble smooth, speckled popcorn and chirongi nuts, which look like large lentils and taste like hazelnuts, are two of the more unusual items you'll find. The front part of the aisle is stocked with an assortment of sweet and savory biscuits, pastries, and candies. Choose from golden pastry rolls stuffed with a spicy-sweet filling, salty crackers, shortbread, sesame brittle, tamarind hard candies, coconut cookies, and white candyballs that look as if they were dipped in stucco.

Enticing smells waft from shelf 3. The scent of curry powder, black pepper, and cardamom mingles with fragrant cinnamon, cloves, and cumin seeds. We are in the spice and seasoning area of the grocery store. Besides the spices, there are dried pomegranate seeds, dried chilies, poppy and sesame seeds, as well as green mango powder, black salt, and tamarind pulp. The unmistakable sulphureous odor in the midsection emanates from small boxes of hing, a smelly resin that adds a subtle truffle-like flavor to foods. You can purchase your spices in large bags, small packets, or spice jars. You can buy them whole, crushed, or powdered.

Around the corner on shelf 4 are yet more spices: ajowan, black cumin, caraway, cassia, coriander, dill, fennel, mustard seed, nutmeg, mace, and turmeric. There are shriveled, dried fruit rinds, which are used as a souring agent with fish, edible camphor, sandalwood, and citric-acid crystals. Half of the shelf is filled with small boxes and packets of ground-spice blends—everything from pickled meat flavorings and seafood spices to mixes for kormas, koftas, and keemas. There are biryani blends, Madras curry powders, and haleem mixes for seasoning cracked wheat or grain stews. Even easier to use are the spice pastes and cooking sauces. You can make everything from Kashmiri-style chicken jalferezi and rogan josh to a fiery vindaloo or Sri Lankan sambol. These days not even Indian cooks have time to handgrind their spices, and they depend on these time-saving powders. You should stock up on spice blends and pastes to make authentic Indian meals quickly.

On shelf 5 are bags of flours and starches. These are used to make bread and as sauce binders or thickeners. Bread is just as important as rice in India. It is eaten at every meal and made fresh from a variety of flours. The lower shelves are piled with 20-pound paper bags of whole-wheat chapati flour. Smaller paper and plastic bags are on the upper shelves, filled with special blends of flours that are milled from dried legumes, corn, millet, and jowar, a type of sorghum. You will also find cracked wheat and cream of wheat here, used in pilafs and puddings. Then there is rice powder, water-chestnut flour, arrowroot starch, and kodri and samo, two grainlike seeds used on special fasting days in place of rice. The small, round, white pearls are made from sago starch and used in puddings and desserts. They are similar to tapioca.

Shelf 6 is where you'll find dals, the dried legumes that are so important to Indian vegetarian cuisine. Packed with protein and flavor, they are used to make thick soups and sauces for rice and bread. Toovar dal is the most popular. It is sold in large 10- to 20-pound cloth bags that fill half the aisle. These yellow, split, pigeon peas are available dried or oiled for longer storage. Smaller bags contain white or dark brown chickpeas, Bengal gram, red lentils, or black lentils which are called urad dal. They are sold whole, split, skinned, or unskinned.

Step around the mammoth rice bags stacked down the center of the store to shelf 7. At the front section are more dals. These include whole or split dried beans and peas, with or without skins. You'll find mung beans, white and green peas, red choli beans, kidney beans, muth, butter beans, and black-eyed peas. The end contains the rice products. Large, unlabeled bags are filled with puffed rice and flat-pressed rice flakes, used in snack mixes. The flakes are also cooked into sweet or savory cereal dishes. There are bags of unhusked paddy rice, or "jav," which is used in puja offerings, and cellophane packages of brittle rice noodles, which are used to make savory snacks.

Another turn and you wind your way past shelf 8. This has a potpourri of products: dried dal dumplings, brown vermicelli sticks, sago chips, and convenience mixes. The back of the shelves are stocked with packages of paper-thin, dried discs that range in sizes from a silver dollar to a saucer. They are plain or flavored with pepper, chili, garlic, or onion. These are lentil wafers called pappadam, and they are toasted or deep fried into crisps and served with chutney. Above them are bags of vadi, hard, fermented dal paste chunks that are used in curries and stews. Mid-shelf are bags of light-brown and multicolored sago starch and potato flour chips known as far-far. When they are dropped in hot oil they puff into light, crispy wafers. Nearby are flat, long boxes of very fine vermicelli, called sevian. They are broken into bits, fried in butter, and cooked in milky puddings. The front of the aisle is filled with boxes and pouches of convenient "instant" mixes for whipping up a full range of snacks or hot, sour lentil soups. Pick from mixes for crispy fritters, pakoras, savory doughnuts, crepe-like rice pancakes, steamed rice or farina cakes. There is also a whole range of South Indian spice powders for making sauces to flavor rice. Dessert mixes to check out include creamy rice pudding, falooda, milk fudges, kulfi, and rasmalai.

Facing shelf 9 the eye is met by rows of neatly stacked canned goods. Cans of vegetables are first: drumsticks, lotus-root slices, pale violet or orange yams, bittergourds, several types of green beans, and bean pod seeds. Then there are curried spinach, mustard greens, and steamed taro leaves rolled up with spices. You will also find ready-to-eat canned curries, dals, yogurt soup with dumplings, peas with cubes of curd cheese, mixed vegetable stews, and spicy lentil soups. More canned goods to consider are cooking sauces, fruit pulps, jackfruit, woodapple cream, creamy cheeseballs in syrup, and crystallized gourd. Canned goods are handy for quick meals and instant desserts.

Also on this shelf are gleaming glass jars of pickles and chutneys. Pungent pickle appetizers are made from chopped green mango or other vegetables and preserved in thick, oily spice pastes. Unusual pickled items that you will see are tart, sour gunda, caper-like kerda, spicy, ground gongura leaves, gingery amba-haldi, and olive pickles. There are also Goan-shrimp balichow pickles in a spicy vinegar paste, bitter hurda preserves, and tart gooseberry pickles. Garlic, onions, tamarind, and ginger also get the pickle treatment. Jam-like cooked chutneys, which are made from spicy-sweet mixtures of mango with raisins and nuts or from plums, tomatoes, or apricots, glow like deep amber. There's even dried coconut chutney in jars and packets of brick red, dried, ground garlic chutney mixed with grated coconut and spices. All these tangy, hot condiments add piquant touches to meals and whet the appetite.

Turn around the corner to peruse shelf 10 and its eclectic mix of sugars, vinegars, essences, food colorings, syrups, and oils. At the far end of the shelf are sweeteners. Those jute-wrapped, flower pot–shaped loaves and golden slabs are boiled down coconut sap or sugar cane juice, used extensively in sweet making. There are also jars of amber honey, bags of lump sugar, and bottles of thick, dark palm treacle. Sour notes are added to vindaloos, sauces, and marinades with vinegar. Choose from clear-coconut or dark molasses vinegars. Nearby on the shelf are tubs of crispy fried onion bits, used for garnishing rice and other dishes. Long cellophane bags enclose translucent colored strips of agar-agar, a gelatin substance extracted from seaweed and used in desserts and milky, sweet drinks for texture. Other oddities include tiny basil seeds that are soaked until gelatinous and added to drinks, gum crystals, dried shreds of maldive fish, and "Bombay duck," another type of dried fish. Mid-shelf you will find tiny bottles of food-coloring powders and scented essences. There are also bottles of rose and orange-blossom waters. These are used to tint and perfume foods. Most are natural and are distilled from fragrant flowers, grasses, and leaves; others are imitation and come in flavors such as banana, biryani, and ice cream. Tall, glass bottles of concentrated cordial syrups are next to the essences. There are fruit flavors, glucose types, exotic sandalwood, khus, and rose syrups, which are thinned with water or crushed ice. Finishing up the front section of the shelf are oils: peanut, sesame, almond, safflower, corn, mustard, and palm. You'll also find massage oils and shelf-stable tins and jars of ghee made from clarified butter or vegetable oils.

You are now near the front of the store, across from cookware and kitty-corner from the Ganesh statue. You will get to know the Rajas' grocery store in more detail as you go through this book. We will use the floor plan just described in each chapter as a guide, referencing where to find a particular item, what it is, and how to use it. If you get lost along the way, just take a look at the floor plan. Enjoy the adventure!

1

Rice & Rice Products

Hindi word for "rice"

Rice is the essential grain of India—the fluffy white mound around which all other dishes revolve. Rice soaks up soups and thin curries in the south and accompanies thick yogurt and cream-based kormas and koftas in the north.

The basis of all Indian meals is rice, bread, or both. In the south and coastal regions rice is eaten at every meal, and it is the rice that is the meal, while the other dishes are for flavoring it. Rice acts as a neutral foil for the highly seasoned, spicy sauces, curries, and soups that are served with it. The traditional way of eating in India is to use the right hand to scoop rice up with bits of food or pieces of torn bread. A mountain of steaming rice is heaped in the center of a plate or a banana leaf and surrounded by other dishes.

Rice can be cooked with spices, raisins, nuts, paneer cheese, lentils, meat, or with vegetables to make pulaos and biryanis. Rice is flavored with tamarind, lemon, coconut, yogurt, and ghee. Split beans are simmered with rice and seasonings to make hearty one-dish meals. Rice is boiled with milk, sugar, and sweet spices to make desserts. Rice is carefully selected depending on its use, with great distinction made between rice that is good for pulao, rice that makes a creamy pudding, or rice that is preferred as a daily table rice.

Besides its role as a staple, there are many ways that rice is used. Rice is soaked overnight and ground with split lentils into a coarse-grained batter. This is used to make thin, crepe-like pancakes and fritters, or it is steamed into spongy cakes. Rice is ground into flour and used as a thickening agent to make dumplings, flat breads, noodles, batters, wafers, and sweets. Rice is pounded and rolled thin to make rice flakes, then is puffed by heat until crispy.

Rice has been cultivated in India for over 3,000 years, and the country is second only to China in production. There are thousands of types with distinct flavors, aromas, and textures that result from differences in climate, soil, and seed stock.

In the typical Indian grocery store one of the first items you will see—or bump into—are the huge, family-size 20- to 30-pound sacks of rice that are near the front door or stacked like sandbags down a central aisle. Look for the more modest 5- to 10-pound bags. There are also small 1- and 2-pound packets or boxes, good for sampling different varieties. There is rice from India, Bhutan, Myanmar, Pakistan, Bangladesh, Sri Lanka, California, Texas, and the Carolinas to choose from. Some are packaged in rough, burlap bags or white, cotton sacks, while others are in stiff jute or plastic bags. Many of the packages are splashed with vivid graphics of animals, flowers, or angels. All of the packages have Hindi or Arabic lettering along with English, which describes the contents. This labeling is important because you can't see through the burlap or jute to examine the grains.

In most Indian grocery stores you will find two main rice varieties: aged basmati and Patna long grain. Perhaps you will find a few specialty rices such as South Indian red or gobindavog. Brown rice is also usually available. Indian cooks prefer white rice, produced by polishing off the outer layers of bran and oil in the husk so that the rice will keep longer. The stronger flavor of brown rice is felt to overwhelm delicate seasonings. To compensate for lost nutrients, protein-rich legume and dairy dishes are eaten with rice. You will also find parboiled (partially boiled) rice, which is not to be confused with American "minute" rice.

Rice is cooked by two methods in India. One is by absorption; the other is by boiling in lots of salted water. Boiling is the preferred method in many parts of India. After boiling until tender, the rice is drained, fluffed with a fork, and drizzled with ghee or melted butter. The leftover water is saved for cooking—or ironing due to the high starch content.

Rice is sacred in India. Raw rice mixed with red powder (gulal) is showered on bridal couples and guests at weddings. In the Hindu tradition rice has always symbolized plenty. A bride will often kick a measure of rice grains across the doorway of her husband's home, symbolizing that she is bringing wealth into the home of her new in-laws.

All rice should be transferred into clean jars or airtight containers. Store it in a cool, dry place so that it will keep for a long time. Refrigerate leftover cooked rice in well-sealed containers, as rices will harden if exposed to cold. Reheat cold rice with a few spoonfuls of water in a microwave or in a covered pot over low heat. Add leftover rice to soups or dals. Sauté it with fresh ingredients, stir-fry it or blend it with yogurt and spices.

Following are the types of rice that you may find in Indian grocery stores, listed in order from the most used and available to the lesser used and harder to find. A mail-order source for unique rices is found on pages 254–55.

Chaawal is raw rice. Bhatt or bhath means cooked rice.

BASMATI RICE

The word *basmati* means "queen of fragrance." It is an aromatic long-grain rice with very slender, pointy-shaped kernels. In India it is prized for its extra-long grains, translucent milk-white color, even size, silky texture, delicate scent, and buttery, nutlike taste. The unique flavor comes from the soil in which the rice grows. Most imported basmati has been aged six months to a year to intensify its flavor and aroma. Basmati is like wine, improving with age. It can be aged up to ten years or more. Older basmati also cooks better, remaining fluffy while new rice becomes sticky and clumps. Basmati expands greatly, especially lengthwise, as it cooks. This creates distinct, dry, fluffy grains. It is the fragrant foundation of pulaos and biryanis and is an ideal daily table rice.

basmati rice

The imported basmati you will find comes from the Himalayan foothills in North India and Pakistan. The best, Dehra Dun, comes from the North Indian state of Uttar Pradesh. Basmati is graded by its percentage of unbroken, long, pointed grains. Patna is a slightly lower grade long-grain rice, grown in the region around the town of Patna in Bihar state in Northeast India. It is labeled "Patna basmati" and is a little less fragrant. Less-expensive, broken-grain basmati is also sold and has the same flavor and fragrance, but it does not have the texture and appearance of whole rice. Due to the aging process all basmati is slightly more expensive than other rices.

Imported brands must be rinsed several times and checked for grit or small particles of stone. U.S.-grown Texmati, Calmati, and Carolina basmati don't need to be cleaned. All basmati rice should be soaked in cold water for about half an hour before cooking. The long, fragile grains absorb a little water and relax slightly for even cooking.

Basmati is found in 5-, 10-, 20-, and 55-pound burlap, jute, or plastic bags. Some bags are lined with an inner bag to retain freshness. Brown, unmilled basmati is also available, but it takes twice as long to cook. For brown basmati, look for the Swad brand in small boxes and 10-pound bags.

Good brands of Dehra Dun (also spelled Dehraduni) basmati to look for are the following: Swad, Shiva, Super Sadhu, SK818 Super Dehraduni, and Lal Quilla Dehraduni NO-1. All of these are in 10-pound bags with stitched-on handles. Other brands of Indian basmati include Chirag Red Rose, Tilda, Shahzada, Abu Adnan, and Super Pari in 10-pound plastic or cloth bags. Then there are Zebra, Polac, Panda, and Tiger brands from Pakistan, all in 10-pound cloth bags. You may also find Elephant brand in 10-pound burlap bags, which has a purple pachyderm on the front of the bag. Also look for Kohinoor basmati, Gold Seal Indus Valley pure basmati and Natraj brands, all in 10-pound bags. For smaller sizes, look for Sadaf brand (which has various spice-flavoring packets included) or Tilda easy-cook brand, both in 6- and 14-ounce boxes. Methods for cooking rice and rice recipes are on page 243.

> The idea of running out of rice is so unthinkable to Bengalis that they cannot verbalize it. When the rice stock is dwindling, they say that the rice is "increasing" in hopes of averting bad luck by using the opposite word. Rice is also associated with Lakshmi, the goddess of wealth and prosperity, and to waste even a grain is believed to insult her. The spirits of departed ancestors are appeased by an offering called a pinda, which is cooked rice and fish mashed into a lump.

GOBINDAVOG RICE

This grain is called the "prince of rice." It is also called kalijira or black rice—because it resembles the shape of black cumin seeds. This is a polished, white, very fancy, small-grain rice that is grown in Myanmar, West Bengal, Sri Lanka, and Bangladesh. The pointy-shaped grains resemble basmati but on a smaller scale. It is

gobindavog rice

often called "baby basmati." It has a delicate aroma and faintly sweet flavor. When cooked the rice is firm yet tender with separate grains. Gobindavog is delicious in rice puddings, biryanis, or as a plain table rice. In Bengal it is fermented to make the summer dish called pantabhat. Leftover cooked rice is soaked overnight, and in the heat it ferments. It is then drained and seasoned with fried chilies, chopped onion, and vegetable curry.

Look for the Shapla brand. It comes in 5-pound off-white, cloth bags with a lotus in a circle logo from Dinajpur, Bangladesh. It is also sold by mail order (see pages 254–55).

Samba rice, from Sri Lanka, is a similar baby-grain rice that is sold in 1-pound plastic bags in well-stocked Indian grocery stores. Another gobindavog rice is Gujarati jeera (jeera means cumin seed) from the Gujarat state in West India, sold in 10-pound, white, cloth bags under the Pexco brand. Ambemohar is a rare short-grain gobindavog rice to seek out. It has roundish grains that are smooth and creamy white. The distinguishing feature is its mangolike fragrance (amb means mango), which remains even after cooking.

CALMATI & OTHER U.S.-GROWN RICE

Calmati is a basmati-type rice grown in the Sacramento valley of California. The grains are not as long or aromatic as Indian basmati. Calmati is a cross between brown rice and basmati. It is sold polished or unmilled (brown). Texmati, and Kasmati, and the long-grain Carolina Gold are Texas grown varieties of basmati. All of these are found in some Indian grocery stores in 2-, 5- and 10-pound bags.

> Rice first arrived in America when a ship was wrecked on a beach in 1685 near Charleston, South Carolina, then a British colony. The vessel was from Madagascar and was loaded with a long-grain indica variety of rice. Once the ship was seaworthy again, the thankful captain gave the local colonists several bags of the unmilled rice, which they planted. It became the first rice grown in America.

RED PATNI RICE

This rice is grown in the coastal, central, and western parts of India and is parboiled, then dried for storage. The short, thick, glassy, and yellowish grains are streaked with red and maroon. It has a nutty aroma, chewy texture and mild, bland taste. It is good for sopping up spicy flavors. Red Patni is also milled into a red flour, used to make a thick batter for pancakes. It is available in well-stocked Indian grocery stores in 1- and 2-pound plastic bags or by mail order (see pages 254–55).

SOUTH INDIAN RED RICE

Rosematta. This is a parboiled red rice grown in Tamil Nadu and Kerala in South India. The plump, long grains have flecks of the reddish outer layer of bran. The grains are yellowish pink because of being parboiled with the red bits. As it boils, a brownish foam rises to the surface. This should be skimmed off. When cooked, the rice expands into fat, rounded grains that remain separate. After cooking, the rice turns whiter with contrasting specks of red. It has an earthy, slightly smoky flavor, almost like red kidney beans. South Indian red rice goes well with strong flavors and hot, spicy dishes. It is also good in pulaos and stews. Look for the Swad brand in 10-pound bags. It is also available in some well-stocked Indian grocery stores in plain plastic bags or by mail order (see pages 254–55).

south indian red rice

BHUTANESE RED RICE

This is a medium–grain, Japanese type of semimilled red rice from the Paro Valley in the Himalayan kingdom of Bhutan. Red rice is a staple grain of Bhutan and has only recently been exported to the United

bhutanese red rice

States. It is partially polished and has patches of the outer layers of red bran clinging to the off-white grains. It cooks in about 20 minutes and is pale-rose colored, soft, and slightly sticky like Japanese rice. It has an earthy fragrance and tastes like brown rice, but it has a slight roasted, nut flavor. It is good plain, with hearty bean and lentil dishes, or in pulaos. It is available in plain plastic bags in well-stocked Indian grocery stores or by mail order. You may also find another red rice grown in the Himalayas, usually labeled "Himalayan red rice." It looks similar to Thai red rice with long, slim, reddish brown, unmilled grains. It has a chewy, nutty flavor and cooks faster than brown rice does because the grains are slimmer. It is somewhat rare in Indian grocery stores, but it is available by mail order (see pages 254–55).

PARBOILED RICE

This is known as siddha in Bengali. The technique of parboiling rice was developed in South India centuries ago—long before Uncle Ben was on the scene—as a way of increasing the nutritional value of polished rice. Unhulled rice is boiled, dissolving the nutrients from the bran into the water. Then it is steamed, forcing and sealing the nutrients back into the heart of the rice kernel. After cooling, the rice is husked and milled to remove the outer layer of bran. Indian parboiled rice has a harder texture than regular rice as a result of being heated, so it actually takes longer to cook. But it fluffs up, yielding a larger volume. American converted or "minute" rice is similar, but it has been partially cooked before milling which is the reason that it cooks quicker.

Parboiled rice grains are glassy, pale yellowish, and slightly dented. Cook as you would any rice, but allow an extra 10 minutes cooking time. Parboiled rice is made from long- or medium-grain rices. A South Indian specialty is pittu, a hot cereal made from raw and parboiled rice that has been crushed into a coarse flour and mixed with freshly grated coconut and water. The thick paste is then stuffed into hollow bamboo molds and steamed upright. The unmolded pittu is served with coconut milk and sugar to start the day on a sweet note. Bash ful, also called kozhul, is a parboiled rice from Bangladesh. It is a blend of medium- and short-grain parboiled rices. Some grains are cream colored with bits of red bran attached. Others are

Food stalls and snack vendors line the grassy perimeters of the entrance gate to Kantagar temple in the northwest region of Bangladesh. Men squat around charcoal fires selling tea, betel, fritters, and packets of pinkish bash ful with various curry sauces. As I settled on the ground to eat, a bird zoomed down and grabbed some rice, flying off to its nest somewhere in the tree above, confirming why picnics here are called choruibhati, or "rice for the sparrows."

slightly translucent with opaque specks. When boiled, a pinkish brown foam rises to the surface and should be skimmed off. The cooked grains are separate and tender. Bash ful is found in well-stocked Indian grocery stores in plain plastic bags or by mail order (see pages 254–55). For regular parboiled rice look for the Par Excellence and Golden Temple brands in 25-pound bags. Also look for Tilda parboiled basmati in 10-pound bags and 6- or 14-ounce boxes.

JAV

jav

This is called phan in Bengali. It is dried paddy rice—rice kernels encased in strawlike, golden greenish husks after harvesting. The rice is not eaten, but is used for puja offerings to Hindu gods. The rice is placed in front of deity figures along with red gulal powder, flowers, and sweets; incense is lit and prayers are chanted. Rice symbolizes fertility and abundance in Hindu tradition. Jav is sold in large 5- to 10-pound bags and convenient 3.5-ounce packets. Look for the Swad brand.

Panicum — Rice-Like Cereal Grains

These cereals are harvested from types of wild, grassy water plants (pani means water), cultivated since ancient times in the Gujarat and Maharashtra states. The cereal grains are threshed from husks just as rice is. They have a somewhat Glutinous texture when cooked. Women cook and eat the seeds several times a year on lunar-related religious festivals. Both types of panicum are good for people with wheat allergies.

KODRI

Varagu or varai. These are small, off-white grains that resemble tiny, pearl barley with a slight indent. Kodri is very nutritious and is cooked like rice, either plain or with ghee and spices. It has a delicate flavor and light texture. It is also roasted and ground with other grains and spices into bhajni flour for breads (bhajni means roasted). Diabetics eat Kodri in place of rice. Look for the Nirav and Swad brands in 14-ounce bags.

SAMO

samo

Morrio. These are tiny, teardrop-shaped seeds that resemble tiny grits. It is cooked and eaten in place of plough-grown rice on special fasting days called Ekadasee. Two times a month, on the eleventh day of the waning and waxing moon, Vaishnavas (members of one of the major branches of Hinduism) observe a non-rice fast and limit physical activities to quiet contemplation and devotional meditation. Women between the ages of sixteen and forty also eat samo once a year on the special fasting day of Sama Pacham. Wash and soak about 15 to 20 minutes before using. Here is how Mrs. Raja cooks samo: Heat oil in a pot. Season it with cumin and mustard seeds. Add garlic and onions and fry until browned, then pour in water. When it boils, add the samo with chopped vegetables. Simmer covered for 20 minutes. Stir in yogurt to serve. Look for the Swad and Nirav brands in 14-ounce bags.

PUFFED RICE

puffed rice

Moori, mumra, murmuras, or kurmura. Harvested rice is dried in the husk until free of any moisture, then it is dropped into an Indian wok that is half-filled with hot sand. The grains explode out of the husks and puff up. They are lifted out with a slotted spoon, straining away the sand and leaving the puffed rice. It is also made commercially. Puffed rice resembles pale, slightly translucent rice krispies. Puffed rice is sold in sealed plastic bags. Once you open a bag, use it quickly as exposure to air removes the crispness. Store in an airtight container.

Puffed rice is mainly used in crunchy snack mixes with roasted nuts, spices, chickpea-flour chips, balls, or noodle bits. It can also be rolled in melted palm sugar and ghee to make sweet, light, crackly balls called kuruma ladoo. Try sprinkling puffed rice over any curry or salad to add a contrasting crunch. Look for the Swad, Bansi, and Laxmi brands in 14-ounce bags. Look also for the Mayur Bengali brand in 7-ounce bags and Patel Brothers in 1- and 2-pound bags. Also, most Indian grocery stores sell bags of puffed rice with no label or just a sticker with the store's name on the bag.

Puffed rice plays a symbolic role in Lahyahome Hindu wedding ceremonies in Western India. The puffy grains (also called parched rice) are thrown into a holy and purifying fire after the couple takes the seven ritual steps (saptapadi) around it. The puffed rice is a sacred offering as rice in all its forms is considered holy. After the ceremony the bride and groom are showered with rice as a symbol of fertility.

Flaked Rice

Poha, pawa, aval, chira, pounded, or pressed rice. Rice grains are husked, cleaned, parboiled and drained. Then they are flattened by large rollers until almost paper thin. The flakes are then dried and packaged. They vary in thickness, depending on the weight of the rollers, and range from thin and almost translucent to the thickness of thin cardboard. Rice flakes are small, oblong, flat, off-white to grayish in color, (or dark pink if made from red rice), have a rough

flaked rice

texture, and resemble torn bits of confetti. They are very light with a bland taste, sort of like baby cereal. Depending on how the flakes are cooked, they can be soft and mushy or crisp and crunchy.

You will find two types of flaked rice: thick and thin. The thick are best for deep-frying as they puff slightly and hold up well without crumbling. The thinner type are best for cooking and making sweets. Look for bags of flakes that are not too crushed or powdery and are stored in an airtight jar. It is best used within three months. Some flakes may be tinted pastel green or pink for use in sweets.

To deep-fry the flakes for snacking, place a handful in a mesh strainer and lower it into very hot oil. The oil will bubble and foam, then settle. The flakes are done when crisp and light golden. Remove the strainer and drain the flakes on paper towels. To make chidwa, the popular snack mix that vendors sell all over India, combine the fried flakes with deep-fried potato shreds (or crushed potato chips), raisins, peanuts, salt, and spices.

To make a spicy cereal, rice flakes are added to a mixture of fried onions, thinly sliced potatoes, and spices. Then it is steamed. Gul poha is a soft sweet made from rice flakes, mixed with grated coconut, palm sugar, and cardamom powder. Chura is a light meal made of flaked rice, cooked with lentils and spices. Phalahar is the Bengali dish of soaked rice flakes mixed with fruit, sugar, and milk or yogurt. Before cooking, the rice flakes have to be washed and drained to soften them. To do this, place the flakes in a sieve and dip them in water just long enough to swish around a few seconds. Be careful with the thin flakes so that they don't disintegrate. Gently press the flakes dry and use in any recipe.

Brands of both thick and thin poha to look for are Swad, in 2- and 5-pound bags, and Patel Brothers in 1- and 2-pound bags. Also look for Maharaja brand red poha in small bags with an elephant logo on it. Swad offers pale-golden poha flakes made from corn in 14-ounce bags. Many stores sell rice flakes in plain, unlabeled bags.

Rice Flour

Chaaval ka atta. Rice flour is powdery and white with a slightly grainy texture like fine sand. It is mainly used as a thickening agent and to make batters and doughs. The texture after cooking depends on how it is used in a recipe. It will be soft and smooth when used to thicken dishes, elastic in doughs, and crisp in batters. When used for thickening, it is used just like cornstarch: the flour is mixed into a little cold water and added to the dish when it is hot, toward the end of cooking. Stir well to make sure that the rice flour cooks evenly without lumping. Rice flour is also mixed with ground black lentils to make doughs for spongy steamed cakes, thin crepes, and the coconut pancakes called appam. Batters made with rice flour are used to coat vegetables for deep-frying, creating a crispy crust. Chawalki roti are flat breads made from a rice flour, ghee, and spice paste dough cooked on a griddle. Rice flour is also mixed with milk, sugar, slivered almonds, and rose water and then heated to make firni, a creamy rice pudding.

After buying rice flour, store it in a dry, airtight container and use within three to four months. You will also find a coarse, ground rice flour called idli-rava or rice sooji. This is labeled "cream of rice," and it is used to make idli, which are steamed, spongy puff cakes.

Brands of rice flour to look for are Swad in 14-ounce or 4-pound plastic bags, Nirav in 2- or 5-pound bags, and Laxmi in 2-pound bags. Idli-rava, cream of rice, is made by Nirav in 2- and 5-pound bags and by Kanaiya, Laxmi, and Swad in 2-pound paper or plastic bags.

> In South India, rice flour is mixed with water to create kolam. This is used to paint decorative motifs on the red, mud floors of homes. Women use rice-flour paste to draw patterns on their foreheads in place of the more usual red dot, which means that one has been blessed by a priest. Kathakali dancers perform while wearing masks painted on their faces with colored rice-flour pastes. When I first went to see a show I expected the dancers to remove their masks at the end of the performance. But as I glimpsed backstage I saw them simply wiping them off!

Rice Khichia

These are round, paper-thin, translucent, rice-flour wafers. They resemble clear-plastic chips and are deep-fried into crispy rice puffs. They are eaten as a snack or mixed into rice and curries. Look for the Nirav brand in plain, cumin, green-chili, or garlic-flavored wafers. Look also for Eastern brand's mint-chutney flavor. Both brands are in 7-ounce bags. Look also for the Deep brand in 7-ounce boxes.

Rice Noodles

Chaaval ke sev or rice sticks. Rice noodles are made from a rice flour dough. The dried noodles are sold in long strips or small coils. They are thin like vermicelli, white, slightly translucent, and very brittle. Rice noodles are mainly used to make sweet or savory snacks. After softening by plunging into boiling water, they are drained, stir-fried in ghee or oil, and mixed with milk and sugar or salt and spices. They are also boiled (for 1 or 2 minutes) and added to milk drinks as a texture ingredient. When the noodles are cooked, they become soft and slippery. Noodle upma, a delicious South Indian breakfast or snack dish, is made by sautéing soaked lentils in oil with mustard seeds and curry leaves until golden, then adding softened, broken bits of rice noodle, then stirring with sugar, salt, and chopped green chilies until soft. Look for the Swad and Sailing Boat brands in 16-ounce bags.

Stocking Up

Choose a rice for your everyday table rice. Basmati is the most versatile and authentic for Indian meals. You might want to have a bag of one of the more exotic rices, such as South Indian red or gobidavong, for a different taste. Add some rice flour as an all-purpose thickener and for making fried foods or pancakes. Flaked rice is handy for a quick cereal or savory snack. Finally, get some puffed rice if you want to experiment with blending your own snack mixes.

2

Breads & Flours

फलोर

Hindi word for "flour"

In the northern and central parts of India, wheat is the staple grain. Here, ground whole-wheat flour, called atta is the basic ingredient in most breads. A vast variety of wheat-based breads are eaten with every meal in the north, while breads accompany rice and curries in other regions. To a person from the north, nothing is more delicious or satisfying than a roti hot off the tava (iron griddle), smeared with ghee or melted butter.

Roti is the general term for bread in India. It is made from a variety of ground grains. Rotis can be thin, thick, chewy, plain, flavored, or stuffed with savory fillings. The most common daily bread is unleavened chapati, made from finely ground whole-wheat flour and water. Different flour mixtures, shaping techniques, and cooking methods produce a wide range of breads with unusual tastes and textures. There are four main types of Indian breads: griddle-cooked, shallow-fried, deep-fried, and baked. While wheat flour is the most commonly used flour, many other grains are ground into flours for use in bread making.

Whole-wheat kernels and flour are the base of several other foods. Coarsely cracked whole wheat is used in pilafs and puddings or is finely milled into semolina and used in savory and sweet puddings. Sevian is a fine vermicelli pasta made from a whole-wheat flour dough. Bread variations that are not based on wheat include lentil wafers and dried dal-paste dumplings.

In India you don't go to the corner bakery for fresh bread. You bring whatever whole grain you want to be ground to the neighborhood mill. Here, two stone slabs called a chakki are used to grind the grain into flour. The flour is used to make fresh, hot bread for every meal. Most Indian groceries sell fresh chapati, corn roti, and naan. Smaller stores receive shipments of frozen breads from bakeries in large cities, so check the freezer case. Frozen bread is fine if it is reheated in a microwave, toaster oven, or oven. Chapati can be heated in a hot, dry, iron pan. Following are some types of breads that you may find in Indian groceries or on restaurant menus.

Griddle Cooked Breads

These are all flatbreads cooked on hot griddles, called tavas, or cast iron pans without any oil. They are made by various national and regional companies. Look also for locally made brands in the area in which you live. Most of them are packaged in plastic bags with anywhere from 5 to 12 pieces. Flatbreads are eaten with meals, used to scoop up foods and soak up sauces, smeared with jam, chutney, or melted butter.

CHAPATI

The daily bread of India, these are thin, soft, unleavened 5- to 6-inch diameter round breads that look like light-brown flour tortillas. Chapatis are made from a whole-wheat atta flour, water, and salt dough. The dough mixture is lightly kneaded, rolled into small balls, rolled flat to the desired thickness, and cooked on a hot griddle for about 1 minute per side. Store-bought fresh or frozen chapati should be reheated and wrapped in a dry kitchen towel to keep it warm during the meal. Brands to look for are Royal, Delicious Foods, Good Life, Kontos Moghul Homemade Taste, and Vegi's Homestyle Gourmet Foods. To make your own chapati, see the recipe on page 242.

DAHI CHAPATI

This bread is similar to regular chapati, but it is made with a yogurt-enriched whole-wheat flour dough. It has a softer texture.

PHULKA

This is extra-thin chapati made with a similar whole-wheat flour dough, but it is enriched with butter or ghee. The main difference is in the size. Phulkas are larger, about 8- to 10-inches in diameter and paper-thin. They are cooked in the same way on a hot griddle but for slightly less time. They also puff up a bit.

GEHUN PHULKA

The word "gehun" means "wheat kernel" and these ultrathin chapatis are made from soaked, finely ground wheat berries that are mixed with whole wheat atta flour and enriched with powdered buttermilk and melted butter or ghee. The paper-thin, light, reddish brown, large, round breads are soft and pliable.

MAKKAI-KI-ROTI

Corn roti or taza makkai roti. These are corn-based griddle-cooked flatbreads that are similar to Mexican tortillas, but they are much thicker. The golden yellow, 5- to 6-inch discs have a slightly sweet flavor and stay moist and flexible after cooking. They are made from a mixture of finely ground cornmeal, whole-wheat flour, fresh corn kernels, water,

makkai-ki-roti

sugar, salt, and ghee. Brands to look for are New York Nan & Spices and Delicious Foods corn roti. Both come with 4 to 5 pieces per bag.

TIKKAR ROTI

This thick peasant-style bread is popular in Rajasthan. It is made from a whole-wheat-and-corn flour dough mixed with chopped garlic, ginger, onions, tomatoes, green chilies, and coriander leaves. The flat, golden brown, round breads are cooked with a little oil on a hot griddle and served with chutney and pickles.

METHI ROTI

This is a soft, yellow, spicy, flat, round bread with chopped fenugreek leaves (methi), chili, turmeric, spices, and salt, added to the enriched flour dough. It is delicious with rice and melted butter. Look for the Good Life brand in

methi roti

8-ounce bags with 5 pieces.

MISSI ROTI

This is a soft, round flatbread made from a mixture of chickpeas and whole-wheat chapati flour. Chopped garlic, onion, tomatoes, or roasted cumin seeds may be added to the dough. Look for the Royal, Kontos, and New York Nan & Spices brands. All come with 5 to 10 pieces to a bag.

MOTI ROTI

This soft, chewy flatbread is like sourdough. The dough is made from all-purpose white flour mixed with yogurt and oil. The dough is lightly kneaded and left to ferment and rise. The slightly fermented dough is then formed into balls, rolled flat, and cooked on a hot griddle. It is good with saucy curries or as a breakfast

In Mysore, I ate elephant-foot wadas, which are large flatbreads that are brown on the outside and golden from turmeric on the inside. They looked like the footprint an elephant might leave in the mud, but they tasted delicious when dipped into soppu pallya, which is steamed spinach thickened with cream and seasoned with mustard and cumin seeds.

bread smeared with fruit chutney. Look for the Moghul brand in packages of 12 pieces.

ROTLA

Rotla. These are hand-patted, thick, hearty flatbreads made from an Indian millet flour called bajri. The millet flour, water, salt, and oil dough is patted into flat discs, which are thicker than chapati, and cooked for slightly less time on a hot griddle. They are pale golden with a rich toasty flavor.

RUMALI ROTI

This is North Indian, very large, round, paper-thin flatbread cooked on an upturned, convex griddle called an ultra tava. The bread is as wide in diameter as a bicycle wheel, and the name means "as thin as a silk scarf." To achieve the thinness, the bread is thrown into the air and nimbly spun and stretched, much like a pizza. Rumali is similar to Middle Eastern mountain bread.

HARI ROTI

This is a light greenish brown flatbread made from whole-wheat chapati flour, boiled and mashed green peas, salt, lime juice, chopped mint, or coriander leaves mixed with oil or ghee and water into a dough. The kneaded dough is rolled into 5-inch circles and cooked on a hot griddle.

KHAKHRA ROTI

khakhra roti

This is a crispy, thin, Gujarati-style bread made from whole-wheat and white flours mixed into a dough with a little oil, warm water or milk. It is then flavored with garam masala. These pale-golden, very thin, round breads are roasted until crisp on a hot griddle. Some are pale greenish with the addition of finely chopped fenugreek leaves. They look like tostadas. Mrs. Raja told me that people from Gujarat carry this roti with them when traveling, as it stays fresh for several days. The bread is eaten with pickles. Look for the Deep brands methi (fenugreek-leaf) khakhra packed in beautiful, paper-covered, 7-ounce cardboard boxes inside plastic wrappers. Look also for the Maya brands plain bread in 14-ounce boxes and Suraji's garlic flavor in 7-ounce plastic packets.

MUGHALI ROTI

Crispy on the outside and soft on the inside, these yeast-risen breads are made from whole-wheat chapati flour, yeast, salt, milk, and a pinch of sugar and aniseed. After rising and kneading, balls of dough are rolled into 5- to 6-inch circles and roasted until light brown on a hot griddle.

BESAN THEPLA

This is a Gujarati-style, soft, flat, nutty-flavored, spicy bread made from dry-roasted chickpea flour, wheat flour, and millet

37

flour mixed with ground spices, minced fresh herbs, salt, melted butter, yogurt, and water. The dough is rolled flat into 6-inch circles and cooked on a hot griddle. Theplas remain moist even when they are cold. They are popular lunchbox and picnic breads in Gujarat.

Pan-Fried Breads

These breads are cooked on a hot griddle or cast-iron pan. They are fried with a little oil or ghee on each side. They form a slightly crisp crust and are soft on the inside. Many are made into sandwiches. Pan-fried breads can be eaten as part of a meal or as a snack with soup and pickles. Stores in any "Little India" will have the best selection of national brands and locally made types. Check to find out what is available.

PARATHA

This is a flat, unleavened bread made from a dough similar to chapati. But the dough has a little ghee or butter added to enrich it, and less water is used, making a medium-stiff dough. The breads are shallow-fried and basted in ghee on a hot griddle. Plain parathas are rolled out,

folded, oiled, re-rolled, refolded, re-oiled, and re-rolled again, creating a multilayered, flaky, puffy, pastry-like, triangular-shaped bread. Look for the Delicious Foods brand in packages of 4, the Hand Made Indo-Pak brand with ten breads, and the New York Nan & Spices brand in packs of 5.

paratha

STUFFED PARATHA

Stuffed paratha is made by rolling two thin circles of dough, placing a filling in the center, pinching the edges together to seal them and rolling the layers together to create a pastry like flat bread, which is shallow-fried in ghee. Following are filling types to look for.

ALOO PARATHA

This is paratha filled with a layer of mashed, spiced potatoes. It is delicious warm or cold. Look for the New York Nan & Spices brand in packs of 5.

ALOO PALAK PARATHA

This is paratha stuffed with a filling of mashed, spiced potatoes mixed with finely chopped spinach or any other leafy green such as watercress, mustard greens, or radish leaves.

In Bengal paratha is known as parota. It is usually a three-cornered, flaky bread cooked in ghee. It can also be circular with five to six layers. If cooked by a top-notch Muslim cook, known as a baburchi, it can be grandiose with sixty or more flaky layers beneath a golden brown crust. Called dhakai parota, this rich bread is eaten throughout Bangladesh with various curries.

MOOLI PARATHA

This is paratha stuffed with a filling of shredded mooli (giant white radish) and garam masala. Look for the New York Nan & Spices brand in packs of 5.

METHI PARATHA

This flaky paratha is stuffed with chopped fenugreek (methi) leaves mixed with chopped green chilies, sugar, turmeric powder, and salt. Look for the Delicious Foods brand in packages of 4 and the New York Nan & Spices brand in packs of 5.

BIRAHI PARATHA

Also called besan or chickpea paratha. This paratha has a nutty flavor from a stuffing of dry-roasted chickpea flour mixed with water and spices.

PURAN POLI

Meetha paratha. Meetha means sweet. This bread is stuffed with a filling of sweet dal. The dal is made from split yellow lentil which is boiled until soft and thickened with water, palm sugar, and cardamom. It is eaten with spicy curries and soups, or it is enjoyed as a treat during the spring festival of Holi.

MAKKAI PARATHA

This is a golden yellow paratha made from cornmeal, whole-wheat chapati flour, palm sugar, finely chopped green chilies, crushed ajowan seeds, oil, and water. The folded, multilayered, pastrylike, triangular breads are shallow-fried in ghee. Melted butter is drizzled over them as they cook, giving them a crisp texture.

PUDLA

This is also called puda. This is a spicy, pancakelike bread made from a batter of chickpea flour and water that is flavored with cumin seeds, turmeric powder, minced chilies, onions, lime juice, salt, and diced tomato. A few tablespoons of batter are spread on a hot-oiled griddle, and the bread is cooked until golden brown on both sides.

Deep-Fried Breads & Pastries

These are breads made from flat dough or stuffed balls of dough that are dropped in hot oil and deep-fried. Some types are sold already fried. Others are sold uncooked in packages to be fried at home.

PURI & LUCHI

These are puffed breads. Puri is made from chapati flour that has just a bit less water, making a firmer dough. Luchi is made from a coarser

cooked puri

wheat flour and semolina dough. It is popular in Bengal. Both types are rolled into small circles and fried one at a time in bubbling hot oil. While cooking, hot oil is constantly spooned over the top of the flatbreads until it puffs up into a steam-filled balloon. It is then gently turned over and fried on the other side until golden brown. They are torn into pieces and eaten with foods. Very small puffed puris, called pani-puri (water puffs) are also sold, usually in plain plastic bags. These are stuffed with boiled potato, chickpeas, and spicy water. Khasta luchi are rich, flaky flatbreads enriched with ghee or oil and pan-fried. Unpuffed puri bread is sold in sealed plastic bags. Look for the Vegi's Homestyle Gourmet Foods brand with 12 pieces to a package. They have to be deep-fried at home, or they can be heated in a dry pan like chapati.

poori bread

DAHI PURI

This puri bread is made with a buttermilk-and-wheat flour dough with coarsely crushed, dry-roasted cumin seeds. Ground black pepper or poppy seeds are added to the dough. They are deep-fried in the same way as puri luchi.

MASALA PURI

These spicy puri breads have paprika, turmeric, ground coriander, and cumin added to the wheat flour dough.

ALOO PURI

This is a silky-smooth puri made with boiled potato, garam masala, ground cumin, and paprika added to the basic wheat flour dough.

TIL PURI

This is a flavorful, nutty puri with ground, dry-roasted sesame seeds (til) and warm milk added to the wheat flour dough.

METHI PURI

This is a puri bread made with a puree of fresh fenugreek leaves, yogurt, turmeric, ground coriander, minced green chilies, and garam masala added to the wheat flour dough.

SAMOSA

These are crispy, deep-fried, triangular turnovers of pastry dough stuffed with a

At the festivals honoring the annual visits of the three goddesses, Durga, Lakshmi, and Kali, their likenesses are placed in pandols, which are canopied platforms where throngs of devotees come to offer prayers and flowers. The 2nd day of Durga's visit is called Ashtami, and it is the most important day of the festival. Durga is Shiva's wife and the goddess of deliverance. People pray to her for help in times of crisis and danger. On this day only vegetarian food is eaten. After the final rituals, which are performed by a priest to syncopated drum beats, golden luchi is eaten with a thick potato curry and dal.

samosa

spicy, minced meat or mashed potato and pea filling. They are good dipped in tangy chutney. Singhara is the Bengali version, which is stuffed with a sweet filling of palm sugar and coconut. In most Indian grocery stores these are sold at the front counter by the piece.

KARANJI

Crescent shaped deep-fried pastries popular in Maharashtra, filled with either fresh gingery peas or a sweet, soft coconut milk, and nut mixture. Karanji is sold by the piece at the front counter of some stores. Modak is a sweet fig-shaped karanji made by folding up the edges of a pastry dough circle with a spoonful of sweet filling in the center up to create a fluted, inverted cone. Because modak is a great favorite of Ganesh, whenever karanjis are being made, an honorary modak is first offered up to him—then the rest can be made in crescent shapes for the mere mortals.

KACHORI

This is a deep-fried, small bread made from a whole-wheat chapati flour dough filled with mashed, cooked, spicy green peas. A depression is made in a small ball of dough, and it is filled with the pea mixture, smoothed over to seal, rolled into a 3-inch ball, and deep-fried until golden brown. It is often sold at the front counter by the piece.

BHATURA

This is a puffed, deep-fried, leavened bread made from fine-grained semolina flour, white flour, yogurt, salt, sugar, melted ghee, and warm water. The kneaded dough is left to sour slightly and to rise. Small balls are

bhatura

rolled into thin rounds and fried in hot oil. The bread sinks to the bottom of the pan, then it bobs to the surface. As the bread rises it is pushed back under the oil with a slotted spoon until it puffs into a steam-filled balloon. It is then turned over and fried until pale golden on the other side.

Oven-Baked Breads

These are breads made from leavened dough and baked in clay tandoor ovens. The round pita-shaped or oblong, thick flat-breads are made by several national brands and in "Little India" bakeries—check to see what types are available in your area. They are served with meals, used to scoop up foods, or are folded around grilled meats or kebabs.

NAAN

This is a leavened white-flour bread enriched with yogurt, eggs, and butter. The dough is kneaded and left to sour slightly and to rise. Then the soft dough is formed into oblong or teardrop shapes and baked in large, charcoal-fired, clay tandoor ovens. Once the clay walls of the oven are hot, the breads are slapped onto the inner walls where they quickly cook, partially puffing as they absorb a smoky flavor. Each bread is pricked with a metal skewer and peeled off the oven wall. Naan breads have a soft center and crisp crust. Look for

naan bread

Vegi's Homestyle Gourmet Foods tandoor naan in 12-ounce packages, Kontos in packs of 10 pieces, the HandMade Indo-Pak brand

tandoori naan bread

with 8 pieces, and the Royal, Swad, and Imran brands' tandoori naan in packs of 8 to 10 pieces. Swad also has wholewheat naan. Naan can be reheated in an oven or grilled on a barbecue grill to add an authentic smoky taste.

GARLIC & ONION NAAN

These variations of naan are made either by brushing the bread before baking or by grilling it with crushed garlic or minced onion with a little salt and yogurt. Poppy or nigella seeds may also be sprinkled on the dough before baking. Look for Vegi's Homestyle Gourmet Foods garlic or onion naan in 12-ounce packages, Kontos onion naan in packs of 10, and Apex garlic and onion naan.

ROGHANI NAAN

The name means "red naan" because the bread is given a brushing of saffron water before baking. The thick, soft breads are brushed with ghee, glazed with a solution of saffron that has been soaked in warm milk, and sprinkled with poppy and sesame seeds before being baked. Look for Vegi's Homestyle Gourmet Foods roghani naan in 2-ounce packages, and for the Swad and Kontos brands in packs of 10.

roghani naan

MASALA NAAN

This is a hot, spicy naan with garam masala, finely minced green chilies, chopped onion, and coriander leaves added to the dough.

PANEER NAAN

This is a naan stuffed with a filling of paneer cheese (Indian curd cheese) flavored with ground coriander and paprika. Balls of naan dough are rolled into thick, 3-inch circles, and the cheese filling is placed in the center. The dough is wrapped up around the cheese, sealing it in. The stuffed ball is then rolled and brushed with oil before baking.

KHASTA ROTI

This is a North Indian, crispy, tandoor-baked bread made from a butter-enriched dough that tastes like pie crust.

KULCHA

Kulcha is similar to naan. It is made from a leavened white flour dough, but it is kneaded with much more ghee. Kulchas are round and can be stuffed with a variety of fillings, like paratha. There is also a square type which is popular in Hyderabad, that is marked with 2 crisscrossed lines made from thumbprints in the soft dough. The plain or stuffed kulchas are baked in an oven, then they are shallow-fried in ghee. Stuffings include spicy potato, spinach and paneer cheese, garlic paste, mint puree or kesari, which is saffron soaked in milk with sugar. Look for the Kontos brand's plain kulcha in packages of 10 and Moghul kulcha in packages of 12.

SHEER-MAAL

This is a Persian-influenced, round, flat bun from Northern India. It is also popular in Hyderabad. Sheer means "milk." This leavened bread is made from white flour, dry yeast, salt, eggs, warm milk, cream, raisins, poppy seeds, butter, and rose essence. After rising, the dough is rolled into thick circles and pricked all over with a fork, brushed with melted butter and a saffron solution, then sprinkled with poppy seeds and baked. The milk makes the bread soft. Look for the Vegi's Home-style Gourmet Foods brand in 12-ounce packages.

Bread Variations

These are not quite breads, but they fall into this chapter because they are bread offsprings—dried dough discs and dried dal-paste lumps—that are eaten as part of a complete meal.

PAPPADAM

Papad, paparh, and appalam. These are round wafers made from a plain or seasoned ground-lentil or mung-bean and rice flour paste. They are rolled paper-thin and dried in the sun. Sizes vary from 6 to 8 inches in diameter to 2 to 5 inch ones. Pappadam is flame-roasted in North India and deep-fried in South India. To flame-roast the wafers, place them on a metal rack several inches above an electric or gas burner. When exposed to heat, they will lighten in color, expand, and become flecked with small, black dots. Move the wafer around very quickly with tongs to cook it evenly and to keep it from burning. Flip the wafer and roast the other side. The finished wafer will be brittle and yellowish with charred specks.

pappadam

To deep-fry pappadam, pour oil a depth of about 1 inch in a pan. When the oil is hot, drop in a wafer. It will sizzle and expand while curling up a bit around the edges. Use a spatula or slotted spoon to press on the surface of the wafer. Within 3 to 5 seconds it will turn crisp and lighten slightly in color. Remove it with tongs, and drain the oil. After roasting or frying, they will stay crisp for 1 to 2 hours.

Pappadam are served as a light bread with meals, crumbled up and mixed into rice. They can also be an appetizer if dipped in chutney. They can also be used as a noodle by softening them in hot water and cutting them into ribbons. Try the strips gently stir-fried with vegetables or dropped into soup. Pappadam ka saag is seasoned, simmered yogurt mixed with roasted, broken wafer bits to make a sort of curry. The wafers are available plain or seasoned with black pepper, chili pepper, garlic, onion, or spice blends in 7- or 14-ounce paper or cellophane packages.

Look for the Apalum, Bikaner, Kharo, Joy, Lijat, Sabras, Shivan, and Shree Mahal Akshmi Madras brands. The Vardan brand is flavored with turmeric. The Testy Maitry is laced with garlic in packages with a smiling cartoon-kid logo. The Welco brand makes mini papads in plain and black-pepper, packed in three rows of 2-inch wafers. The Swad brand has an extensive range of mini cocktail-sized papad in cumin, chili, Punjabi, spicy punch, garlic, and black-pepper flavors.

VADI

Wadi or bori. These small, hard, dal-paste chunks are made from fermented, dried, split, yellow mung-bean, soy, or chickpea-flour pastes. Some have spices added to them. They range in color from brown to bright yellow and in size from large nuggets to small Hershey's kisses. Phulbori are white droplets made from split and skinned urad dal. The paste is whipped to make them airy and light. Vadi are cooked in a curry gravy like dumplings, or are added to stews and soups. To cook, soak the vadi in hot water for about 20 minutes and drain. Sprinkle with lemon or lime juice and a little water. Add salt, pepper, spices, chopped onion,

and garlic and let the vadi sit a few minutes to absorb the seasonings. Fry some curry powder in a little oil and add the vadi chunks with some peas or diced potatoes. Cook it until soft.

You can also sauté the soaked chunks in oil with cumin seeds, salt, and chopped onions, then add some water and cook until soft. Small ones can be fried until crispy. Crumble them over cooked, leafy greens or other vegetables. They have a long shelf life and are

vadi chunks

Rathajatra, the 1st festival of the monsoon season, celebrates a story about the young Lord Jagannatha. The town of Puri has the biggest festival. Each year gargantuan, wooden chariots containing images of the three deities from the story are rolled out of the temple. Devotees drag the chariots about a half mile to Gundicha Ghar (Garden House). Legend has it many people used to throw themselves under the wheels hoping to go to heaven, hence the word juggernaut. Perhaps so many fried pappadams are eaten on this day because of their resemblance to the chariot wheels.

handy to have for quick, nutritious meals. Look for the Raj Mahal brand's caramel colored soya chunks in 8-ounce plastic bags and the Bansi Deep brand's soya, chola (chickpea), and moong (mung-bean) vadi in 7-ounce bags. Look also for the Swad brand's chola, moong, soya nutrella, Punjabi, and Gujarati (these two are spicy) wadi in 7- and 14-ounce bags. Many markets sell them with just the store's name on the bag.

Flours & Starches

The following flours are listed from the most popular to the least used varieties. Most flours are sold in 1- to 5-pound plastic or paper bags, except for chapati flour that is also found in 20-pound paper bags. Flours and starches should be stored in airtight containers in a cool, dry place. They can last for up to four months. If you live in a warm, humid climate, it is best to store them in the refrigerator in tightly sealed containers to prevent weevil infestation.

ATTA FLOUR

Chapati or durum wheat flour. This is a finely stone-ground, sifted, whole-wheat flour made from a low-gluten wheat. Wheat has been cultivated in India for thousands of years, and much of it is grown in the northern Punjab region, often called the breadbasket of India. The entire soft, golden brown wheat kernel, including the bran and germ, is milled almost to a powder. The light-tan or buff-colored flour makes delicate flatbreads that shape easily and cook quickly.

atta flour

In Indian grocery stores, atta flour may be labeled 80/20 or 60/40, the higher number referring to the proportion of whole meal to white flour. These are special bread-making blends. Regular whole wheat flour will not work for Indian breads because it has a higher gluten content, making heavy, dense chapatis. Atta flour's texture is much softer, making it easier to knead and roll. You can substitute a mixture of two parts all-purpose white flour and one part whole-wheat flour if atta is unavailable.

Atta is used to make chapati, roti, paratha, and puri breads. It is also used in steamed cakes, as a thickener in sauces, and in some milk desserts. Fish fillets and vegetable cutlets are rolled in it before deep-frying to give a crisp coating. A dough made of atta flour, called dum, is used to seal cooking pots as their contents steam over low heat. Atta flour is also used in cakes, pastries, and batters. Atta flour is sold in large 20- to 55-pound, brown or white, heavy, paper bags, that are stitched closed across the top. It is also in smaller plastic or paper bags. Look for the Chirag, Golden Temple, Laxmi, Meera, Taj Mahal, and Janta House of Spices brands. The Nirav and Swad brands come in 5-pound bags.

LADDOO FLOUR

This is also spelled "ladu." This is a coarsely ground, whole-wheat flour used for some breads and sweet balls, called ladoos, that are made from fried, wheat-flour droplets mixed with sugar and ghee. This flour is a creamy brownish color with a slightly granular texture as it contains more bran. It can be used for all unleavened breads, but they will be thicker and heavier than breads using atta flour. Some flours are labeled laddoo-magaz, which means that it is a blend of split chana dal (small chickpea) and whole-wheat flours. Besan laddoo is a coarse chickpea flour. Both are used for breads and sweets. Look for the Nirav, Kanaiya, Jalpur, Laxmi, Swad, and Ghanti Chhap brands' wheat laddoo flour in 2-pound plastic bags. The Ghanti Chhap brand has laddoo-magaz flour in 2-pound bags, and Swad offers ladu besan flour in 2-pound bags.

HALIM

These are whole-wheat kernels. They are crushed to make cracked wheat, and they are cooked whole in pilafs and grain stews. Haleem is a Pakistani dish made with whole- and cracked wheat cooked with lamb or chicken, spices, and several pulses (usually chickpeas, mung beans, and red lentils). Melted ghee is stirred into the thick, hearty stew. It is garnished with chopped onions and coriander leaves before serving. A favorite dish of South Indian Muslims is kiskiya, a whole-wheat porridge cooked with minced meat and spices. Halim is found in the refrigerator case to prevent the oil in the kernels from turning rancid. Look for the Laxmi and Swad brands in 2-pound plastic bags.

CRACKED WHEAT

Lapsi. Also called dalia, it is similar to bulghur. Lapsi is made by crushing or cracking raw, whole-wheat kernels into small, hard, light-brown bits that are rough and uneven. When wheat is made into flour, the sifting process leaves some broken grains behind. These are collected and sold as cracked wheat. Lapsi is sold in three grades: fine, which is used for tabbouli-like salads with minced fresh herbs, medium, which is for milky puddings and coarse, which is for pilafs. Cracked wheat is very nutritious and has a wheaty aroma, a grainy, chewy texture, and a hearty, nutty taste. Try sautéing cracked wheat in ghee, then cooking it with milk and sugar. Lapsi kheer is a sweet coconut-milk pudding. You can make a simple breakfast porridge by cooking cracked wheat with water, salt, and a little butter until the grains are soft, which takes about 20 minutes. It is also cooked with spices and vegetables for savory pilafs. Partially boiled cracked wheat can be added to batters for pancakes and fritters, adding taste and texture. Look for the Laxmi and Swad brands. Store it in an airtight jar, and use it within four months.

SEMOLINA

Sooji, rava, or rawa. Semolina is made by processing the creamy colored grains of hard endosperm (the inside of the wheat kernel) that are sifted out of durum wheat during the milling process. Semolina is granular. It is available in fine, medium, or coarse grains. When cooked, semolina has a smooth, slightly grainy texture and bland taste, good for both savory and sweet dishes. Cream of wheat is made from farina, which is milled from soft wheat (not durum) with added salt and preservatives. This can be substituted in recipes for semolina, but it will not have quite the same quality. Semolina is cooked

semolina

with spices, nuts, diced vegetables, and water until it is thick and fluffy to make upuma, a South Indian breakfast dish that is garnished with grated coconut and chopped coriander leaves. Semolina is also boiled with milk, sugar, and raisins to make puddings. It can be roasted in ghee and mixed with sugar to make sooji halwa, a thick sweet. Rava dosa are thin pancakes and rava idli are small, steamed cakes made from semolina and rice flour batters. Small amounts of semolina are often added to deep-fried bread doughs such as puri as it helps the breads rise and stay puffed longer. Look for the Nirav, Jai Swami, Laxmi, Maharaja, and Shashi brands of fine and coarse sooji in 2-pound paper or plastic bags. Store it up to four months in an airtight container.

SEVIAN

Semolina is used to make prasad, which is a religious ritual. It is cooked with other pure ingredients such as ghee, milk, palm sugar, and bananas. A little of the prasad mixture is wrapped in banana-leaf parcels, and after it has been offered to a deity or priest to sanctify it, the blessed prasad is distributed to devotees at religious gatherings. It can be eaten at the temple or taken away to share with others. Other prasad foods include sweets and fruits.

This is ultra-thin, wheat-flour vermicelli. Sevian is a fine, hard, pale, golden brown noodle that is sold in sticks about one foot long. Sevian has a cookielike aroma and flavor when it is fried in ghee or dry-roasted. It is used in sevian kheer, a milk pudding made by sautéing bits of noodle with cashews and raisins in ghee until golden, adding milk and sugar, and boiling until the sevian is soft, which takes about 10 minutes. It is delicious warm or chilled and sprinkled with more nuts. A traditional treat that Muslims eat to break the Ramadan fast is a dish of sevian cooked in milk with saffron and nuts. Sevian is also added to clear soups and pilafs. You will find the fine skeins packaged in long cellophane bags or cardboard boxes with colorful paper labels. It is also sold roasted or in broken bits. It will keep for about four to five months. Look for the Ahmed, Chirag, Laziza, National, and Sadaf brands in bags. Also, Elephant brand's plain or roasted sevian is in 7-ounce boxes, and the Zaika brand's roasted sevian is in 7-ounce bags.

MAIDA OR MAITHA FLOUR

This is unbleached, plain, white, all-purpose flour. It is made from the endosperm and is mainly starch—all the germ and bran have been sifted out, leaving a refined white, soft flour. Maida flour is good for obtaining a smooth, elastic texture. It is used to make cakes, pastry dough for samosas and naan, or pan-fried puffed breads. It is also combined with whole-wheat pastry flours to get the texture needed for chapati and other Indian flat-breads. Look for the Jalpur, Nirav, and Swad brands in 2-pound bags.

BESAN FLOUR

Chana, patani, Bengal gram, or chickpea flour. This pale, yellow, high-protein flour is made from a small, yellowish or brown type of chickpea. It has a matte texture, earthy aroma and slightly nutty, rich flavor. Besan flour is used in curries as a thickener and to make batters for pakoras and bhajis, which are deep-fried vegetable fritters. It is used in breads, blended with other flours, and used as a stuffing for birahi paratha. Besan flour is roasted and cooked with palm sugar and ghee to make fudgelike sweets with a crispy, melting texture. Besan flour dough is squeezed through a press into hot oil to make chips, noodles, beads, and swirls for snack blends. Besan beads, called boondi, are used in sweet ladoo balls. The flour is blended with yogurt and cooked with spices to make kadhi, a thick soup floating with dumplings. Pithla is a besan flour sauce that is eaten with rice or bread. It is made like polenta, by slowly adding and constantly stirring the flour into spiced, simmering water or buttermilk until it thickens. Indian women use besan flour mixed with milk as a cleansing face mask. Besan flour will keep in an air-tight container for up to six months. Look for the Chirag, Eastern, Ghanti Chhap, Laxmi, Maya, Meera, Nirav, Shiva, and Swad brands in 4-pound bags. Besan flour is used in the onion bhaji recipe on page 240.

> During rationing in the 1940s in India, semolina and cake flour were scarce, so besan flour was used to make dishes like waffole, which are steamed, shredded, cabbage-besan squares. Traditionally, the thick, ginger-spiced, buttermilk-besan flour batter was steamed over the embers of a coal stove (shegdi) in a flat, heavy-bottomed pan called a langdi. A flat tava piled with hot coals covered it. Nowadays it is cooked in a steamer, and the sweet-and-sour cake is cut into squares and garnished with chopped coriander leaves, shredded coconut, and a squeeze of lime.

besan flour

MAGHAJ FLOUR

This is coarsely ground chickpea flour used in some breads, sweets, and stuffings. Look for the Swad brand in 14-ounce or 4-pound bags.

Besan Flour Blends

DOKLA FLOUR

This is also called dokra flour. This is a mix of besan and rice flours. It is used to make steamed, cornbread-like cakes called dhokla. Look for the Nirav, Jalpur, Swad, and Chanti Chhap brands in 2-pound bags. Dhokla cakes are a specialty of Gujarat. The word "dhokla" means "to fool someone" because, while vegetarian, they have an almost meaty flavor from the fermented dokra flour. Dhokla shops dot the streets of towns in Gujarat, where people line up for piping-hot, steamed cakes that shopkeepers bring out on huge trays.

ONDHWA FLOUR

This is a blend of besan, rice, and black-lentil flours, used for breads, batters, pancakes, and steamed cakes. Look for Kanaiya, Jalpur, and Nirav brands in 2-pound bags and Swad brand in 14-ounce or 4-pound bags.

DAKOR GOTA FLOUR

This is an instant fritter mix made from a blend of besan and wheat flours with salt, ground red pepper, coriander, and spices. It is blended with water and a little oil into a dough, shaped into balls or patties, and deep-fried. Look for the Rasraj brand, which comes in mild or hot, in 1-pound white boxes.

BAJRI FLOUR

This is millet flour or kurakkan. It is milled from bulrush, or pearl millet that grows in cylindrical ears on stalks. It is cultivated in the driest regions of India and Pakistan. It is the staple grain of Gujarat, where it is used to make batloo, which are flat, griddle breads pocked with depressions made by the cook's thumb. Bajri grains are tiny and teardrop-shaped in a mix of greenish gray and bright yellow. The flour is gray with a nutty aroma and slightly bitter-sweet taste. It is often combined with wheat flour to make breads or cakes. Bajri flour gives a soft, dry base to baked goods, and it is gluten free. Rotla is millet flatbread. Thalipeeth are yellow pancake-like breads made from a seasoned millet flour and yogurt batter tinted with turmeric powder. Look for the Nirav, Meera, Ghanti Chhap, Swad, and Laxmi brands in 2-pound paper or plastic bags. Store in the refrigerator in an airtight container for up to two to three months.

bajri flour

RAJI FLOUR

Nachna or red millet flour. It is milled from finger millet, a rushlike sedge with slender spikes that resemble cattails covered in tiny yellow seeds. It produces small, round grains with a reddish purple coat. Raji flour is grayish. It is blended with other flours in breads. A popular

South Indian pudding, raji puttu, is made by mixing a little water and salt with the flour until it resembles bread crumbs. This is mixed with grated coconut, sesame seeds, palm sugar, fried cashews, and cardamom powder. Then it is steamed. The cake is crumbled and then

served with melted ghee. Malted raji is a beverage powder that is mixed with powdered barley, sugar, and cardamom. Called Ragimalt, a few teaspoons are blended into a cup of warm or cold milk. Look for the Lakshmi brand in 7-ounce blue-pink boxes. For raji flour, look for the Swad and Nirav brands in 14-ounce bags. Store it in an airtight container. It can be refrigerated for up to three months.

ragimalt

JOWAR FLOUR

This is juwar or cholam flour. This is milled from pearl-like grains that grow in stubby ears on a tall sorghum type of plant. The tiny, greenish tan grains have a slight indent on one side, sort of like a kernel of corn. Whole, dried jowar grains are also sold. They are usually found in the refrigerator case. To use jowar, soak and boil it like rice, or use it in soups and stews. Jowar flour is creamy white to yellowish, and has a dry, wholesome taste. It is used to make jowar breads, called bhakris, which are cooked on a griddle and served with coconut, garlic, and dried, red-chili chutney. This is the common man's staple in rural Maharashtra, where jowar is less expensive than wheat.

Jowar flour is also used to coat foods before frying to give them a crispy outer shell. It can also be used in place of rice flour to make dosa (crepes). When kneaded with hot water into dough, it makes tasty chapati. Batta kaap are crispy, fried potato snacks made from thick slices of peeled potato that are dusted in jowar flour, seasoned with chili powder and salt, and deep-fried. Look for the Jalpur, Nirav, and Swad brands in 14-ounce, 2- or 5-pound paper or plastic bags. Whole jowar grains are sold in 1-pound bags under the Vardan brand. Refrigerate both the grain and the flour in an airtight container for up to three months.

CORNMEAL & CORNSTARCH

In India, corn is called maize. After all, it was introduced by the Portuguese. It is grown mainly for grinding into a mealy flour, called makkai ka atta. When the dried kernels are coarsely milled, cornmeal is produced. Finer milling produces cornstarch. Cornstarch, also labeled as corn flour, is white, powdery, and very soft. It has a mild taste. When it is dissolved in water and heated, it turns translucent. It is used to thicken curries without altering the color or flavor. Cornstarch boiled with milk and sugar sets to make creamy puddings. It is always first dissolved in a cold liquid to make a smooth paste. Then it is added to the hot liquid to cook it. Cornstarch is made by Nirav and Swad in 2- to 5-pound bags.

Cornmeal is coarse, grainy, and light yellow. It adds a chewy, homey texture to breads and pancakes. It is also used to coat foods for frying, producing a crisp crust. Cornmeal is added to batters for fritters and some vegetable dishes for texture. Pithachi mirchi is green bell peppers cooked with spices, dry-roasted cornmeal, grated coconut, sesame seeds, and a little water into a thick stew. Look for the Swad and Nirav brands.

Legume Flours

In India any dried bean, pea, or lentil is called dal. While chickpeas are the most commonly used dal for besan flour, several other dried legumes are also made into flours and used to add flavor, texture, and nutritional value to breads, batters, pancakes, and fritters. Following are dal flours found in Indian grocery stores. All will keep 5 to 6 months if stored in a dry, cool place in airtight containers.

MATHA FLOUR

This is a flour ground from moth dal, which are tiny, olive brown, seedlike beans similar to mung beans. Look for the Kanaiya, Sun, and Swad brands in 2-pound bags.

MOONG FLOUR

Also called dhamta flour, this flour is made from dried, skinless, split, and ground mung beans. It is often used as a thickener or to dust foods for deep-frying and to make dal-paste vadi chunks. Look for the Jalpur, Swad, Sun, Nirav, and Laxmi brands in 2- to 5-pound paper or plastic bags.

MUTTER BESAN

This is a pale yellowish or off-white flour made from dried, ground, yellow split peas. It is used in deep-fried snacks, breads, and as a thickener in curries and sauces. Look for the Sun brand.

URAD FLOUR

urad flour

This is also called papad flour as it is used to make pappadam wafers. Urad flour is made from dried urad black lentils that have been skinned and split. They are then ground, producing a slightly grainy white flour (only the skins are black, once removed the legumes are off-white). Urad flour is mixed with rice or wheat flour to make dosa crepes, uttappam (thick pancakes), steamed idli cakes, and roti breads. A whipped paste made of the flour is used to make phulboris, which are small, white, dried dumplings. Look for the Nirav, Jalpur, Laxmi, Swad, and Sun brands.

BUCKWHEAT FLOUR

Singoda flour or kutu atta. Buckwheat is not a type of wheat or a true grain, although it is milled and used as such. Buckwheat is a triangular-shaped seed from a cereal plant in the rhubarb and sor-rel family. The hard outer shell of the notched seeds are removed, leaving the triangular seed, or groat. Roasted groats may be famil-iar to you as kasha. Unroasted buckwheat groats are ground into a slightly gritty flour with gray flecks of the hull mixed with the grayish tan flour. It is highly nutritious with a strong, nutty flavor. Since it contains no gluten, it is always mixed with other flours or cooked with green bananas or potatoes in bread and cake doughs. Buckwheat dishes are eaten during special fasting days when grains are to be avoided. It is used to make kotu pakora raita, which are puffy, deep-fried buckwheat fritters mixed into spicy yogurt. Seasoned buck-wheat flour batter is used to coat half-cooked potato slices. Which are deep-fried to make koto aloo pakoras. Buckwheat flour is often found in the refrigerator case to keep it from turning ran-cid. It can be refrigerated in an airtight container for up to four months. Look for the Swad and Laxmi brands.

buckwheat flour

RAJAGRO FLOUR

Amaranth flour. This is made from tiny, pale yellow seeds of the leafy, green amaranth plant. The whole seeds are called rajgira, and they are cooked as a cereal or added to pilafs. The seeds are ground into a buff-colored flour with a faintly grassy, earthy flavor. It is high in protein, low in fat, and contains very little gluten, so it is added to other flours in bread doughs and batters. Rajgira seeds are sold by the Swad brand in 7- and 14-ounce bags. For rajagro flour, look for the Swad and Nirav brands.

SINGHAR ATTA

This is water-chestnut flour. Also called paniphal, this is a grayish, powdery flour made from water chestnuts, which are harvested from the lakes of Kashmir. The sun-dried, shelled tubers are ground into flour and used in batters, flatbread doughs, and sweet puddings. The flour gives a lovely sheen to the liquids that it thickens and a crunchy texture to foods that are coated in it and deep-fried. Dishes made with singhar atta are also suitable for no-grain fasting days. Look for the Swad brand in 14-ounce bags.

TIKHOR

This is arrowroot starch. This is a fine, white, powdery starch extracted from the rhizomes of a tropical plant with arrow-shaped leaves. The rhizomes are crushed and washed in water to obtain a milky liquid. The dried liquid yields fine grains of starch that are used as a thick-ener like cornstarch in sauces and glazes. The advantage is that arrow-root starch thickens at a lower temperature. It is also used as a binding agent. For example, it is used in mashed lentil and potato patties for deep-frying or in vegetable cutlets. Look for the Swad brand in 14-ounce plastic bags.

Sago

Sabudhana. Also called javvari. Sago pearls are small, hard, white balls made from the starch that is extracted from the pith of the sago palm, which is similar to tapioca. When sago is cooked, it changes from opaque white to translucent. The taste is bland with a creamy, slippery texture. Sago is used to make sabudhana kheer, a milk pudding flavored with cashews and cardamom. Subudhana khichdi is a savory fasting dish eaten from June to September when devout Hindus eat no meat or fish. This dish is made from sago, root vegetables, peanuts, and green banana. Sago is cooked with spices, palm sugar, roasted peanuts, and grated coconut. It is served hot, sprinkled with lemon juice.

Sago is also soaked until mushy and made into sweets, or it is kneaded with seasoned mashed potatoes into a dough, shaped into patties, and pan-fried. In South India, sago starch is used to make small pappadam wafers, called sabudhana poha, or papad that look like transparent cornflakes and are sometimes tinted pastel colors. Just before serving they are deep-fried into crispy puffs. Look for the Ashoka and Swad brands. They are also often found in unlabeled, clear-plastic bags. Sago pearls are sold by Maya, Swad, and Patel Brothers brands in 2- to 5-pound bags.

Sago Starch Products

FAR-FAR

You will see some other dried products based on sago starch. What looks like dull brown pasta shells, macaroni-like tubes, and colored, flat, square chips are dried far-far made from sago starch and potato flour dough. There are also multicolored, round and star-shaped, hollow tube bits. These are made from tinted sago starch and potato flour dough squeezed through a special press, cut into little segments, and dried. Both types are dropped into hot oil where they instantly puff up. Far-far is eaten as a snack and served like pappadams with meals.

far-far

It is sold in plastic bags. Look for the Virani brand's round tube bits or flat, square chips and for the Ramdev brand's stars or squares. Look also for Laxmi Fry 'Ems colored bits, Ashoka spiced-potato pappad chips, Maya shell pappad, Mayur yellow tubes, and Patel onion-flavor pipes in small bags.

SAGO PAPPAD

These are thin, crispy, white and multicolored, round wafers with a nubby texture. They are made of sago starch, rice flour, and tiny sago pearls. They are deep-fried into puffy pastel crackers, eaten as a snack, or served with meals. You may find translucent, crosshatched,

sago pappad

brownish chips made from sago starch and potato flour, which are also deep-fried into puffs. Look for the Swad, Lion, or Maya brands in cellophane-wrapped rolls of about 14 round wafers. Look also for the Nirav brand's potato wafers and jeera (cumin) far-far in 7-ounce bags.

FALOODA SEV

These look like thick, pastel strands of cellophane that are wound into loose coils in small plastic bags. The stiff, noodlelike strands are made from tinted sago starch and are used to make the favorite dessert drink of Indian Muslims and Parsis. Falooda is a cold milky beverage that is made from sweetened milk flavored with rose cordial syrup (called sharbat gulab) mixed with falooda sev (soaked in hot water about five minutes to soften), and bits of agar jelly or subja (soaked basil seeds). The final touch is to float a scoop of vanilla ice cream on top. Look for the Sai Kripa and Swad brands.

Stocking Up

The larger the store, the better the selection of fresh breads. But most stores have the basics. Choose a package or two of fresh chapati, plain or stuffed roti, and a pack of puris to fry at home. Stock up on packages of frozen naan—they keep well and you can just reheat the number of pieces that you need. Naan can also be used as a base for pizza. Try grilling naan or melting cheese on a piece under the broiler. Add some packets of pappadam or far-far for snacks and a bag of vadi nuggets for quick meals. Cracked wheat and semolina are handy to keep in stock for cereals, pilafs, and puddings. Finally, depending on how ambitious you are, you might want to pick up some chapati or a flour blend and try making your own breads.

3

Legumes & Dals

Hindi word for "dal"

In India, dal literally means "split beans," but it is a generic term used to describe all dried legumes and pulses: peas, beans, and lentils. Dal also refers to the cooked dish of legumes or beans that accompanies most Indian meals. Dal-based dishes provide essential proteins and are one of the cornerstones of Indian cuisine. They are eaten every day at almost every meal. You will find whole or split dals, with or without skins. You will also find polished lentils, called dhuli or washed dal. Most dals have a mild but distinct taste and texture. Dals are very versatile and are used in main-dish meals, soups, stews, snacks, and sweets. Dals are a sauce for rice and a dip for bread. Some kinds are germinated to produce sprouts or are fermented, puffed, or fried. Dals absorb the flavors that they are cooked with—from subtly seasoned oils to complex, fiery-hot masalas.

Dal can be a thin broth or a thick stew. In North India, dals are thick and hearty for scooping up with bread; those made in the south and eaten with rice are thin and soupy. Split dals cook much faster and produce a creamier texture than whole ones. Most dals must be soaked in cold water for several hours or overnight to soften them before cooking. The consistency of dal depends on how much water they are cooked in. Never add salt or acid ingredients such as lemon juice, vinegar, or tomatoes to dal while cooking, or they will never become tender. Add the salt or acid substance at the very end, once the dal is soft. The last step in making dal is to stir in seasoned oil or ghee. This is called tempering, or vaghar. A few teaspoons of oil are heated in a small pot with mustard or cumin seeds. When the oil starts popping, fresh curry leaves or whole, dried chilies are added. When the oil smokes, a pinch of hing (asafoetida) powder is added (it helps reduce gas), and the smoky oil is poured into the dal. The dal should sit covered for a few minutes to let the vaghar settle and to release the flavors of the spices. Before serving, the dal is stirred to mix in the seasoned oil. You can remove the whole chilies if you want—they are very hot if you bite into one.

Dal is eaten with other foods as part of the meal, but it can be served as a first course, like soup. Dried legumes have a long shelf life, but older ones will take longer to cook. Buy ones that look smooth, not shriveled. All imported dals need to be carefully picked to remove any small stones or bits of twig. Dals have a prominent place in Indian grocery stores. Bags of various types, ranging from small, pink lentils to black urad dal are neatly stacked on shelves. Many grocery owners have their dal bagged with stickers with just the store's name and dal type. Nationally distributed brands that carry most every kind of dal include Swad, Chirag, Nirav, Kishan, Laxmi, Patel Brothers, and Vardan. The bags are clear plastic so that you can see the size, shape, and color of the dal. Bag sizes range from 1 to 5 pounds, except for the very popular toovar dal, which is found in 10- to 20-pound burlap or cloth bags. After purchasing, transfer dals to glass jars. They can be stored for up to six months. Following are the dals found in Indian grocery stores, listed from most popular to lesser used.

TOOVAR DAL

Toor, arhar, yellow lentil, or pigeon peas. They are sold skinned and split into two round halves. Toovar dal is the most widely used dal in India. You will find two types: dry and oiled. The oily kind look glossy and are coated in castor oil to preserve them for long storage. They have to be soaked in hot water and rinsed before using. Dry and oiled types taste the same. Toovar dal is pale yellow to gold, and it has a

toovar dal

pleasant, slightly sweet, nutty taste. It cooks fast and is highly digestible. Soak the dal for 3 to 5 hours before cooking. It is usually cooked whole, but it can be pureed after soaking to make batters. Toovar dal is a staple of South India. It is used in sambhar, a spicy dal, and vegetable soup. Masala dal is a thick, hearty toovar dal cooked with chopped onions and seasoned with garam masala. Mooli dal subzi is toovar dal cooked with finely chopped white radish and spices. It can also be cooked with grated coconut and tamarind paste or with shredded carrots and spices. A squeeze of lemon and chopped, fresh coriander leaves are often used to garnish the dal after the seasoned oil is mixed in. Toovar dal is used in the rasam soup recipe on page 252.

BENGAL GRAM

Channa dal or Gram lentil. This is the most widely grown dal in India. It is a matte-yellow color and resembles toovar dal, but it is slightly larger with a stronger flavor and a sweet, nutty aroma. Bengal gram should look plump and bright yellow. Soak it for 8 hours or overnight before cooking. These legumes cause the most flatulence, so they are always cooked with a pinch of hing. They can be simmered with chopped onions, spices, tangy tamarind, or garlic. They can also be cooked with meat in spicy curries such as dal gosht. Bengal gram is often stewed with vegetables, especially bottle gourd and squashes. Cooked with palm sugar and ground into a paste, it is made into sweets or used as a stuffing for pancakes called puran poli. It is also puffed, becoming light, porous, and crunchy with a roasted-nut taste. This is added to snack blends. In the southern state of Kerala, a harvest festival, Onam, is celebrated in September with water carnivals, parades, boat races, and much feasting. A delicious Onam dish is channa dal payasam, a sweet made by cooking gram lentils, palm sugar, grated coconut, cashews, and raisins in ghee. In general, gram lentils are associated with festivals in India.

Onam is the symbolic day that the good king of old, Mahabali, returns from exile in the nether regions to visit his beloved people. Colorful floral decorations are arranged each morning in family courtyards to welcome the king. The city is lit up at night with strings of lights that look like electric jasmine garlands. Keralites sport new clothes, visit friends, and exchange gifts. The week of events culminates in a grand parade that is led by gold-clad elephants and by a troupe of young men in white uniforms holding aloft a rainbow of silk umbrellas.

KUBLI CHANNA

White chickpeas, Punjabi channa, chole, or garbanzo bean. These are large, spherical, creamy tan peas with a peak at one end and an indent at the other. It is the most important legume grown in India. It has a thick, wrinkled skin that comes off during soaking and cooking. Chickpeas have a strong nutty flavor and creamy texture. When soaked (8 hours or overnight), they nearly double in size. They are boiled whole before using in curries, rice pulaos, stews, salads, or chutneys. Chickpeas absorb the flavorings and spices that they are cooked with and are delicious with garlic, onions, and chilies. They give any dish they are added to a thick, creamy consistency. They can be used in yogurt-based salads (raitas), in tossed green salads, or as a garnish sprinkled over rice or vegetable dishes. Puree them with garlic and spices to make dips, and add them to soups and stews. Channa Chor is a crunchy snack made of toasted, flattened chickpeas flavored with black salt, red pepper, and citric acid.

kubli channa

A Sikh favorite at special festivals is choley-bhature. This is chickpeas cooked until creamy with spices and eaten with bhature, which are huge, round puffs of deep-fried bread. You may also see dried, pale green, small chickpeas. These are called green choliya and are dried, immature chickpeas. They have a delicious fresh pea like taste. Soak and cook the same as you would chickpeas. They are good in salads or plain with a little butter and salt. Look for the Nirav brand's choliya in 2- or 5-pound bags. All the major brands have white chickpeas. They are used in a chickpea curry stew recipe on page 245.

> The first day of Barsha, the Bengal monsoon season, is celebrated with kichuri, a special dish of rice, lentils, and spices (khichdi or kichidee elsewhere). Kichuri is associated with rain and is made anytime there is a heavy downfall. Each grain of rice and lentil should be fully cooked yet remain distinct, not mashed together, which takes careful watching of the pot. The British kedegree, the mixture of rice, smoked fish, and hard-boiled eggs eaten for breakfast, is based on kichuri.

KALA CHANNA

These are wild peas or black chickpeas. They are a cousin to white chickpeas and have the same shape, but they are smaller and dark brown. After harvesting, they are sun-dried until dark reddish brown. They have thick skins, a strong earthy aroma, and a pleasant, nutty taste. Kala channa is sold whole and needs to be soaked overnight before cooking. Kala channa is cooked with ginger, garlic, chilies, grated coconut, and spices into a thick stew. It is eaten with bread or rice. The peas color the liquid that they are cooked in, resulting in rich, brown curries. In October the festival of Dussera is celebrated, honoring the goddess Durga. Women dress in their best sarees, and families attend music, dance, and theatre programs. Each region makes special Dussera feast foods. In Maharashta, a small, puffed, puri bread made of rice flour is served with spicy, kala channa curry that is topped with roasted coconut chips.

MASOOR DAL

masoor dal

These are red lentils. Whole lentils with brownish green skins are called matki or bagali. There are also whole or split, skinless, salmon pink lentils. They are small, flattish, and round. Split red lentils have a delicate, nutty flavor. The whole ones are chewier with a musky, earthy taste. When cooked, they turn golden yellow. Split red lentils are the fastest-cooking dal and only need to be rinsed. They cook in about 20 minutes. Whole ones take longer to cook, but soaking several hours reduces the cooking time. Red lentils are often cooked, mashed, added to minced-meat curries, and seasoned with strong flavorings such as ginger, garlic, fenugreek seeds, tamarind, and curry leaves. They can also be sprouted and cooked. Skinless, whole, or split red lentils are versatile. They are good cooked with onions, grated coconut, and spices, or with chopped vegetables into thick, creamy soups or stews. Red lentils are used in the dal recipe on page 244.

URAD DAL

This is black gram or black lentil. It is sold in three forms. Whole ones, called sabat urad, are small, oval-shaped, ivory lentils with gray-black skins used in curries and vegetable dishes. Split, skinless ones, called white gram, are creamy white. They are used in purees and soups or are ground into flour for breads, crepes, steamed cakes, and sweets. Split ones with skins are called chilke urad, and they are used the same as the skinless ones. They are grayish with flecks of dark green and have black skins. No soaking is needed for urad dals. They cook quickly, in about 25 minutes. Black lentils with skins have a strong, raw, earthy smell and a rich, heavy flavor. Split, skinless ones have a floury aroma and bland taste.

All types, especially split ones, release an unctuous, gluey liquid that gives the finished dish a thick, creamy texture. Split black lentils are cooked with rice or added to seasoning oils, then browned with mustard seed, spices, and chopped onions to add a nutty taste and chewy texture to vegetable dishes. Dal makhani is a smooth, rich dish made from whole urad dal cooked with black-eyed peas and cream that is garnished with spicy, fried onions. In North India, black lentils are cooked whole, often

urad dal

combined with red kidney beans, to make the Punjabi festival food maa di dal, a rich dish served with plain rice and butter. In South India, black lentils are ground and blended with ground rice which is then fermented. The batter is used to make dosa (crepes), uttappam pancakes, and idli (steamed cakes). For a dosa recipe, see page 241.

MOONG DAL

These are mung beans. Whole, tiny, oval beans with olive green skins are called sabat moong. They have a stronger flavor than split ones. They are chewy with an earthy flavor and are mainly used for sprouting and in thick dals, which are served with soupy vegetable dishes. Soak whole ones 5 to 6 hours before cooking. Split moong dal without skins are light yellow and flattish. They don't need to be soaked and are easy to cook and digest. The split beans are boiled and mashed in porridges, soups, stews, and sauces. They become somewhat glutinous when cooked, lending a creamy texture to dishes.

To make pancake and fritter batters, the split beans are soaked overnight and ground with water, or after soaking and draining they are deep-fried and added to crunchy snack mixes. Moong dal kitchri is rice cooked with split mung beans. They are also cooked with ghee, sugar, nuts, and spices to make sweets. Split mung beans with skins are called chilke moong and are mainly used in vegetable curries and chutneys. Unskinned, split mung beans are also used to make tangy khata moong. Boiled beans are mixed with buttermilk or yogurt blended with garlic paste, salt, turmeric, cumin, and lemon juice. It is cooked uncovered (to prevent curdling) until creamy, which takes about 20 minutes.

DRIED PEAS

There are two varieties of dried peas: green (pattani) and white (wantana). Skinned and split peas are called muttar or matar dal. Vantana are whole peas, which are also used for sprouting. Whole ones are round, slightly wrinkled, and yellowish white or olive green. Split peas are two rounded halves. When cooked, dried peas are chewy with an earthy taste. Avoid buying discolored, soft, or shriveled peas. They should be even in color and very hard. Soak 8 to 12 hours before cooking. The peas absorb water and swell. They then can be used in soups, curries, or salads.

Split peas are cooked with garlic, grated coconut, and spices. The mixture is added to rice dishes and pulaos or cooked with grated potato, cream, and spices to make malai muttar. Whole, soaked, and

dried peas

drained peas are deep-fried and added to crunchy snack mixes. Whole peas are often cooked with cubes of paneer cheese or chunks of potato, or they are sprouted and added to stir-fries with spices and fresh vegetables. To sprout dried peas (or any bean), soak them 8 to 10 hours, place them in a colander lined with paper towels, and cover them with more towels. Pour several cups of water over them, which will drain off. Cover the colander with a plate to eliminate light. Pour more water over the peas three times a day to keep them moist. In about three days they will sprout to 1 inch in length. Rinse and simmer them in water with a pinch of salt and baking soda, covered for about 1 hour.

KIDNEY BEANS

These are called rajma. They are large, dark, maroon beans with an almost meaty aroma and a full, chewy flavor. The thick skin has a slightly sweet taste. Rajma beans should be bright in color, shiny, and smooth. They take a long time to cook, even when soaked overnight. For convenience you might want to substitute canned beans. Kidney beans must be carefully cooked because the skin contains a toxic resin. This is eliminated by boiling them rapidly for 15 minutes, then simmering them until they are tender and completely done. Many Indian cooks use pressure cookers to ensure this and to reduce cooking time.

Cooked kidney beans are delicious with onions, lamb, and tomatoes or in vegetable curries and salads. Try them in a salad with chopped red onion and coriander leaves. Toss the salad with lemon juice and a pinch of sugar, then cover it in oil seasoned with mustard seeds and curry leaves. In Kashmir roadside stalls sell Kali dal to

kidney beans

Today in Bombay lunch is delivered by a vast network of dabbawallas, which are fleets of men in white dhotis and Ghandi caps. Over 1,000,000 specially marked dabbas, or "everhot" tiffin carriers, are collected from suburban housewives and transported to the desks of office workers for the noon meal. Tiffins are round, metal, stackable containers that are clamped together by a handle. Each tier holds rice, a favorite dal, and curries. The dabbawallas then reverse the process, returning the tiffins to the owner's homes after lunch. The word "tiffin" comes from the slang British word "tiffing" which means eating or drinking between meals.

devotees visiting the temple there, which is dedicated to the goddess Vaishno Devi. Kali dal is a creamy, kidney-bean, black lentil curry that is spooned over rice and sprinkled with chopped coriander leaves. Some grocery stores also sell a lighter red, slightly smaller type of kidney bean. Nirav has both kinds. Look for Swad, Patel Brothers, and Vardan for dark red beans.

BLACK-EYED PEAS

These are lobia or cow peas. Husked and split, they are known as chowli dal. They are medium-sized, buff-colored, kidney-shaped beans with a small dark spot, or "eye," on one side. They have fairly thick skins, a subtle, nutty aroma, a creamy, rich, earthy, almost buttery taste, and a creamy texture. Buy plump, smooth, unbroken beans. Old ones have a brownish tint and are wrinkled. Soak them overnight before cooking. They can be cooked with grated coconut and curry leaves, which is South Indian style, or with mustard seeds, chopped onion, ginger, and garlic as in the north. Whole ones are added to vegetable curries, while split beans are used in soups or stews to add a creamy consistency. Black-eyed peas are also added to rice pulaos and salads. Dried, split ones are ground into flours for batters. Black-eyed peas are a favorite fasting food on days when only pure, unspiced foods are eaten, because they taste delicious and rich without any seasonings. They are equally in demand during celebration feasts, when they are added to spicy curries.

black-eyed peas

MUTH DAL

Moath, matki, mot, tepary, and dew bean. These small, elongated beans have a brownish green skin and yellow interior. They are sold whole or split, with or without skins. Split ones are yellow and look like smaller mung beans. They have a strong, earthy aroma and a rich nutty flavor. Because muth beans are so small, they have to be carefully examined for small particles or stones. They do not need to be soaked, and they cook in a little over an hour. Muth is cooked with grated coconut and spices, or it is boiled and pureed into thick soups. Sprouted muth is stir-fried with spices. It is eaten with bread or as a snack mixed with crunchy, toasted sevian noodles. Soaked, drained, and deep-fried muth is enjoyed as a crunchy snack or sprinkled over curries.

PAVTA BEANS

These are lima or butter beans. They are large, off-white, flattish, kidney-shaped beans. They have medium-thick skins, a pleasant, nutty smell, a buttery flavor and a smooth texture. Avoid buying ones that are discolored or broken. Soak them overnight before cooking. They are good cooked with grated coconut, red chilies, and tamarind, then garnished with crispy, fried garlic. Try them combined with eggplant, potatoes, or meat in curries. Or use them in thick stews. Pavta patties are made from boiled lima beans kneaded with mashed potatoes and spices into a stiff dough,

shaped into flattened balls, rolled in flour, and shallow-fried until crispy and golden.

pavta beans

They are delicious dipped in hot, sweet tamarind chutney. Lima bean dishes are often served at South Indian wedding banquets.

Hindu wedding feasts in South India feature a long parade of vegetarian foods that are served to hundreds of guests on individual banana leaves. A constant procession of servers brings out dish after dish, starting with a small sweet that is followed by nine or more courses. The meal includes a variety of pickles, mounds of rice, seven vegetable dishes, lima beans, dal, pappadams, yogurt salad, and a rice pudding.

VAL

Valor, lablab, and hyacinth bean. These are small, oblong, plump, creamy, buff-colored beans with a thick, white, ridged stripe on one side. They come from the flat pods of valor green beans. The dried beans are sold whole or split, and they must be soaked overnight before cooking. Val has a nutty aroma a creamy texture and a slight, but not unpleasant bitter taste. The thick, chewy skins should be rubbed off after soaking.

val

Val is cooked with spices and vegetables in curries or with grated coconut, palm sugar, and ginger. It is also sprouted and added to soups or salads. In the Gujarat state, val is a favorite with the mostly vegetarian population. Soaked, sprouted val is stir-fried with chopped green chilies and grated coconut, or is cooked with eggplant, drumsticks (long-bean pods), and spices, then eaten with chapatis.

RED CHORI

red chori

These are adzuki beans. These are small, oval, dark, reddish brown beans with a strong, unusually sweet flavor and a creamy texture. They have to be soaked for 5 hours or overnight before cooking. They can be used in place of mung beans or whole urad dal in any recipe. Red chori is good cooked with spices in pulaos or vegetable curries. It is also boiled and pureed in thick soups sprouted and added raw to salads, or stir-fried with spices and fresh vegetables.

KULITH

This is horse gram. This hardy legume is grown in many regions of India, and it is a staple of farmers' diets, providing essential proteins. Kulith are small, oval-shaped, and reddish gold with a slight greenish tint. They look a little like masoor lentils, but they have a stronger flavor and the aroma of fresh-cut hay. Soak them for 8 hours before cooking. Cook with grated, roasted coconut and crushed black pepper or fried garlic, mustard seeds, and spices. Kulith saar is a thin, hot, sour soup made with water that the gram has simmered in. The soft, cooked beans are used in vegetable curries. Soaked, sprouted kulith is stir-fried with grated coconut and spices, or it is added to salads and curries. Dried kulith is ground into a grayish brown powder and made into thick soups served with rice and ghee.

Stocking Up

Stock up on several dals for a full range of tastes. Toovar dal is the workhorse of the Indian kitchen. Add some to your shopping cart to use in dals, soups, curries, and batters. Chickpeas are a must for thick stews, salads, and creamy dips. Add a bag of quick-cooking red lentils or mung beans. Then select a pea or bean—green peas and black-eyed peas are good choices—and experiment by choosing a new dal, such as val or muth, on each trip.

Making dal from dried legumes and pulses takes some time for soaking and cooking, but the taste is worth it. Play with various seasonings and spices to create mild, creamy dishes or peppery-hot, richly flavored dals. Once the beans, peas, or lentils are soaked and boiled, you can use them in many dishes and taste combinations. Cooked Dals develop with age and taste even better a day or so later. You might want to cook a large batch and freeze half of it in plastic containers. Just thaw and reheat it for quick meals.

4

Spices & Seasonings

Hindi word for "spices"

Indian food uses more spices than any other cuisine, with a dozen or more often used in one recipe. Many spices are native to India, which is the largest exporter of spices in the world. But "spicy" does not have to mean "hot." Vivid flavors characterize Indian foods, but chili levels are adjusted to suit personal tastes. It is the skillful use of spices that transforms ingredients into a synthesis of complex, aromatic, and delicious dishes.

Indian cuisine is as varied as the geography of the country, with great regional differences reflected in the dishes from each area. Many of the same spices are used, but they are manipulated differently. In the north of India, whole spices are dry-roasted, then ground, and added while cooking. In the south whole and powdered spices are blended into a wet paste and used in cooking. Cooks in the north add a pinch of garam masala (a blend of ground spices) at the end of cooking. Cooks in the south finish off a dish with a seasoning of curry leaves, mustard seeds, and dried chilies sizzled in coconut oil.

Spices are used whole, ground, fried, or roasted. They are also mixed in yogurt as marinades. One spice can alter the flavor of a dish, while combinations of several in varying proportions will produce totally different flavors and textures. Spices in the Indian grocery store include dried berries, bark, seeds, roots, rhizomes, leaves, flower buds, and chilies. Each spice has its own unique culinary and medicinal property. Some are used mainly for flavor, others for their aroma. Many are ground into powders, others are used whole. Some season meat or bread dishes, while others go with delicate fish or vegetables. Several, such as saffron, cinnamon, and cardamom, are used in both savory dishes and desserts. The same spice may be roasted, ground, or popped in oil for different flavors within the same dish.

Seasonings add depth, subtle tastes, and aroma. These range from a tangy green-mango powder to a pungent-smelling, powdered resin called asafoetida (hing). Seasonings are combined with spices to create richly layered flavors and fragrances. In India cooks usually buy whole spices and grind them at home on stone slabs. It is, however, much more convenient and quicker to buy ready-ground spices. Indian grocery stores stock a full range of both whole and ground spices and seasonings. You can purchase electric spice grinders in the cookware aisle if you want fresh-ground spices. All spices should be transferred from bags or packets to clean, airtight jars and then stored in a cupboard away from light. Some companies sell spices in plastic shaker jars. Whole spices will keep fresh for about three months to a year. Buy ground spices in small packets or jars to retain freshness, and use them within three to four months. For some recipes the spices need to be roasted. To dry-roast spices, add them to a heavy pan that is set over low heat. Roasting brings out the flavor. Stir the spices constantly and remove them from the pan once they smell fragrant, as scorching turns them bitter.

Brands that package most of the following spices are the following: Swad (in 14-ounce bags and 3.5-ounce shaker jars), Nirav (in 7- and 14-ounce bags), Maya (in 7-ounce shaker jars), Patel Brothers (in 2- and 4-pound bags), Suraj (in 7-ounce packets), Sona (in 7-ounce bags), Chirag (in 3.5-ounce packets), Laxmi (in small packets), Jayshrees (in small packets and 14-ounce bags), Eastern and Diamond (both in 7-ounce bags), and Nishaka and Kishan brands (both in 14-ounce bags). Other brands for specific seasonings and spices are listed under the individual heading. Rather than mentioning every popular brand under each heading, refer back to this page to check the major brands that are available. Stores stock several brands, but not all of them, depending on their distributor. Medical uses are at the end of each heading.

AJOWAN

This is also called ajwan, ajwain, carom seed, or bishops weed. It is made of tiny, very pungent seeds of the lovage herb. It is closely related to caraway and cumin. The small, brownish, oval, ridged seeds look like miniature cumin seeds with fine bits of stalk attached. The

ajowan

taste is sharp and slightly bitter with thyme, pepper, and oregano overtones. The fragrance is similar to cumin. Ajowan is used sparingly due to its strong flavor. It is often added to dals or dishes made with chickpea flour to aid digestion. The seeds are used in breads, vegetable pickles, green beans, and root vegetables. Its bitingly hot taste is mellowed by cooking with other ingredients. Ajowan is also added to batters for frying fish. It adds zing to deep-fried, crunchy snacks like chickpea flour sticks and potato balls. Ajowan contains thymol, an antiseptic, and it is chewed to ease stomachaches, flatulence, and diarrhea. The seeds are sold whole or powdered. Look for the TRS brand in 3.5-ounce packets with a green label.

ALLSPICE

Kababchini. This is made of the small, dried, unripe berries of a tall evergreen that is indigenous to the West Indies, but which is grown in Kashmir and other parts of India. The berries are picked when green, and they turn dark purple as they dry. Allspice has the flavor and fragrance of cloves, nutmeg, black pepper, and cinnamon rolled into one spice. The dried berries are about 1/4 of an inch in diameter with a slightly textured surface. The ground spice is fine and rust colored. Allspice has a sharp, mildly sweet flavor that adds a warm note to dishes. It is mainly used in North Indian cuisine, and it is the secret ingredient in many rich curries and biryanis. Allspice is used in spice pastes for grilled chicken and kheema tikki, a minced lamb patty. It is also used in relishes, chutneys, and preserves or to scent and flavor tea. The whole berries are crushed or powdered before using. They may be added whole to biryanis, but they are not eaten. Allspice helps relieve diarrhea and flatulence.

AMCHOOR

Also called khatai powder, amchur, or green-mango powder, this is powdered green, unripe mango. In Hindi, aam means mango and choor is powder. It also comes in dried slices. Raw, sour green mangoes are peeled, sliced, and dried in the sun. It is sold as light-brown, shriveled slices that look like pieces of wood or as a dark tan, lumpy powder with a sweet, musky, raisin aroma. Both have a tart flavor and are used as a souring agent in dals, soups, vegetable dishes, chutneys, and pickles. The dried kind has to be pulverized to use. Amchoor can be added to a dish either before or after the main ingredient is added to hot oil. When added before, it imparts a deep flavor; if added afterward, the taste is more subtle.

Amchoor is also sprinkled over meats to tenderize them prior to cooking, and it is added to the crumb coatings for fried fish. It is delicious fried with cumin seeds, turmeric, and chopped green chilies to flavor cauliflower or potato dishes. Okra is slit and stuffed with a bit of amchoor powder and garam masala. Then it is braised. Amchoor powder is the main ingredient in hot and sour chaat masala. It adds a special tang to snack salads called chaats. It is added to samosa and to savory pastry stuffings. The powder is sold in small packets and boxes, while slices are sold in plastic bags. Both will keep up

amchoor

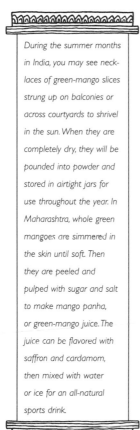

During the summer months in India, you may see necklaces of green-mango slices strung up on balconies or across courtyards to shrivel in the sun. When they are completely dry, they will be pounded into powder and stored in airtight jars for use throughout the year. In Maharashtra, whole green mangoes are simmered in the skin until soft. Then they are peeled and pulped with sugar and salt to make mango panha, or green-mango juice. The juice can be flavored with saffron and cardamom, then mixed with water or ice for an all-natural sports drink.

to a year if stored in a clean dry jar. Look for the National Foods brand's khatai powder in boxes and for the Sinha Trading Company brand in packets. Look also for the Swad brand in small jars and 7-ounce bags and for the Eastern brand in 7- and 14-ounce plastic packets. Amchoor powder is used in the chaat masala recipe on page 237.

AMLA

Also known as nellikai, emblica, or Indian gooseberry, this is the dried fruit of a small deciduous tree grown all over India—and in the Rajas' garden to the side of the store. It is very important in India as a rich source of vitamin C and in herbal treatments for both the body and hair. The pale green, lobed, translucent, sour berry is sometimes available fresh, but it will mostly be found in dried form. You will often find bags of shriveled, roundish, flat pieces in the ayurvedic section. They are dark golden on the interior with a blackish brown skin and dark seeds. There can also be chopped, pitted bits in bags. The pieces and bits have to be soaked for 2 hours before using. Reconstituted amla has a

amla

sour, tingling taste. It is used as a souring agent in soups, curries, and dals. The fresh berries are made into chutneys, sweet-sour preserves, and herbal tonics.

ANARDANA

This is made of dried pomegranate seeds. Small, sun-dried kernels of a wild Indian pomegranate, called daru, are used as a souring agent. Anardana has a sour smell and a tangy, slightly dry, astringent taste. It is available as whole seeds or powdered. The hard, wine-colored, sticky seeds cling together and have to be coarsely ground before using. The

anardana

powder is lumpy and reddish brown with the texture of dried tea leaves. Either form adds tang to curries, dals, chutneys, and vegetable dishes. Channe ki misal is a Punjabi-style chickpea-potato salad flavored with chopped onion, minced red chilies, ground pomegranate seeds, black pepper, salt, and lemon juice. The seeds are also added to lamb dishes or sprinkled on yogurt salads as a garnish. The seeds are soothing to the stomach and good for the heart. Look for Ahmed whole seeds in small boxes and the TRS brand in 3.5-ounce plastic bags. For the powdered form, look for the A-1A, Badshah, MDH, or Shan brands in small boxes or packets.

ANISEED

Vilayait sanuf. This is made of tiny, oval sage and khaki seeds from an herbaceous plant with clusters of lacey, white flowers. It has a strong, aromatic, sweet-licorice flavor with a slightly bitter, zesty bite. When dry-roasted, which increases the fragrance, the taste becomes bittersweet. Aniseed is used to heighten the flavor in meat curries. It is sizzled in hot oil and poured over dals and vegetable dishes as a finishing garnish. Aniseed is sold both whole and powdered. The powder is used in desserts or added to coffee and tea. It is chewed on its own or blended with fennel and roasted coriander seeds in breath-freshening mixtures. Aniseeed is a digestive and diuretic when simmered in boiling water for a few minutes and sipped. Longer boiling destroys the digestive properties. It is also used as an insecticide.

aniseed

ASAFOETIDA

asafoetida

This is also called hing or perukaya. It is made of dried resinous gum from the rhizomes of several species of ferula, a giant fennel that grows in India, Iran, and Afghanistan. The name comes from the Persian word "asa" for "gum" and the Latin "foetidous" for "stinking." Because of its incredibly pungent and offensive smell, it is aslo referred to as "devils dung." It is the product of a tall, smelly herb with strong, carrot-shaped roots. In the spring, just before flowering, the stems are cut near the root. A milky sap flows out and is collected over a period of three months. This is sun-dried into solid lumps. The fresh resin is pinkish tan, changing with exposure to oxygen to a milk-chocolate color.

It is sold in pure lumps, tightly wrapped in paper or a tin box. A powdered version is sold in small plastic containers, packets, or shaker jars. There are two types: finely ground mustard yellow powder and sandy brown, coarse granules. The powder types are milder. They are cut with rice flour and turmeric. The granules are ground lumps. To use the lump type, chip off a tiny bit and crush it in a mortar with a pestle. To use the powdered type, lift a small pinch out on the tip of a blunt knife and add it the cooking pot. You can also press a small piece of the pure resin into the inside lid of a pan in which you are cooking food. The steam melts the gum, permeating the food with its flavor.

Asafoetida smells like very rotten eggs due to its sulfur compounds. It is a very powerful seasoning. Just a pinch imparts a truffle-like essence to any dish it is added to and rounds out the flavor. The strong smell fades with heating. Asafoetida dissipates gas from legumes and beans, making them lighter and more digestible, so it is often added to dals. Hindu Brahmins and Jains use it in place of the prohibited garlic and onions in their cooking, as it adds a similar pungency. In the days of moghul rule the court singers of Agra and Delhi would arise at dawn, swallow a spoonful of asafoetida mixed with ghee, and practice along the banks of the Yamuna River. It was believed that asafoetida enhanced the singers' melodic voices.

It is especially good in potato, lentil, or chickpea dishes. It is often added to pickled vegetables. Asafoetida helps flatulence and respiratory problems such as asthma and bronchitis. Brands to look for are Vandevi in small, blue-and-yellow packets, L.G. Laljee Godhoo & Co in small, white plastic shakers, Cobra in little, round, yellow plastic boxes, and Sonali in white, round plastic jars with green caps. Let your nose guide you in this section of the store—you can't miss the pungent fumes. Asafoetida is used in the chaat masala recipe on page 237.

BLACK CUMIN

black cumin

Shah zerra, siyah, kala jeera, and royal cumin are some of the names for this spice seed from a wild-flowering herb that grows in the mountain regions of North India. The ridged seeds are dark-coffee brown to blackish, and they are slightly smaller and thinner than its close cousin, cumin seed. Black cumin is mainly used in the cuisines of Kashmir, Punjab, and Uttar Pradesh. During monsoon season a traditional folk cure for the aches and pains of the flu, kalo jeera bharta, is concocted with black cumin. The spicy-hot relish is made from roasted black cumin, crushed and fried garlic, and green chilies ground into a paste. It is mixed with mustard oil and salt, eaten with plain rice, and washed down with hot, cumin-infused tea.

It has a distinctive herbaceous aroma and a complex bittersweet taste with caraway overtones. It is more expensive than regular cumin, and it is used dry-roasted and ground in small quantities. Black cumin seeds are used in spice mixtures to flavor dals, curries, pulaos, and biryanis. It is also used in cooling digestive drinks. The roasted, ground powder can be sprinkled over yogurt soups or raitas. It is sold whole or ground. Look for the Laxmi and Maya brands in small packets.

BLACK SALT

Kala namak. This is also called saindhav or rock salt. Black salt is mined from soft-stone quarries in central India. The irregular crystals, which range from translucent amber to dark reddish brown, have smooth, glossy surfaces where cleaved. Finely ground, powdered black salt is pinkish gray. It is rich in minerals and has a smoky, sulphureous aroma and a tangy taste. Black salt brings out and heightens flavors in foods. It adds zip to a multitude of deep-fried snacks and chaats, such as hot, sour, and savory salads made with seasonal vegetables, tossed with spices, and smothered in hot, sweet, and tart chutneys.

black salt

Black salt is also added to chilled yogurt raitas and salads. Try it sprinkled on slices of tart green apple or mango. On hot days, nimbu sharbart, a sweet, sour, salty, spiced lemonade is made from lemon juice, sugar, and black salt to combat dehydration. Both crystalline and powdered black salt are sold in small packets, shaker jars, or boxes. The powdered salt is the most convenient to use, but it is not quite as flavorful as the whole crystals. The powder tends to be a little gravelly, as bits of earth clinging to the crystals get ground with it in processing. The crystals have to be dissolved in liquid or crushed in a mortar and pestle before using. Black salt will last forever if stored in a clean, dry container. It is recommended for people with high blood pressure or on low-salt diets because it does not increase the sodium content of blood. It also helps ease heartburn and flatulence. Look for the Deep brand pure powdered black salt in 4-ounce packets with a green label. Also Swad brand in 7-ounce packets. Black salt is used in the chaat masala recipe on page 237.

CAMPHOR

Kacha karpoor. Pure, edible camphor is a crystalline compound that resembles coarse salt. It is made from a steam distillation of the aromatic leaves and wood of cinnamomum camphora, an evergreen tree that grows in China and India. The spice is sold wrapped in paper in small boxes, jars, or packets. It has a strong, slightly sulphureous, cardamom aroma. Tiny pinches of it are used as a flavoring agent in milky desserts and sweets to add aromatic fragrance. Look for the Swad brand in 3-ounce jars. You will also find inedible camphor lumps. These are burned in puja fires (arti) to add fragrance.

CARAWAY

Siya jeer. These small, elongated, curved, ridged seeds are brown, hard and sharply pointed at each end. Caraway is a close relative of cumin, dill, and fennel. Caraway seeds have a dill-like, pleasant smell and an aromatic, sharp, slightly bitter, stinging taste. When chewed they leave a warm feeling in the mouth. Caraway is sold whole and ground. It is mainly used in North Indian cuisine to flavor bread, cakes, and paneer curd cheese. Caraway complements meats and poultry. It is added to rice pulaos. Caraway seeds are chewed to freshen the breath and to aid digestion. It is considered a cleansing tonic for the kidneys, and it relieves flatulence and nausea. The essential oil is used in mouthwash and to scent soaps.

caraway

CARDAMOM

green cardamom

Elaichi and kapulga. There are two distinct types of cardamom. One is the oval, light green pod, which is also chemically bleached and sold as white cardamom, and the other is a larger, dark brown, beetle-shaped, wrinkled pod called kali illaichi, or black cardamom. Both are members of the ginger family. The best cardamom comes from Kerala in South India. Green cardamom is often called "queen of the spices," and it is one

black cardamom

of the most valued and costly spices in the world. Only saffron and vanilla are more expensive. Not to worry, the small packets sold in Indian grocery stores will not cost you more than a few dollars. Green cardamom pods are picked just before ripe and then dried. The light green pods encase fifteen to twenty small, round, black seeds that are slightly sticky and cling together. The seeds are ground into powder or coarsely crushed to release their volatile oils. This also releases a strong camphorous fragrance. The flavor of cardamom is sweet and zesty with a hint of eucalyptus. For subtle flavor the whole pods are added to rice pulaos, simmered dishes, puddings, and sugar syrups. It is best to lightly bruise whole pods first so that their fragrance will permeate the dish.

Freshly ground cardamom is used to flavor both savory and sweet dishes. It is added to rich curries, biryanis, and desserts. Tea and coffee are spiked with cardamom. Green cardamom is sold ground or in pods. Buy whole pods with the freshness sealed in. Ground cardamom rapidly loses its aroma and flavor. Look for plump, evenly colored pods. To remove the seeds for grinding, toast the pods in a dry pan. Split them by gently thumping them with a pestle. Remove the seeds and pound them into a fine powder. If you purchase a large bag of pods, store them in the freezer and use as needed. Some stores also sell small amounts of decorticated cardamom (seeds only) or cracked seeds, but they are much more expensive.

Black cardamom is available as seeds in the pod or ground. The large, oval, dark brown pods are never used in sweet dishes as it has a hot, peppery, medicinal flavor. The whole pods are slightly crushed to release the warm aromatic flavor, and they are added to biryanis, pulaos, and meat curries. Look for the Ravi and Swad brands' black elcha in 7- or 14-ounce bags.

Cardamom is used to relieve stomach disorders and is a digestive. Gargling with cardamom-steeped water helps a sore throat. Drinking it in tea eases a headache. Cardamom pods are chewed after heavy meals as a digestive, and the seeds are added to breath freshening mixes. All the major brands package green cardamom pods, seeds, and powder.

Keralu came into existence, the legends say, when the god Parasurama hurled his axe into the raging sea, forcing it to retreat. The land uncovered was Kerala, a place born of the sea and blessed with an abundance of foodstuffs and spices. Kerala's economy is based on over 350 miles of curving, palm-shaded coastline with its bustling harbors, intricate system of backwater canals, and mountain-fed rivers. Exports include coconut products, tropical fruits, seafood, coffee, tea, black pepper, cashews, cinnamon, and the world's finest cardamom.

CASSIA BARK

Jungli dalchini, or Chinese cinnamon. Cassia bark comes from a tall, tropical, flowering laurel tree that is native to

Myanmar, China, and Northeast India. The tiny, yellow flowers produce a small fruit, which is dried and sold as cassia buds. The rough, corky bark of the tree is harvested just after the monsoon season when it is easy to peel off. The outer part is scraped off, and the remaining bark is dried into large curls, which are called quills. Cassia bark is dark reddish brown on the outside and lighter and smooth on the inside. It is often confused with cinnamon, and some countries export cassia bark as cinnamon. It smells like cinnamon, but it is much harder and rougher. The taste is bittersweet and astringent. It is sold in small, curled pieces or ground. Don't try to grind the bark yourself because it will break the blades of your food processor or spice

> Bengal is the only part of India where food is served in separate courses. The order is based on age-old beliefs that relate to the aid of the digestive process. Bitter leaf and gourd dishes come first, followed by fish fritters, plain rice, dal, chutney, fish soup, vegetable curries, and fish that is often eaten by so-called vegetarian Brahmins. Finally, there is a sour ambal relish as a palate cleanser, and the meal concludes with a milk-based sweet.

grinder. Cassia bark or powder is used to flavor curries, rice, and vegetable dishes. It goes especially well in lamb dishes and rich biryanis. Cassia bark is not used in desserts due to its bitterness. Cassia buds are also used in cooking. One little, tan bud is often used to fasten betel leaf envelopes like a button.

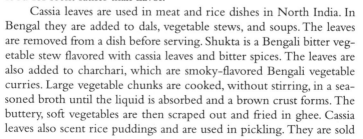

cassia bark

CASSIA LEAF

Tej patta. Also called Indian bayleaf, these are the large 4- to 8-inch-long, dried, brittle, light tan leaves of the same tropical laurel that produces cassia bark. The trees grow in the hill stations of Northeast India at high altitudes. Small branches of the leaves are dried in the sun and tied in bundles to be sent to market. The leaves resemble large bay leaves but have a totally different flavor. They are fried briefly in a little oil to release the pungent, sweet, woodsy aroma that has a hint of cinnamon. The leaves are added to food for scent rather than flavor.

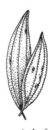

cassia leaf

    Cassia leaves are used in meat and rice dishes in North India. In Bengal they are added to dals, vegetable stews, and soups. The leaves are removed from a dish before serving. Shukta is a Bengali bitter vegetable stew flavored with cassia leaves and bitter spices. The leaves are also added to charchari, which are smoky-flavored Bengali vegetable curries. Large vegetable chunks are cooked, without stirring, in a seasoned broth until the liquid is absorbed and a brown crust forms. The buttery, soft vegetables are then scraped out and fried in ghee. Cassia leaves also scent rice puddings and are used in pickling. They are sold whole or in pieces. Look for leaves that are even colored and free of mold. Cassia leaf-steeped water relieves diarrhea and flatulence.

CAYENNE PEPPER

Psi hui. This is the well-known red powder made from sun-dried red chilies. The very hot, almost seedless, thin-skinned chilies are usually lightly roasted before being ground. Cayenne is named for the city of Cayenne, which is in French Guiana on the northeast coast of South America. In the spice trade it is known as "ginnie pepper." It is a long, thin, curved, red berry, as are all chilies, that tapers to a pointed tip. It no longer grows in French Guiana but it is cultivated in many other places around the world, including Louisiana (where Tabasco is made), the Caribbean, Europe, Africa, India, Thailand, Korea, Japan, and China. The peppers traveled in the holds of Portuguese ships and were planted wherever the sailors went, spreading this gift to the world.

Depending on the type of chili used, the powders range from reddish orange to brick red, but they are all extremely hot. India is the largest exporter of cayenne, much of it coming from Rajasthan where the chilies are dried in huge, red mounds in the blistering heat. Cayenne powder is sold in various-sized bags, packets, and shaker jars. Cayenne is used in almost all spicy, savory dishes in India, from dal and curries to korma sauces and tandoor meats. Try cayenne and salt sprinkled over fried wedges of potato or mixed into a chilled yogurt raita. Cayenne is used to relieve sinus problems and bronchitis. It reduces inflammation, relieves lung congestion, and strengthens the heart. Take a teaspoon with honey when you have a cold.

The prophet Mohammed, founder of Islam, was a spice merchant before he heard Allah's higher calling. As a young man he worked with Meccan spice traders, eventually becoming a partner in a Mecca shop. He traded exotic spices from faraway lands and essential oils for perfume. He had a successful and lucrative spice business established long before the Muslim religion spread along the spice routes to India, Indonesia, Malaysia, and Sri Lanka.

CELERY SEEDS

Ajmud. These are tiny, light, tobacco colored ridged seeds. They come from Indian celery, which is a descendant of a wild herb called smallage. The seeds have a strong celery smell, a bitter, slightly cuminlike flavor, and a sharp bite. Celery seeds are sold whole because they are rarely used in ground form. They go well with tomatoes and are used in tomato-based curries, sauces, soups, and salads. They are often sprinkled over breads before griddle-cooking or baking. Try the seeds sizzled in oil to release the aroma or blended into yogurt or salad dressings. Celery seeds are a tonic for asthma, and an infusion of the seeds in hot water is used to calm the nerves. They are added to commercial birdseed. The essential oil is used in making celery salt, a common Western seasoning.

CINNAMON

Dalchini. This is known as kurundu in Sri Lanka, which is the world's largest producer of what is considered by connoisseurs to be the finest cinnamon in the world. Cinnamon is the dried inner bark from the cut upper branches of a tropical laurel tree that is native to Sri Lanka. The trees are cultivated on huge plantations there. Its botanical name is cinnamomum zeylanicum, a reminder of the Dutch name for the island, Zeilan, which later changed to Ceylon. Cultivated trees are kept pruned to keep both the shoots narrow and easily accessible and the bark thin and soft. The bark is harvested after the monsoon season, when the trees' aromatic oils are at their peak, and then taken to a processing plant. The outer bark is scraped away and the paper-thin inner bark is peeled off. This inner bark rolls naturally into quills. As it dries, smaller pieces are fitted into larger ones until a 3-foot "pipe" is formed. These pipes are tied together in 300-pound bundles for shipping. During grading some quills break and are sold as quillings.

In India you can have your horoscope cast the old-fashioned way: by kili josyam, or parrot astrology. Men squat along busy streets with their trained green parrots in cages, while nearby, several cards with pictures of various deities lie face down. To determine your future, the bird is released from its cage, and it grabs one of the cards with its beak. Each of the deities matches a chapter in an ancient text written by a sage. Perhaps the parrot's diet of birdseed laced with celery seed has something to do with its psychic ability.

Sri Lankan cinnamon is buff colored with a rich, fragrant aroma and a sharp, sweet aromatic flavor. The cinnamon from Kerala in South India is mahogany colored, tightly rolled, and shorter. Both types are available as sticks (quills), quillings, and ground. When buying cinnamon sticks, make sure that there are no broken or chipped ones. It is best to grind cinnamon at home because the powder loses its aroma and flavor fairly quick. Cinna-

cinnamon

mon is added to both savory and sweet dishes. It flavors pulaos, biryanis, rich curries, meat dishes, and desserts. It is an essential spice in garam masala, the secret spice blend that is used in many Indian recipes. Tea and coffee are often laced with cinnamon. All true Sri Lankan curries, fiercely hot or mild, include a cinnamon stick simmered in the sauce. Cinnamon infused in hot water relieves nausea and stimulates digestion. It is also used in incense, toothpaste, and perfume.

CITRIC ACID

Nimbu ka sat or limbuphool. Also called sour salt, this is either fine, white, shiny powder or large crystals of natural citric acid that are extracted from lemon juice or made by fermenting glucose. Citric acid has no aroma and a sour taste. The powder is mixed with water to make homemade curd cheese or brushed over the surface of cut fruits to prevent them from darkening. The small, white crystals are ground with sugar, salt, spices, and green-mango powder to be sprinkled over fried snacks. It is also added to snack blends such as chidwa or Bombay mix. It

citric acid

provides a sour taste without moisture. Citric acid is sold in small packets or jars. Look for the Gul Bahaar and Swad brands in 3.5-ounce packets of crystals or for the Ziyad brand in 7-ounce jars.

> It is interesting to note that Pierre Poivre, an artist, scholar, and naturalist who traveled widely in the Far East, was hired by the French East India Company in 1748 to gain a piece of the lucrative clove trade. His name, Poivre, was especially auspicious for someone going into the spice trade. The French word for grocer is "epicier" and originally came from the English "pepperer," or spice merchant. In the Middle Ages a grocer sold only spices. In France, merchants whose specialty was the pepper trade were called poivriers.

CLOVES

Laung. Cloves are dark brown, nail-shaped, dried buds of a tropical evergreen that is native to the Moluccas, or Spice Islands, which is now a part of Indonesia. Interestingly, the name comes from the French word "clou," which means "nail." The French were once the biggest importers of the spice, using it in perfume and to flavor foods. Cloves are dried, unopened flower buds that grow in small clusters. The full-grown, green buds are sun-dried until dark brown and hard. The buds have a long cylindrical base, crowned by a small, light brown ball, encircled by the 4-spiked calyx. Cloves are very aromatic with a slightly numbing, sharp, warm flavor. They are used sparingly as the strong flavor can overpower a dish.

Cloves are sold whole and ground. Ground cloves are one of the spices in garam masala, and they are added to many other spice blends. In India cloves are used in meat, rice, and some dessert dishes. Cloves add a spicy note to North Indian pulaos. Try stir-frying shrimp with cloves, turmeric, cayenne, black pepper, ground coriander, and minced onions. Garnish the shrimp with chopped, fresh coriander leaves. The cloves are not actually eaten, but removed or pushed to the side of the plate. Cloves are a favorite toothache remedy, and they are used to relieve nausea and indigestion. They are often chewed after a heavy meal.

cloves

CORIANDER SEEDS

Dhania. Also called sookha or sabut, these are the small, dried, pale, grayish, round spice seeds of coriander, an aromatic herb. The seeds have a pleasant, sweet smell and a clean, lemony flavor with pine and pepper overtones. They are sold whole, crushed (kuria), or powdered. Coarsely crushed and ground coriander seeds are used extensively in Indian cooking. It is a major component of many ground spice mixtures, curry powders, and curries. The flavor complements many foods without overpowering the other flavors in a dish. When used whole the seeds are fried in oil to release the volatile oils. Before grinding or crushing, the seeds should be gently dry-roasted to bring out the flavor. Grind or crush just the amount you need so that it is fresh. Powdered coriander seed tends to be stale and musty tasting. The ground, roasted powder is added to curries, soups, chutneys, and yogurt-based drinks and salads. Whole or crushed seeds are added to dals, biryanis, and pickles. An infusion of the seeds in hot water helps reduce fevers. It also aids digestion, reduces flatulence, and eases headaches. When you have a bad cold or the flu, drink tea made with crushed coriander seeds and fresh ginger-root slices. Dhana dal is made of split, flat, roasted coriander seeds. It is chewed as a breath freshener.

coriander seeds

CUMIN SEEDS

Jeera, zeera or safed zeera. These are small, elongated, curved, ridged, pale-ochre to olive-green seeds of a plant in the parsley family. Cumin seeds have a distinctive, earthy, peppery fragrance and a warm, toasty, slightly bittersweet flavor. It is available whole or ground. Cumin seed is one of the most widely used spices in India. The seeds are used in rich meat curries in Kashmir, in hot coconut curries in the south, and in the fish dishes of Bengal. The combination of ground cumin and coriander seed makes dhana-jeera, one of the essential spice blends in Indian cooking.

cumin seeds

To make your own cumin powder, dry-roast the seeds until they darken. Then crush them in a mortar and pestle. Roasting enriches the earthy flavor and fragrance. Most Indian curries begin by sizzling cumin seeds in hot oil before the other ingredients are added. Cumin seeds are used in dals, soups, curries, and meat or vegetable dishes. Roasted cumin powder is sprinkled over salads or blended into yogurt raitas and drinks. A refreshing sweet-sour digestive drink, pan jeera (cumin water), is made from tamarind juice and water blended with sugar, salt, and dry-roasted cumin powder. The drink is garnished with a lime slice and mint leaves. Cumin seeds ease indigestion and flatulence. The spice is steeped in water and taken for colds and fevers. With honey added it soothes a sore throat.

CURRY POWDER

The word "curry" may have come from the Tamil word for sauce, "kari." Curry has come to mean almost any gravylike, spiced dish from India. The original, mild to hot, aromatic, yellow spice powder was blended from freshly roasted and ground spices. In South India this spice mixture, or masala, is made from cumin, black-mustard seeds, fenugreek seeds, dried chilies, curry leaves, black peppercorns, coriander seeds, and turmeric, which gives curry powder its characteristic yellow hue. Commercial curry powders are pale imitations of the real thing, and no self-respecting Indian cook would use them. Cooks in India do not use just one generic blend of curry powder for all dishes. They change the mixture, depending on what is being cooked. For example, different spice blends are used for a fish or meat dish. Meat dishes generally have cinnamon, cumin, and cardamom. Fish dishes use fenugreek and curry leaf.

Curry powder is used in curries, soups, and dals. It is also used as a seasoning for fried fish and meat. Khari is a thick buttermilk or yogurt sauce for moistening and flavoring rice. It is made from curry powder and chickpea flour blended with water. It also flavors samosa fillings. Curry powder is either dry-roasted, or it is made into a thick paste with a little water, then fried with oil and onions to release the fragrance. When you need curry in a hurry, use the commercial blends. They are available as hot or mild in bags, packets, tins, or shaker jars. To make your own South Indian-style curry powder, see page 238. Commercial brands include Agmark, Banana Leaf, Bolsts, Mehran, Rajah, Sonali, Vardan, and Vafa.

By the end of the 19th century, ready-made curry powder was being sold in Indian towns. Then an Englishman named Sharwood dined with the maharajah of Madras, who told him about a shop owned by a famous maker of curry powder. Mr. Sharwood visited the shop and learned the Madras curry powder formula. While in Bombay he had tasted a condiment known as chatni, a sweet-sour pickle that he called chutney. He returned to London with a license to import these two specialties. Soon both Sharwood's curry powder and chutney were available throughout Europe.

DILL SEED

Sowa or surva. These are light brown, flat, oval seeds from an herbaceous plant. Dill seeds are aromatic and similar to caraway in taste, with a sharp, tingly, faintly citrus flavor. Dill is mainly sold whole, but it may be found ground. It is best to buy whole seeds and crush them just before using to release essential oils. Dill seeds are used to flavor breads, soups, and sauces. They are used in meat, vegetable, and lentil dishes. They flavor some cakes and pastries. Dill seeds are especially good in lamb or spinach dishes. Dill is used to relieve stomach aches, flatulence, and nausea. A hot infusion of the seeds with honey is effective for colds. Dill water is taken by women after childbirth.

DRIED CHILIES

Sabat lal mirch. Sun-dried pods of a variety of chilies fill a large section of the Indian grocery store. Drying chili peppers concentrates

dried round chilies

their power, making them fiercely hot. They vary from bright red to dark reddish brown. They range from 1 to 3 inches in length. Kashmiri chilies are large, dark red, and short. Dubby chilies are finger-length and crinkled. Sannam chilies are bright red, long, slim, and smooth. There are cherry-sized, round Tinnevelly chilies. There are stubby, pointed Goan chilies. There are lantern-shaped, volcanic Habanero chilies. And there are heart-shaped, orange red, crinkled Dundicut chilies from Pakistan.

Large chilies tend to be slightly milder than the small ones. Most of the intense heat is in the seeds. If the seeds are removed, the chilies' fire is tamed. You can poke a small opening with a sharp knife near the chilies' top and shake out the seeds. Be careful when handling chilies or wear rubber gloves, as the oils can burn or irritate your eyes and skin. Dried chilies can be used whole or broken into pieces in dals, soups, and curries. Whole chilies are often soaked before using. This softens the skin and reduces the pungency. Soaked chilies are pounded to a paste before cooking. They add a deep red color and kick to curries. Dahi chilies have been soaked in a mixture of yogurt and salt, then sun-dried until pale to dark brown. To use the chilies, fry them in oil until blackened and crisp to make chili tairu, which is crunched like pappadams with rice.

Whole, dried chilies are dry-roasted until brittle, then ground to a coarse powder and used in spice blends. They can also be used as a condiment, mixed with salt and sprinkled over dishes. Crushed chilies are also available. They are very hot because the dried seeds are mixed in equal amounts with the flecks of dried skin. Both whole and crushed chilies are fried in oil or ghee with other spices, then added to cooked dishes as a final seasoning. They are sold in various-sized plastic bags and will keep up to a year if stored in a dry, dark place. You may also find packets of stuffed chilies. These are large, split green chilies, about 3 inches long, that are stuffed with a spicy dal paste and dried. To use, soak until softened and sauté in oil. They are eaten as an accompaniment to meals. They are also pickled. Chilies stimulate the appetite, destroy toxins, and purify the blood. All chilies are high in vitamin C. For stuffed chilies, look for the Mayur brand in 3.5-ounce bags. For round Tinnevelly chilies, look for the Chirag and Bansi Deep brands in small bags. The Chirag, Swad, and Laxmi brands offer various types of whole and crushed chilies in packets and bags that range from 7 ounces to 25 pounds.

dried chili

FENNEL SEED

Sanuf. These are the dried seeds of a large, dill-like, perennial plant that has clusters of tiny, yellow flowers. The seeds are the ripe, dried fruit of the flowers. The ridged, greenish-yellow seeds look like large, curled cumin seeds and are very aromatic. They have an intense, sweet, licorice flavor with a zesty bite, which turns mellow and bittersweet when roasted. The best quality comes from Lucknow. It is called lakhnavi sanuf and is olive green. Fennel seeds are sold whole or ground. Look for evenly colored seeds that are not broken. Avoid bags that contain a lot of stem bristles. Fennel seeds add richness to meat and fish curries, zing to vegetables, and sweetness to desserts. They go especially well in lamb or potato dishes. Malpuri are golden, crispy sweets smothered in a fennel flavored sugar syrup. Gaja are flaky diamond-shaped deep-fried pastries flavored with crushed fennel seeds. Refreshing drinks are made with fennel infusions. The seeds, plain or candy-coated, are offered as a breath freshener after meals. Fennel seeds are a digestive, stimulate the appetite, and help the body digest fatty foods. Fennel water makes a good eye wash. For roasted and dried Lucknow fennel seeds, look for Swad brand in 7- and 14-ounce packets. All the major brands have regular fennel seed.

FENUGREEK

Methi or ventayam. These very hard, square, angular, ochre seeds are actually a sort of tiny, dried pea from the fenugreek plant. The seeds are legumes. The plant produces slender pods containing about 20 seeds each. The dried seeds are used as a spice. They are sold whole, crushed (kuria), and ground. The seeds have a deep groove along their length and smell like curry. They have a bitter, burnt, sugar flavor and are a powerful spice. The flavor is tempered by frying them in

fenugreek

oil for a few seconds or by dry-roasting them. Be careful not to let them turn reddish brown and burn, as this intensifies the bitterness. After roasting the seeds are easy to crush. Roasted, ground fenugreek is an essential component of curry powder. It is added to the hot spice mixture, muligapuri, which is eaten with griddle breads. Whole or crushed seeds are used in hot and sour soups, dals, vegetable and bean dishes, pickles, and fish or seafood curries. Ladoos are sugary balls of besan flour flavored with fenugreek. In South India it is used in batters, breads, chutneys, and lentil dishes. In Kashmir, lamb is stewed with fenugreek and ginger, then eaten wrapped in thin breads with kebabs. Fenugreek seeds add a sweet aroma and fragrant flavor to simmered kadhi (yogurt curries). Fenugreek seeds aid digestion and relieve diarrhea and chronic coughs. It is believed that fenugreek seeds promote lactation. Recent research shows that they may lower blood cholesterol and blood sugar. Fenugreek extract flavors imitation maple syrup. Look for the Dishaka brand in 14-ounce bags.

KASHMIRI PLUM

Alu bukhara. This is a small, wine black, wrinkled, dried plum that resembles a small prune. The semisoft flesh contains a large, light-brown pit. It is slightly sticky with a raisin aroma and tart, sweet taste. The plums are grown in Kashmir and Pakistan. They are sun-dried until shriveled after picking. They are used whole in

kashmiri plum

biryanis or are added to curries and slow-cooked meat

dishes as a souring agent. Watch for the pit when eating dishes that contain the plums. They are also used in chutneys and pickles. They are sold in plastic bags. If stored in an airtight container in a cool, dry place, they will keep for up to a year. Look for the TRS brand in 7-ounce bags or for the Swad brand in small packets.

KOKUM

Black deshi. Also called cocumful and fish tamarind, this dried, sour fruit rind of gamboge, which is also called butternut berry, is a bright orange yellow fruit of a large evergreen tree, Garcinia purpurea. The fruit is about 1 inch in diameter. It turns deep purple when fully ripe and has five to eight large seeds. The ripe fruits are picked, the rind is removed, it is soaked in juice from the pulp, and it is sun-dried. It may also be dried over wood smoke to make a black, tart, smoky seasoning called kodampoli, which is used with fish in South India. Unsmoked kokum is dark purplish black, semisoft, and slightly sticky with curled edges. Kokum and kodampoli both need to be rinsed, sliced, and soaked briefly. Kokum can stain your clothes, so handle it with care. You may also find halved, dried, dark, reddish brown curled pieces with seeds visible in the chambers. This is called cocumful. It has to be soaked until soft before using, which takes about half an hour.

All types are used as an acid ingredient, infusing a tart, fruity flavor to dishes. When cooked, it imparts a lovely lavender color to foods. It smells sour but tastes fruity. Buy the darkest rinds as they have the best flavor. Kokum is added to fish and seafood curries. It is also used in pickling and preserving fish. Kokum juice is rubbed onto fish to remove fishy odors. The sourness of kokum balances sweet, coconut-based curries and adds acerbity to fish curries, cutting the fattiness of oily fish like tuna and mackerel. Kokum is also added to sweet-sour dals, and it is cooked with okra and root vegetables. Solkadi is a soupy, pink curry made from simmered coconut milk that is tinted and flavored with kokum, salt, garlic, and coriander leaves, then spooned over rice. Kokum also is used in fruit juice punches. The rinds are steeped in sugar syrup and diluted with water to make amruthkokum, which relieves sunstroke. Look for the Suraj brands cocumful (halved dried fruits) in 3.5-ounce bags. Laxmi has 7-ounce plastic-wrapped packets of the rind. Swad has both types in small packets.

kokum

MACE

Javiti. This is the lacy, scarlet membrane that envelops the hard kernel inside the nutmeg fruit. The mace, or aril web, is removed, pressed flat, and dried. As it dries it changes from bright tangerine to a dull orange or sandy brown. Mace is sold whole as aril, cut into slivers called blades, or ground into a yellowish brown powder. Mace has a sweet perfume that is similar to nutmeg and a bittersweet, delicate flavor. Mace is hard to grind because it is oily, so it is roasted until brittle, then ground with other spices. It is one of the spices in garam masala. Mace blades are added to spicy curries, meat dishes, rice pulaos, and biryanis. It infuses desserts with a fragrant aroma. The blades are removed before serving. Mace powder is used in creamy, milk-fudge sweets. A few mace blades boiled in water and steeped about 10 minutes eases nausea.

> Mustard seeds are believed to ward off evil, so Indian mothers cancel any negative forces floating around their children by praying over them with a fistful of the tiny seeds.

MUSTARD SEEDS

Rai or sarson ke beenji rai. These tiny dark seeds are from an Indian mustard plant. They are essential to Indian cooking. They are used in pickling and season everything from a simple dal to complex curries. The seeds range from brownish purple to reddish brown and have a sharp, bitter taste. When mustard seeds are added to hot oil, they sputter and crackle, giving off an acrid aroma and developing a mild, nutty sweetness in the process. Mustard seeds are only used raw in Bengal, where they are ground with water, chilies, and ginger into a paste. This is added to sinus-blasting, bitter vegetable stews, soups, and fish dishes.

Mustard seeds are sold whole or split. The split seeds are called mustard dal or kuria. They are also powdered and crushed into a moist paste. Whole seeds, split seeds, and ground powder are sold in bags, packets, and jars. The paste is found in large glass or plastic jars, often in the pickle section of the store. The tiny, split seeds look like miniature yellow lentils and are used in pickling, as is the powder. The thick, yellow-red paste is a blend of split mustard seeds and spices in mustard oil. It is used in pickling, fiery marinades, and fish curries. Whole mustard seeds are popped in oil to start a recipe and in seasoned oils poured over finished dishes. Sizzled mustard seeds are also blended into yogurt raitas. Most Indian cooks use only brown mustard seeds, but you can substitute the pale tan variety, which is also sold in Indian grocery stores. They are less bitter and milder in flavor. Mustard seeds stimulate the appetite and are good for the skin.

mustard seeds

NIGELLA SEEDS

Kalongi, Calonji, or charnushka. These are very tiny, pointy, black seeds of a small herb that is related to a popular garden plant, love-in-a-mist. The herb's pale blue flowers ripen into capsules that are collected, dried, crushed, and sieved to obtain the seeds. They are often called onion seed because of their flavor. Nigella seeds have an aromatic, nutty, faintly bitter, distinct onion taste. The seeds are sold whole in small packets. They are roasted and crushed or ground just before using, or they are sizzled in hot oil before the other ingredients are

nigella seeds

added. They impart an onion flavor to breads, yogurt raitas, salads, vegetables, lentils, and chutneys. Marinate some shrimp or fish chunks in a vinegar and turmeric solution, and lightly stir-fry it with nigella seeds, garlic, chilies, and curry leaves. Sizzled nigella seeds, cumin, and mustard seeds are delicious when mixed into grated white radish as a salad. Try the fried seeds sprinkled over steamed greens or baked potatoes. The seeds are a part of panch phora, a Bengali spice blend. Nigella seeds stimulate the appetite. A paste of the seeds is applied to skin blemishes and is said to relieve the sting of a scorpion. Look for the Sugam brand in 3.5-ounce packets.

NUTMEG

Jaiphal. This is the fragrant nut that is found in the center of the ripe, apricotlike fruit from a tropical evergreen grown in Indonesia, the West Indies, Sri Lanka, and India. The nut is encased in a shiny, brittle outer shell wrapped in a lacey web of aril, from which mace is produced. Once dried the shell is cracked open and the nut removed. Dried nutmegs are oval, slightly shriveled, and dusty brown. The interior is light-brown and speckled. Nutmeg has an intense, sweet, peppery, citrus aroma and a bittersweet flavor with fruity overtones. Nutmeg is sold whole or ground into a deep brown powder. Buy whole nutmeg, which is sold in packets or jars, and grate shavings off as you need them—the taste is incomparable. Powdered nutmeg quickly loses its aroma and flavor. In India nutmeg is used to flavor meats, curries, rice, and desserts. It is one of the essential spices in garam masala and other spice blends. Powdered nutmeg is sprinkled over rice and milk puddings, and it is used in milk-fudge sweets. Nutmeg is used medicinally for indigestion, rheumatism, and insomnia—it contains a mild hallucinogen (myristicin) that induces sleep. A paste of nutmeg powder is applied to skin blemishes. It is also considered, though not proven, to be an aphrodisiac.

> Along with cloves and black pepper, nutmeg was involved in the volatile wars of the spice trade. The Dutch controlled the Mollacus, or Spice Islands, and jealously guarded the secrets to growth and cultivation of the trees. The Dutch drove out the Portuguese, gaining a monopoly on nutmeg production and marketing that lasted for 200 years. During this reign the Dutch destroyed nutmeg that was found growing elsewhere. Eventually the British drove them out, and the humble nutmeg tree has since been transported throughout Indonesia and other tropical growing regions.

nutmeg

PAPRIKA

Deghi mirch. This is a red-orange powder made from dried, seedless, ground, ripe, sweet peppers grown in Kashmir. These chilies are similar to the ones used in Hungarian paprika. Because it contains no seeds paprika adds sweetness and a bright, red color to chilies but no heat. Paprika is fried in oil with other spices to release the aroma and temper the rawness of the powder. Paprika is used in dals and sauces in North India. It is sold in cans, packets, and spice jars. Be careful not to confuse paprika with the other red powder—fiery cayenne! Look for the Rajah brand in small cans and for Swad in 14-ounce jars and 7-ounce bags.

PEPPERCORNS

Black pepper is the world's most popular spice. It provided the heat in Indian food until chili peppers arrived on the scene in the 16th century. There are three forms of peppercorns that are obtained from a tropical vine that is native to India's southwest Malabar coast. Black pepper, known as kali mirch, is the dried berry of the vine. It is picked unripe and sun-

white peppercorns

dried until the skin becomes black and shriveled. This is the most commonly used pepper. It has a penetrating, aromatic fragrance and spicy, hot taste. Dried black peppercorns are sold whole, crushed (kuria), or ground. The aroma and flavor of freshly ground peppercorns is intoxicating. Buy large Tellicherry or Malabar peppercorns and grind them in a spice grinder or peppermill. Tellicherry peppercorns are the largest of all, and they are allowed to ripen longer and mature in flavor. Pepper flavors almost every curry, soup, and dal in India, and it is added to numerous spice blends. Whole peppercorns are sizzled in hot oil, then roasted and ground with coconut, spices, and a little water into a paste for grilling meats. Ground pepper is also added to tea.

White peppercorns, called safed mirch, are obtained by allowing the berries to nearly ripen on the vine. After picking they are placed in sacks and soaked in slow-flowing water for about a week, after which the skins are rubbed off. The flavor is in the outer skin while the pungency lies in the core, so white pepper is hotter but less aromatic. It is sold whole and looks like small, gray balls. It is also ground into a soft, pale, gray powder. White pepper is used in pale sauces to avoid speckling. Look for MDH white-pepper powder in small boxes.

Green peppercorns, called badi mirch, are the soft, immature berries, which are

> In Tamil Nadu, split yellow lentils are cooked daily to make sambhar, a hot and sour stew. When legumes cook, a thin liquid rises to the surface of the pot. This is skimmed off and seasoned with tamarind, ground black pepper, and spices. The thin broth came to be known as milagu tannir, which in Tamil means pepper water. A visiting Englishman was served this soup and mispronounced the name as mulligatawny. Thus an Anglo-Indian legend was born, eventually becoming the national soup of India.

picked in garlands off the vines. They are mild with a fresh, caperlike flavor. They are sold pickled in vinegar, bottled in brine, or dried. They are mainly used in canning and pickling. Look for the Ashoka brand's pickled green peppercorns in 11-ounce jars.

POPPY SEEDS

Khus khus. Called posto in Bengali, the poppy seeds used in India are small and ivory to pale yellow. They come from the capsules of opium poppies from which all the opium has been extracted. When cooked, white poppy seeds have a nutty aroma and flavor. They are always sold whole. Poppy seeds are used powdered, wet-ground, or whole. They are also dry-roasted or sizzled in oil to bring out the seeds' flavor. Because they have a high oil content, it is best to store them in an air-tight, refrigerated container. When lightly roasted and ground with other spices, they are used to thicken sauces, curries, and kormas.

In Bengal, wet-ground poppy seeds thicken bitter vegetable soups and stews. In Goa the seeds are roasted and ground with toasted coconut, chilies, and spices to make complex crab and shrimp curries called xacuti. Poppy seeds are used whole in some dishes for their grainy texture, or they are roasted and sprinkled over vegetables, salads, and breads. The seeds are also added to minced meat and kebab mixtures. Khus khus puri are puffy breads rolled in poppy seeds before deep-frying. Poppy seeds reduce fevers, inflammation, and stomach irritations. They are also considered to calm the mind and stimulate digestion.

SAFFRON

Zaffron or kesari. These are the handpicked stigmas, or threads, that are collected from the flowers of the saffron crocus. Saffron is the world's most costly spice due to its scarcity, fragility, and flavor. In India, saffron is also used in ceremonial worship. The golden color signifies enlightenment, illumination, and wisdom. Religious streaks on the forehead are made from saffron paste. Statues of Hindu deities are anointed daily with saffron paste to scent and decorate them. Saffron is also used as a dye to color the golden robes of Hindu and Buddhist priests. To produce 1 pound, 70,000 pale-purple flowers must be plucked at dawn just as the blossoms open, which is during the 2 weeks in late October that they bloom in Kashmir. Next, the 3 fragile threads of each blossom have to be carefully removed and dried. The dried stigmas are deep red and very brittle.

Saffron threads are sold in loosely matted, small amounts in little plastic or glass containers. They should be sealed, dated, and labeled to prevent adulteration. Saffron is also sold powdered, but steer clear as it has probably been cut with turmeric. The best saffron comes from Kashmir and is called mogra cream. The saffron in most Indian grocery stores comes from Mancha, Spain, which is also of very high quality. Saffron has an acrid, slightly sweet,

saffron

musky aroma with a strong, bittersweet taste. Saffron enhances savory and sweet dishes. A few strands are soaked in a small amount of warm water or milk, and then added along with the liquid to the dish. Saffron adds a fragrant richness to rice, braised chicken, spiced lamb, koftas, and milky desserts. Strained mango juice is flavored with saffron water. Saffron-infused biryanis and pulaos are served for special occasions.

Saffron is used to treat hypothermia during the winter in the Himalayas, and it is a digestive stimulant. Some believe it to be an aphrodisiac. Although it is expensive, it is affordable to use, as just a few threads flavor and color a dish. A small, flat box of about a gram of saffron will not be more than a few dollars. Look for the Swad brand in 1- or 2-gram plastic containers. Look also for the Gathering of Saffron brands pure Mancha saffron in 1-gram boxes tied with a red string.

SANDALWOOD

Chandan. Sandalwood is obtained from the ochre-brown sandalwood tree, which is native to Mysore and Tamil Nadu. It is the most prized wood in India. It is used for temple carvings and is the source of one of the most expensive fragrant oils in the world. In India small amounts of the wood and essence are used in cooking. In addition to its musky, faintly pine-floral-citrus scent, it is considered cooling to the body. In hot weather the essence, ruh chandan, is mixed with sugar syrup to form the base for icy drinks. Small bits of the wood tied in a muslin cloth with crushed cardamom pods are boiled in milk to flavor milk-fudge sweets. Sandalwood pastes are applied to the skin to counter the effects of tropical heat. You will find pure sandalwood powder, small chips, pure oil, or essences in Indian grocery stores. Look for the Swad brand's powder in small packets and for Sreemani's sandal powder in little, paper-wrapped, round containers.

sandalwood

SESAME SEEDS

Til. These are small, flat, creamy-white, teardrop-shaped seeds from the sesame plant. The more earthy, bitter, black seeds are not used in Indian cooking. When dry-roasted, white sesame seeds have a nutty, sweet flavor and turn golden brown. The seeds are sold whole. As the seeds contain over 50 percent oil, store them in a dry, cool place in an airtight container. Moisture will cause the seeds to clump. Sesame seeds are sprinkled over breads before baking. Roasted seeds are sprinkled over yogurt raitas and vegetable dishes. Til chutney is made from roasted sesame seeds, peanuts, garlic, and grated coconut, all coarsely ground in a blender with salt and a little tamarind. The chutney is delicious on rice crepes, on bread, or as a dip with pappadam crisps. Many sweet treats feature sesame seeds. The seeds are considered to have warming energy. Sesame sweets are eaten to celebrate winter festivals where children exchange sesame candies. In South

India newlywed brides are decorated with ropes of candied sesame pearls, bracelets, and hair combs.

STAR ANISE

star anise

Anasphal. This is the dried, eight-pointed, star-shaped seed pod of an Asian magnolia, which is native to China and Vietnam. Star anise is mahogany in color, and each tiny, canoe-shaped star point holds a beadlike seed. It has a sweet, aromatic anise flavor and is sold whole. Star anise is added to rich biryanis, rice casseroles layered with spiced lamb and fried onions, slivered nuts, and soaked saffron threads. The pods are removed before eating or pushed to the side of the plate. It is also added to minced-meat curries and stews. Star anise is chewed to freshen the breath and to aid digestion. It soothes the stomach and is used to flavor cough syrups.

TAMARIND

Imli. This is the fruit pulp obtained from the bean-like hanging pods of the Indian tamarind tree. The 4- to 6-inch-long, knobby, curved pods are cinnamon brown and fuzzy. This brittle shell encloses dark brown, sticky pulp and large brown seeds held together by a fibrous husk. Tamarind is an acidic ingredient, milder than lemon and sweeter than vinegar. The pulp has a tangy, apricot-date flavor and fruity aroma. The whole pods are sometimes available. Processed tamarind is sold in three forms: thick, pressed slabs of pitted and unpitted pulp, jellylike concentrate, and powder, which is used dry or mixed into a paste with water. Tamarind extract made from the pulp or concentrate has a tart, sweet-sour, fruity taste.

tamarind

To make extract to use in recipes, soak a hunk of the tamarind slab in hot water. When it softens, mix it into a mushy paste and press it through a sieve over a nonmetallic bowl with your fingers or the back of a spoon. The fine pulp and juice will pass through, leaving behind the fibers and seeds. Be sure to collect the thick, strained paste that is stuck to the underside of the sieve. Any residue can be frozen or saved for polishing brass. The concentrate should be diluted with water into a medium-thin paste. Tamarind extract is used in hot and sour soups, dals, sweet chutneys, tart dipping sauces, vegetable dishes, and curries. In Madras, Tamils cook fish in a spicy tomato-tamarind paste and coconut milk. Meethi (sweet) chutney is made from tamarind and palm sugar boiled until thick and simmered with chopped dates, salt, cayenne, and cumin powder. This dark, sweet, tangy mixture goes with everything from samosas to yogurt raitas. It is used as a dip or drizzled over breads, pastries, and fried snacks.

In India tamarind vendors ply their goodies to school children, who love fresh tamarind pulp with salt and chili powder as a snack. Tamarind cools the system, cleanses the blood, and is a mild laxative. Look for the Tamicon brand's concentrate in 8- and 14-ounce plastic tubs (beware the hermetically sealed inner lid under the red cap that

you have to puncture to squeeze out the concentrate). Look also for the Kishan and TRS brands in 7-ounce cellophane-wrapped blocks and for Dri Tam in 7-ounce boxes of instant powder.

TIRPHAL

This is made of the dried buds of the tirphal tree. These gnarled trees grow deep in the forests of West India, in Karnataka and Maharashta. The small berries ripen in monsoon season and are picked by October, then they are sun-dried until they split open. The small seeds inside are removed and discarded. The dry, dark, brownish black shells have a light-tan interior and a rough, spiny exterior. They resemble Sichuan peppercorns. Tirphal has a pungent, woody aroma and a sharp flavor with a bitter, biting aftertaste. It is not a commonly found ingredient. Triphal is sold and used whole. The tiny buds are always quickly dry-roasted (they burn easily) to release their aromatic oils and then added after the main ingredients. Tirphal is mainly used in fish curries or is added to lentil, bean, and pea dishes. Lima beans are delicious when cooked with grated coconut and a tamarind-chili paste, then flavored with tirphal and garlic. Tirphal aids digestion of legumes and is an antiflatulent.

tirphal

TURMERIC

Haldi or manjul. This is the ground, dried root stem of a member of the ginger family. Turmeric has a pungent, acrid, scorched-earth aroma and a musky, bitter taste. It is sold ground and as whole, dried roots. Turmeric is the soul of Indian cuisine. It is blended with other spices into curry powder and tandoori pastes. It is used in almost every dal, meat, fish, and vegetable dish (except for leafy greens as they will discolor and taste bitter). Turmeric is a preservative and is used extensively in pickling. It is used to thicken, color, and flavor foods, especially festival rice and biryanis. Turmeric is often rubbed on fish steaks before pan-frying them.

But be careful, the color leaves a long-lasting stain. When added to the oil before the main ingredients, turmeric imparts a deep yellow color and pungent taste to the dish. Added afterward, it infuses a subtle flavor and a light-lemon color. The powder should be dry-roasted before adding to curries and sauces to release the aroma and temper the bitterness. Turmeric powder is mixed into a paste and used as a quick antiseptic for minor burns and wounds. Chefs often use it to stop bleeding when they knick themselves. It is a cleansing spice and a blood purifier. It is also antibacterial, which is another reason that it is rubbed on fish before cooking.

Stocking Up

Essential spices that you will use over and over include cardamom, cayenne, coriander seeds, cumin seeds, dried chilies, mustard seeds, black pepper, sesame seeds, tamarind, and turmeric. If you like strong, pungent, or tart flavors, get amchoor, asafoetida, black salt, fenugreek seeds, and kokum. Curry powder is handy for quick curries. Saffron is worth the small expense for the rich fragrance and golden color that it adds to foods.

After browsing through the incredible array of spices, no doubt some will have slipped into your shopping basket. Back home, a few whiffs will conjure up the exotic world of far-flung spice islands and crowded bazaars. With an abundant supply of spices you have the intrinsic elements to make seductively flavored meals. Without spices one cannot even imagine Indian cuisine. Once sought by Europeans to flavor and mask the odor of rotting meats, spices now add sparkle and a rich dimension to the foods they infuse, scent, and flavor.

5

Spice Mixes, Powders & Pastes

Hindi word for "spices"

Spices and spice blends are the heart and soul of Indian cooking. Every Indian dish is flavored with a distinct blend of spices. Simple dishes may use just a sprinkling of popped mustard seeds and turmeric but a rich North Indian meat curry may use a blend of fifteen different spices. Traditionally, these mixtures, known as masalas were ground at home, fine tuned for specific dal, meat, vegetable, or fish dishes. While it is satisfying to roast and hand grind spices, it is time consuming and not always practical. It may even put you off from trying an Indian recipe.

Luckily, Indian groceries stock a vast selection of ready made spice blends, both powdered and in pastes. There are dozens to choose from—including biryani blends, tikka mixes, and kebab spices to garlic, ginger, and vindaloo pastes. These are handy when you crave an exotic curry in a hurry or want to try a spice blend without purchasing all the individual spices needed to make it. There are also classic and regional blends to select from. Powdered spice blends are sold in small 2- to 3-ounce boxes and 7-ounce pouches. Transfer them to clean, dry jars and they will keep up to a year. Pastes are found in glass or plastic jars, on the spice shelf near the powders. In some stores, pastes may be on the same shelf as the pickles and chutneys.

First we will take a look at classic and regional spice blends and flavoring powders. Next are spice mix blends you will find, brands that make them and what they are used for. Finally we will examine spice pastes and cooking sauces and brands to look for.

Classic Spice Blends

CHAAT MASALA

chaat masala

Chaat literally means, "to lick" in Hindi. Chaats are snacks or finger licking foods and light salads made from seasonal ingredients. They are mouth watering combinations of tastes, textures, and flavors—fried bits of puri, cubes of potato, and tart chunks of fruit, for example. The essential seasoning to these combos is chaat masala, a tantalizing tangy, salty, and spicy blend. The distinctive chaat flavor comes from smoky black salt, green mango powder, and ground cumin. Other spices in the blend include asafoetida, ginger, mint, cayenne, ajowan, black pepper, and pomegranate powder. Chaat ingredients are tossed with the masala and smothered in sweet tamarind or mint chutney, yogurt, or chili sauce. Aloo chaat is one of the most popular, made from cubes of boiled potato tossed with chunks of tomato and chopped chilies. Fruit chaats are made from a mix of ripe and sour fruit chunks. Look for MDH Chunky Chaat Masala in 3.5-ounce green boxes. Also Shan, A-1A, National, and Badshah brands in small boxes. To make Aloo chaat, see the recipe on page 237.

DHANSAK MASALA

A blend of sweet and hot spices used to make the richly layered dish of India's Parsi ethnic group, reflecting their Persian ancestry. Dhan means rice and sak is the dal and lamb that go with it. The masala consists of ground cinnamon, cardamom, cloves, cumin, black pepper, coriander seeds, red chilies, ginger, nutmeg, and star anise. To make dhansak, lamb is cooked in a thick sauce with the spice mixture and stirred into cooked, split yellow lentil dal. This makes the sak and can be eaten as is with bread. To complete dhansak, a fragrant spiced pulao is made and served with the sak, minced meat kebabs and a salad made from chopped onion, tomato, and

Parsis are Zoroastrians who fled Iran in the 8th century due to religious persecution. Their language agility and business savvy led to wealth, as they became shippers and merchants. Others became grocers, opening small shops offering exotic imports like cheese and chocolates. Parsi cuisine is a blend of Persian influences, the sweet and sour flavors of Gujarat, and Western ingredients. Parsis are well-known for lavish wedding feasts called lagan nu bhonu. At these patra ni macchi is a must—pomfret coated in a green coriander-coconut chutney and steamed in banana leaf packets.

herbs. Look for Badshah brand in small boxes. If you can't find it, substitute garam masala with a pinch of nutmeg and star anise powder.

GARAM MASALA

Garam means "warming" and this classic blend of spices is the preferred blend in the cold winters of North India where it originated. Garam masala is not fiery hot and is often mistaken for curry powder, although it is a brown powder. Curry powder seasons food at the beginning of cooking. Garam masala, however, is added as an additional seasoning, sprinkled over many dishes after cooking to give extra fragrance and flavor. Every Indian cook has their special recipe, but the basic combination includes coriander seeds, cumin, and cardamom, black pepper, cloves, cinnamon, and nutmeg. The overall taste is slightly sweet. Garam masala adds aromatic warmth sprinkled onto dals, vegetables, curries, cooked fish, meats, salads and yogurt. It is sold in vacuum-sealed tins, jars, packets, and bags. Look for Rajah brand in cans, MTR, MDH, and Shan brands in small boxes, and Kissan, Nirav or Swad brands in 7- and 14-ounce packets or small jars. To make garam masala, see the recipe on page 237.

garam masala

MADRAS CURRY POWDER

The classic, pungent, deep yellow spice blend, originally from Madras in the State of Tamil Nadu. It is made from dry-roasted, ground coriander seeds, turmeric, red chilies, cumin, fennel, and fenugreek seeds, black peppercorns, triphala, cloves, cassia bark, and dried curry leaves. The spice powder is then pureed with crushed garlic, ginger, and a little vinegar to make a thick paste used in curries and sauces. It is sold in tins, packets, and boxes. Look for D&D Madras Gold brand and Genuine Ship brand in tins or Poonjiaiji's Ship brand in small boxes.

PANCH PHORA

Also spelled panch phoron. A 5-spice seed blend indispensable to the cuisines of Bengal and Bangladesh. It is made from equal amounts of fennel seeds, brown mustard seeds, nigella seeds, fenugreek seeds, and cumin seeds. Panch means "5", thus the name. The seeds can be ground, but panch phora is mainly used unground. The flavor is bittersweet with an aromatic, earthy aroma. To use, put the amount of mix needed for a recipe into a small jar and shake the seeds so they are evenly mixed. The seeds are sizzled in hot oil to release the flavors before other ingredients are added. This blend is used in dals, fish dishes, vegetable soups, stews, and curries. Ghanto is grated or finely chopped vegetables cooked with panch phora, ground spices, and ghee. Murighanto is fish heads cooked with the five spices and rice. Panch phora can easily be made by blending equal amounts of each of the five spice seeds. Look for Maya and Chirag brands in small packets.

SAMBHAR & RASAM POWDERS

Sambhar powder is a South Indian blend of spices used to flavor a dal of the same name. Sambhar dal is a thick vegetable and split yellow lentil stew flavored with tamarind and sambhar powder. The powder is made from dry-roasted mustard seeds, fenugreek seeds, cumin seeds, dried red chilies, black peppercorns, coriander seeds, dried curry leaves, turmeric, and asafoetida ground with a small

sambhar powder

amount of fried split lentils. The rich, reddish gold powder is sold in small boxes and larger pouches. The powder is mixed with water and simmered with chopped vegetables and a little lemon juice or tamarind and cooked yellow lentil dal is stirred in. Garnish with fried curry leaves and chopped fresh coriander leaves.

Rasam, which means "essence" is a close relative of sambhar, but thinner and served as a spicy soup. Rasam powder is made from the same sambhar blend with additional chili and tamarind and a small amount of sautéed lentils. To make rasam, blend the powder with water, and simmer about 20 minutes with some chopped tomatoes. The thin broth is served with rice, fried snacks, and steamed rice cakes or rice crepes. Look for Nirav, Swad, Madhur, A-1A, Badshan, Gits, MDH, National, and Shan brands for both in small boxes. Also Sri Ganeshrams 777 brand Madras sambhar powder in small round cardboard containers with a yellow paper label and Agmark brand in small yellow tins.

TANDOORI MASALA

The brick red spice blend of Punjab. It has a fragrant spicy aroma and hot, salty, and sour taste with strong cumin and coriander seed overtones. Dry-roasted cumin and coriander seeds, cinnamon, cloves, cayenne, ginger, turmeric, mace, and salt are ground to a fine powder. Red food coloring powder is added to most blends, creating the red-orange color. Meat, poultry, and seafood are marinated in a mixture of yogurt and tandoori masala and baked in clay or regular ovens. The powder can be fried in hot oil before the main ingredients or along with them in curries and vegetable dishes. Add a bit of tandoori masala to potato dishes and cream based sauces or curd cheese curries for flavor and color. Try

The Punjab is known as the granary of India, where the cuisine is robust, bread-based, and spiced with tandoori masala. In the Punjab, huge clay ovens, half-buried in the ground, are fired with coals lit at the bottom. Tandoori food became hugely popular after the partition of India, when Punjabi refugees from the northwest fled to Delhi. The basic Indian menu the world over is based on this original formula of North Indian fare: tandoori meats and bread, kebabs, pilafs, creamy kormas, minced meat keemas, and buttery vegetable and bean dishes.

mixing a little of the powder with sour cream or mayonnaise for a spicy dip. It is sold in tins and boxes. Look for Rajah brand in large and small tins and Shan, MDH, Badshah brands chicken tandoori masala in small boxes.

S p i c e M i x e s

There are many different spice mixes packed into small, colorful boxes or pouches on the shelves of Indian groceries. In the Rajas' store they fill half of shelf 4. The pictures or photos on the labels depict the vast number of delicious dishes you can make using the pre-ground blends and give a clue to what the spices are used for—chicken, fish, lamb, kebabs, or meatballs. Check the labels for a listing of all the spices in each masala. If you get your kormas and keemas or koftas mixed up, the following guide will set you straight.

Widely distributed brands that offer all of the following spice mixes are: A-1A, Badshan, Chef's Pride, Eastern, Madhur, MDH, National, and Shan. They are in small boxes and recipes are included on the side panels or on papers inside them, but reduce the amount of oil many recipes call for—often several cups! There is also MTR and India's Spice'N Flavor brands in 7-ounce thick paper, foil-lined pouch bags.

Other brands you may see, which make a smaller range of spice powders are: Khanum, Kusum, Palat, Poonjiajis Ship brand, and Ramdev brands in small boxes. Ahmed brand has a line in very small 1.7-ounce boxes wrapped in cellophane. Rather than list all the brands after each heading, refer to this section for brands to seek out.

ACHAR GOSHT MIX

Achar means pickle and gosht is meat. This spice blend, popular in Bhopal is for lamb braised with green chilies and pickling spices—turmeric, ground mustard seeds, coriander, and salt. The tangy, spicy stew is eaten freshly cooked or stored and eaten several days later. The meat is cooked in the spices with mustard oil.

ACHAR MASALA

Pickling mix. Split, skinned black mustard seeds, called raina or kuria are blended with chili powder, salt, and split coriander and fenugreek seeds, and ground black pepper. The coarse orange-red powder is mixed with mustard oil for pickling. Look for Jalpur brand in boxes and Sugam brand in 7-ounce bags. Also available as a moist paste with oil added—look for Maya brand in 16-ounce jars. Split and powdered mustard seeds are also sold for pickling. Look for Maya brand split seeds in 10-ounce shaker jars and Patel Brothers in 2-pound bags. Swad has mustard powder in 7-ounce bags.

achar masala

BALTI GOSHT

Spice mix for a sort of Indian stir-fry in a spicy sauce from the northern most region of Pakistan, called Baltistan. Meat, seafood, or vegetables in any combination are fried with the spices, chilies, chopped tomatoes, ginger, garlic, and vinegar and are simmered with water until tender.

balti gosht

BHUJIA SPICE MIX

Spicy potato curry blend. Boil peeled, sliced potatoes in water with the spice mix and diced tomatoes until tender, then stir in chopped green chilies and coriander leaves and mash a few of the potatoes to make a thick stew.

BOTI KEBAB MASALA

Cubes of lamb or other meat are marinated in yogurt mixed with the masala, then grilled or baked in a tandoor (or other oven).

CHANNA MASALA

Blend of spices for flavoring chickpeas. It can also be used in dals or with bean and vegetable stews and has a tangy, hot, and spicy flavor. Good for making aloo chole, spicy potatoes, and chickpeas. Spices include ground coriander seeds, red chili, turmeric, cumin, black salt, and green mango powder.

CHAPPLI KEBAB

Spice mix for Peshawari style meat patties. Minced meat is kneaded into a smooth dough with the spice and flour mix, finely

diced onions, chopped chilies and crushed garlic and fresh ginger. The meat mixture is formed into thin, flat patties with a slice of tomato pressed onto one side before deep-frying until brown and crispy.

chappli kebab

> A Balti is an all-in-one curry and the name means both the style of cooking and the pan it is cooked in, which is better known as the karahi or Indian wok. A branch of the Silk Route crossed Baltistan on its way to India, and this diversion became known as the Spice Route. The earliest settlers were Tibetan nomads and from them Buddhism entered China from India, and Lamas, Tibetan holy monks, were selected and educated. Later nomadic Hindu tribes moved in, followed by the Chinese, then Muslim invaders, all leaving an impact on the cuisine.

CHICKEN JALFEREZI

Spice blend for a mild, creamy Kashmiri-style cooking sauce for stir-fried chicken, named after Colonel Frazer of the British Raj army. The mix is made of ground sweet peppers, coconut powder (or lactose), chili powder, black pepper, and turmeric. To use, mix the spice powder with water and rub over pieces of chicken. Mix chopped onion, green peppers, and chilies into some yogurt. Heat oil

chicken halferezi

and cook some crushed tomatoes until they form a paste, add masala covered chicken pieces and fry until liquid is absorbed, then stir in yogurt mixture, cover pan and simmer about 15 to 20 minutes.

FISH MASALA

Good for fish, shrimp, lobster, and crab, this is a fragrant spice blend of garam masala, cardamom, green mango powder, black cumin, mace, nutmeg, black salt, ginger, and paprika. Use to make sauces for fish and seafood curries.

fish masala

DEGHI MIRCH MASALA

Deghi Mirch Masala is simply made of ground up sweet red peppers. It's better known as paprika.

EGG-TOFU MASALA

Blend of spices for making hard-boiled egg curry and seasoning scrambled eggs. Also used to make paneer cheese, tofu or vegetable curries, and can be used as a spice rub for grilling or baking vegetables. Key spices are ground red chilies, turmeric, fennel seeds, cardamom, cumin, star anise, and nutmeg. Only offered by India's Spice 'N Flavor brand in 7-ounce pouches. Palat brand has egg masala for egg curries. To use, brown chopped onions in oil, add the spice mix, salt, vinegar, and water and bring to boil—add halved hard-boiled eggs and simmer until the sauce is thickened.

egg-tofu masala

FRY GOSHT MASALA

Powder made from ground coriander seeds, paprika, black cumin, and other spices used for flavoring fried lamb or other meat. Dredge the meat pieces in the mix and fry or use the spice blend to make a sauce to pour over fried meat.

haleem mix

HALEEM MIX

Spice blend for making a thick stew of cracked wheat or other grains and lentils popular in Pakistan and with Indian Muslims. Use the mix fried in oil and add soaked wheat or barley and lentils, add water and simmer until thick and tender, then mash and serve garnished with fried onions, sprinkle with garam masala, and pour ghee over it. Yogurt-marinated chicken or lamb can be cooked in the stew, making a rich one dish meal. Key spices in the pungent blend are red chilies, paprika, turmeric, ginger, and garam masala.

HUSSAINI KEBAB MIX

Spice mix for seasoning lamb cubes before grilling on skewers. The meat chunks are marinated in a mixture of yogurt, lemon juice, garlic, ginger, and other spices, skewered and grilled. The kebabs are served in a creamy sauce made from simmered milk, cream, and ground almonds or cashews.

JAFFNA CURRY MIX

Sri Lankan curry powder with a sweet spicy taste, made from ground cinnamon, fennel seeds, fenugreek seeds, and cloves, cardamom, and cumin. Jaffna is a city on the north tip of the island.

JEERA SIP

Jaljira. Jeera means cumin and this is a tan colored powder mixed with water to make a tangy, salty, and spicy cooling cumin drink. The blend is made from green mango powder and ground cumin, citric acid, salt, caraway, black pepper, ginger, chili, cloves, and asafoetida. You can sweeten with sugar. Serve with crushed ice.

KADHAI MASALA

A kadhai is an Indian wok and this is a chunky spice blend for stir-fried chicken or vegetable dishes. Kadhai khana (food) is very popular along the Northwest frontiers, bordering Pakistan. The coarsely ground mix contains crushed coriander, fennel, mustard and fenugreek seeds, ground red chilies, cumin, black pepper, ginger, dry mango, bay leaves, cassia bark, and star anise. To use, fry onions in oil, add spice mix, chicken pieces or vegetables with some water and chopped tomatoes and simmer, covered until tender. Only made by Poonjiaiji's Ship brand in 3.5-ounce green boxes.

kadhai masala

KALEJI MASALA

Spice blend for liver kebabs. Small squares of liver are marinated in a mixture of yogurt, ginger-garlic paste, and spices, then skewered and grilled. Main spices in the mix are garam masala, ground coriander seeds, cumin, and red chilies.

The chicken was first domesticated in the Indus valley and was brought to Persia once commercial contracts were made, arriving in Greece in the 5th century B.C. A variety of wild fowl, probably descendants of the russet-colored Malaysian mound-bird, were tamed, not as a meat source, but for use in divination rituals. Eventually certain breeds evolved and both the meat and eggs became a part of the diet.

KEEMA SPICE MIX

Blend of spices for ground or minced meat curries. Keema means anything finely chopped or grated, including vegetables. The ground meat or grated vegetables are browned in oil with chopped onions and garlic, and then the spices are stirred in with a little water to make a sauce and are simmered. A creamy keema sauce can be made by adding yogurt or cream with the spices. A keema kofta is kofta patties or balls simmered in a creamy keema sauce.

KOFTA SPICE MIX

Spice blend for ground meatballs in a rich sauce. Koftas can also be cheese balls (malai kofta), potato balls, croquettes, vegetable patties, or dumplings. The sauce is made from fried spices blended with yogurt. The koftas are simmered in the sauce. Nargasi koftas are hard-boiled eggs encased in a spiced ground meat paste, deep-fried, and simmered in a mild curry sauce. Goshtaba are velvety smooth meatballs in a light, Kashmiri-style cardamom-laced sauce. Arooq are deep-fried spicy patties made from minced lamb, chicken, or fish in a spicy sauce.

KORMA

Quorma or khorma. A spice blend for a specific style of cooking—slowly braising chicken, meat, or meatballs, in a spicy, cream based sauce to make a thick curry. Sour cream, yogurt, coconut milk, or cream can be used, blended with the spice mix, and simmered with the meat.

korma

KUNNA MIX

Spice blend for stewed lamb curry (matka gosht) or shab deg, Kashmiri-style beef shin stew. Heat oil, fry chopped onions and garlic with pieces of meat and spice mix, add water and cook over low heat 6 to 8 hours. Dissolve some flour in a cup of water, add to pot, and cook another 30 minutes until thick.

MURGHI MASALA

Murgh means chicken and this is a spice mix for tandoor baked chicken. Marinate the meat in a mixture of yogurt and three spice powder and bake in a very hot oven. Each brand has its own spice blend and other chicken recipe suggestions.

NIHARI SPICE MIX

A spice blend from Lucknow in Uttar Pradesh for slow-simmered lamb shank stew or brains. Whole shanks or nallis are cooked in a moghul-influenced creamy sauce made from ground almonds or cashews, kewra (screwpine) essence, ginger, garlic, and spices.

PANI-PURI MASALA

Pani means water, puri are small Ping-Pong-ball-sized, deep-fried, puffed breads, also called gol gappa or puchkas. The mix is a blend for making flavored water. The crispy puffs are stuffed with chickpeas, filled with the water and popped in the mouth. The mix includes powdered coriander, cumin, salt, citric acid, cumin, and chilies.

pani-puri masala

PASANDA MASALA

Spice mix for making Kashmiri-style lamb kebabs. Pasanda means delicious pieces. Half-inch thick slices of leg meat are pounded with a mallet until thin and are smeared with the spice mixture and grated, raw papaya to marinate several hours. The pasandas are then rolled up, secured with string, pan-fried, then grilled until reddish brown. In Pakistan pasandas are a specialty, made with beef.

PAYA MASALA

Also called nahari or narahari masala, this is a blend of spices for lamb trotter stew, a specialty of Hyderabad. Trotters (lamb feet) and tongues are boiled with spices, then slowly simmered overnight. The slightly gelatinous mass is eaten for breakfast with kulcha bread.

ROGAN JOSH MIX

Also called Kashmir korma spice mix. Rogan means fat and josh means heat. Traditionally, fatty meat on the bone was used in this dish and the meat was slow cooked in its own fat, with extra added. Today rogan josh gets its flavor from the lavish use of spices. This is a spice blend for lamb cooked in a thick North Indian Moghul-style sauce made with yogurt, tomatoes, onions, and ginger. Fry the spices in oil, add the meat and yogurt and simmer.

SHAMI KEBAB MASALA

Spice mix for minced lamb patties. These delicate, crumbly patties are made from ground lamb cooked with red lentil dal and spices and ground into a fine paste. The paste is shaped into patties and pan-fried until golden brown, then garnished with sliced onions and chopped mint.

SINDHI BIRYANI

Spice mix for Sindhi-style hot and spicy meat, fish, or shrimp cooked with rice. The meat or seafood is cooked in a pot with the spice blend

sindhi biryani

and covered with a layer of soaked basmati rice, sprinkled with oil, and slowly steamed until the rice is tender. The rice and meat are mixed together just before serving. The Hindu Sindhis migrated to Bombay from Pakistan when India was partitioned and are famous for their cuisine.

SURTI JIRALU POWDER

An ochre-colored powder similar to chaat masala but saltier, popular in Gujarat. It is a blend of ground rock salt, cumin, black salt, chili, turmeric, ginger, and asafoetida. Use it sprinkled over yogurt, in lassi yogurt drinks, and on crispy fried breads, salads, and slices of fruit.

surti jiralu powder

TIKKA MASALA

Tikka is derived from the Hindi word tukra, meaning pieces. This is a spice mix for boneless cubes of meat, chicken, or fish, or minced meat kebabs grilled on skewers over coals. Spices include ground cardamom, cumin, turmeric, nutmeg, and paprika. Blend the spice mix into yogurt and marinate the tikka cubes before grilling. Tikka boti are kebabs of lamb and malai tikka means grilled kebabs served in a spiced cream sauce.

Sindhis are Hindus who originally came from Sind State in southwest Pakistan, bordering Rajasthan. As they were under Arab and Mughal rule for centuries, the Muslim influence in their food is strong. Yet Sindhis managed to retain their distinct cuisine and traditional dishes after migrating to Bombay and other parts of India. Many Sindhis are vegetarians and all are recognized as great gourmets, renowned for their halwas, sweets, and pappadams.

VINDALOO MASALA

A blend originating in Goa. Vindaloo comes from the Portuguese word vindalho, meaning with vinegar and garlic. Vindaloo is a hot, sweet and sour curry made with the spice mix blended with tamarind and a little vinegar. The mix contains ground red chilies, ginger, garlic, coriander and cumin seeds, black peppercorns, and cinnamon. In Goa vindaloos are made with pork and seafood, but you can use any meat or vegetable.

You may also find Bombay biryani spices, broast masala for making a sauce for roast chicken, kat-a-kat spices for offal, stew masala, bihari kebab blends for barbecued meat strips, sabzi (vegetable) masala, fry meat spices, hunter beef masala, seekh kebab spice mixes and fried chop spice blends. Try what ever looks good to you.

Spice Pastes & Cooking Sauces

These are labor saving, moist spice pastes, and coarse purees of garlic and ginger, two much used ingredients in Indian cuisine. Many popular powdered spice blends like tandoori, tikkas, kormas, and rogan josh are also sold as pastes. Refrigerated, the pastes keep several months and are often fresher tasting than dry spice blends. The intricate and complex flavors of Indian foods are at your fingertips any time with some of these pastes in stock. You will also find some exotic sambols and convenient cooking sauces. Most spice pastes and cooking sauces are found in the section with powdered spice blends or on the shelf with pickles and chutney. Some garlic and ginger pastes will be in the refrigerator case.

AMBUL THIYAL MIX

A Sri Lankan specialty made of ground kokum (sour fruit rind), black pepper, red chilies, cinnamon, and dried curry leaves. Use this dark, pungent paste in fish or seafood curries. It has a spicy and tangy flavor. Look for Larich brand in 13-ounce glass jars. The same brand also offers crab curry mix, a paste made from ground red chilies, fennel seeds, cumin, red rice, salt, ginger, dried curry leaves, drumstick leaves, garlic, palm oil, and tamarind.

DO PIAZA COOKING SAUCE

Do Piaza is an old Moghal term meaning something added to or cooked with a meat dish, for example lamb simmered with spinach. Today it describes a dish cooked with extra or "double" the amount of sliced onions. Do Piaza is an Indian Muslim dish, also popular in Bengal that was once ruled by a Muslim Moghul. The thick red, mildly spiced sauce is made from pureed cooked onions, tomatoes, and spices and is used for simmered lamb, chicken, or beef dishes. Sauté some chicken, pieces in oil with garlic and onions, add cut up potatoes and the sauce, simmer until the chicken is tender and sprinkle with garam masala for a delicious Bengali dish. Look for Pataks brand in 15-ounce jars.

The little teardrop-shaped island of Sri Lanka seems to drip from South India's eastern tip. The cuisine is a mix of Sinhalese and Tamil traditions with Dutch, British, and Portuguese influences. Staples include rice, curries, coconut, chili, and dried fish sambals. Both fresh and salted fish, vegetables, and meat are made into sour tamarind and spicy coconut milk curries, classified by color. Black curries are dark brown and intense, made from complex, roasted spice blends. Red curries are fiercely hot and spicy while white curries are milder and coconut based.

JALFEREZI COOKING SAUCE

A thick, pale yellow, creamy paste used for a Kahmiri-style pan-fried chicken dish. The sauce contains coconut milk, ground sweet peppers, garam masala, turmeric, cumin, garlic, and ginger and has a mild, sweet spicy taste. To make chicken jalferezi, brown pieces of chicken in ghee or oil with some chopped green peppers and add the sauce, thinned with a little milk or water, simmer until the chicken is tender and serve garnished with fried onions. Look for Pataks brand in 14-ounce jars.

KATTA SAMBOL

Also called seeni sambol, this is a Sri Lankan dark red, thick paste used for cooking or as a condiment. It is made from pureed fried onions, maldive fish, chili powder, sugar, salt, and vinegar. Maldive fish is cured, smoked, and dried bonito crushed into small pieces.

katta sambol

The tangy, spicy hot paste is used as a thickening and flavoring agent in vegetable curries or as a sauce, like ketchup. It is good mixed into plain rice. Look for Daffys brand in 14-ounce jars and Larich brand in 13-ounce bottles.

SAAG COOKING SAUCE

A thick, North Indian-style cooking sauce made from pureed spinach, onions, garlic, chilies, and spices. The thick, dark green, medium hot sauce is used to make aloo palak, potatoes cooked in spinach sauce, and is simmered with cubes of fried paneer cheese to make palak paneer. Murgh shahi saag is boneless pieces of chicken cooked in the sauce with tomatoes. Good heated and served over rice. Look for Pataks brand in 14-ounce jars.

saag cooking sauce

GARLIC PASTE

A coarsely ground paste of peeled, crushed garlic cloves, preserved in salt and oil. Not quite as flavorful as fresh minced garlic, but easy to use—many Indian recipes start off with minced garlic and ginger and chopped onions fried in oil. Refrigerate after opening. Look for Maya brand garlic paste and red chili-garlic paste in 14-ounce jars, Swad brand in 7-ounce jars and Poonjiaji's brand in 32-ounce jars. Also Indian Condiment brand in 10.5-ounce jars and Aki's in 8.8-ounce jars.

garlic paste

GINGER PASTE

A thick puree of peeled, ground ginger root preserved in salt and oil. Less aromatic than fresh ginger, with a slightly processed taste, but handy to use. Ginger paste should be fried with the other spices in a recipe in a little oil. Ginger paste can be used in any recipe requiring fresh minced ginger—except for ginger tea, which is made with fresh slices. Refrigerate after opening. Look for Maya, Poonjiaji's Sangam Mart and Swad brands, as well as Nirav brand ginger and ginger-garlic paste in 7-ounce jars.

Cooking Pastes

You will find jars of popular cooking pastes and sauces in the same section as the spice pastes. There are mild, medium-hot and extra-hot Madras curry pastes, balti paste for one-pan simmered meals, thick tangy kebab pastes, rich, sweetly spiced Moghali pastes for meats, and

tandoori paste

biryani pastes for seasoning the meat or vegetable layer of rice casseroles. You can also select from vivid red tandoori and tikka pastes for grilling or sautéing meats and seafood, fiery hot, tangy vindaloo pastes, and Kashmiri masala, rich with garlic and spices. There is also aloo mattar paste for potato and pea curries and pulao masala paste for flavoring rice. Cooking sauces include rogan josh, rich creamy coconut korma sauce, and a tangy coriander and lemon flavored tikka masala for grilled or sautéed chicken. Most have cooking suggestions and recipes on the label. Brands to look for are Maya, Laxmi, Ashoka, and Pataks in 8- to 14-ounce glass jars. Curry King offers a thick golden curry sauce and spicy tomato paste for cooking vegetables and chicken in 25- and 12-ounce jars; also Calcutta masala, a light cream and tomato simmer sauce, Bombay curry and Kashmiri marinade sauce, all in 16-ounce jars.

Stocking Up

When shopping for spices, you will see many Indian housewives stocking up on those handy little boxes of spice mixes and so should you. Even restaurants use them. Keep a full range on hand for meat, fish, bean and vegetable dishes, and use to add authentic flavor without the chore of hand-grinding each spice. Experiment to find a blend you especially like—and don't feel the mix can only be used for the suggested dish—try with other ingredients too. You might also want to pick up a box of chaat masala (one box lasts for a long time) for tossing together tangy vegetable or fruit salads. Sambhar powder is great to have for dals and soups and garam masala for sprinkling over finished dishes. Stock up on jars of cooking sauces and pastes for pulling together an easy grill or quick curry.

6

Aromatics & Herbs

Hindi word for "herbs"

One of the most distinctive aspects of Indian cuisine is the blending of seasonings. These seasonings range from fresh herbs and aromatic rhizomes to fierce chilies and fragrant leaves. This medley of ingredients, each with an explicit taste, constitutes the rich fusion of Indian flavors. Herbs add aroma, flavor, and color. Essential oils in the leaves, stems, or roots release aromas and flavors when sizzled in hot oil. The abundant use of pungent chilies, fragrant curry leaves, and fresh, sharp ginger characterizes many curries and dals. Mint defines the taste of chutneys and raitas (yogurt salads). Fenugreek leaves are used as both an herb and a leafy green. Citrus juice adds tartness and accents other flavors in a dish. Many herbs and aromatics are native to India, while a few come from far away.

It is hard to imagine Indian food without chilies. Today, India is the largest producer and major exporter of this treasure in the world. You will find several types of chilies, aromatic herbs, leaves, and ginger in the produce section of the Rajas' grocery store. The herbs are arranged in neat piles and bundles in baskets or small plastic baggies, which retain the freshness. In general, most herbs will keep for about a week if stored properly. After purchasing herbs, wipe off any moisture with a paper towel, then wrap them in cloth to absorb any condensation. Unwrap and keep them in an airtight bag or container in the refrigerator. Other storage tips for specific herbs will be included in this chapter.

AMBHALDI

Zedoary. This is also called white turmeric or mango ginger. A close relative of turmeric, it is the rhizome, or root stem of a plant with long, fragrant leaves. There are two types: one is small and chubby like ginger and is also known as curcuma-amada, while the other is long and slim like turmeric. They both have a thin, light-tan skin and a pale, lemon-yellow, hard interior. Ambhaldi has a distinct, ripe-mango smell

ambhaldi

when cut and a crisp, gingery-sharp, slightly bitter taste. Chop, slice, or mince it. Then fry it in oil with spices to flavor soups, dals, curries, and vegetable dishes. It is also pickled with chunks of green mango, or it is made into a hot, sour relish made of the finely ground root mixed with minced ginger, garlic, green chilies, and salt. Ambhaldi adds flavor and a warm, yellow color to dishes, but it is used sparingly as the taste can be overwhelming. It can also stain clothes and fingers, just like turmeric can. Look for plump roots with no sign of shriveling. Store it refrigerated for up to two weeks. Ambhaldi purifies the blood, is an antiseptic, and helps a cut stop bleeding. A paste of the ground root is blended with cream as a face mask for clear, shining skin.

BETEL LEAF

Piper betel. This is a thick, glossy, bright-green, heart-shaped leaf from a creeping vine that is related to pepper. In India it is called paan. The term also refers to the leaf envelopes of betel chew or quid. Fresh paan leaves are sold at the front counters of most Indian grocery stores and in paan shops. Betel chew is served after a meal, with each person wrapping their own parcel from an array of fillings in a compartmented box. A basic paan consists of a fresh betel leaf dabbed with slaked lime (chuna) and kattha, a vermilion paste made from a type of acacia wood. Shavings of dried betel nut are piled on. A pinch of tobacco might be added. The leaf is then deftly folded into a triangle and chewed. At festive occasions many other spicy and colorful ingredients are added. These include cardamom, fennel seeds, colored shreds of coconut, tiny sugarballs, cloves, ginger, preserved rose petals in syrup, menthol paste, and gold-flecked saffron jelly. Paan is chewed as a breath freshener, a digestive, and an antacid. It is also said to be a mild stimulant. Many

betel leaf

Indians have reddish orange stains on their lips, tongues, and teeth due to the addictive habit. In India I often had to dodge flying betel spittle. After masticating, orange betel-juice wads are unceremoniously spit out by the chewer, leaving bloodlike stains where they land.

CHILIES

An old legend in Northeast India connects paan ingredients to the characters in a bloody drama. Having no food to serve their guest, a poor couple kill themselves out of shame. Realizing that he was the cause, the guest kills himself too. A robber stumbles upon the scene, cleans up, and hides. The betel nut, which is chewed first, represents the husband since his blood was shed first. The lime paste represents the wife, and the betel-leaf wrapper stands for the guest, whose arrival wrapped the house in tragedy. Tobacco leaves used to wipe stains from the mouth represent the robber.

Lal mirch (red) and hari mirch (green). Indian food is a delicious blend of heat, fragrance, and flavor. The heat comes from chilies that contain varying degrees of hotness depending on size, shape, or color. In general, the smaller and greener the chili, the hotter it will be. Red chilies are ripe versions of green chilies, thus they are slightly less hot. Chilies have a strong, sharp aroma and range in taste from mild to volcanic. In hot countries like India, chilies are eaten to cool the system. Capsaicin (the heat compound that makes chilies hot) dilates blood vessels to increase circulation and perspiration. The most common are slim, tapered, finger-length chilies that are fire-engine red, yellowish green, and bright green. These are hot but not overwhelming. The medium-length, plump chilies can be yellow, pale orange, red, or green. The slightly larger, smooth, thick, round bright-green serrano chili is a bit milder than the stubby, dark green or red jalapeno, but both are packed with heat. The very hottest is the tiny, basmati-shaped kunkuni, or naga chili which is found in red and green and is also called the "bird dropping" chili. These searing, hot babies are munched whole with meals and used in cooking. The mildest are 5- to 6-inch-long, pale yellow banana chilies, which are often used as a vegetable when stuffed with spice pastes.

The heat comes from the whole chili, but the tip is the mildest. The area where the seeds attach to the membrane is the hottest. Any chili will lose fire when the seeds are removed. Slit the chili lengthwise and rinse it under running water, being careful not to let the chili oils irritate your eyes or skin—wearing rubber gloves helps. If you find a chili is too fierce, drinking water or beer only spreads the oils around your mouth. Dairy products neutralize the capsaicin, so try milk or yogurt to extinguish the flames. Sugar also helps.

Various types of fresh chilies are used in almost every savory dish in India. They are pounded into pastes for curries, sauces, and marinades. They are chopped and sizzled in oil with spices to begin a recipe or cooked in seasoned oil to finish a dish. Chilies add punch to dals, soups, rice, vegetables, meat, or fish. They are used in pickling and preserving foods. They add heat, aromatic flavor, and bring out the flavors of foods that are cooked with them. Indian food shouldn't scorch your taste buds, but tantalize and excite them. Look for crisp, firm chilies that are not shriveled. They will keep for several weeks if kept dry in a paper or plastic bag and refrigerated.

CORIANDER LEAF

Hara dhania or cilantro. One of India's favorite fragrant herbs, this is used as parsley is used in the West. It has flat, fan-shaped, ruffled leaves with a distinctive aroma of citrus, pepper, and ginger. It has a pungent, zesty flavor. Chopped coriander leaves season curries, soups, dals, rice, and vegetables. They garnish everything from fried chicken to cold drinks and yogurt salads. The leaves are pounded with salt and lemon juice or with spices and grated coconut to make pesto-like chutneys and dips. For a creamy dip, blend the chutney with sour cream or mayonnaise.

Chilies are often called chili peppers although they are in no way related to peppers. When Columbus set sail in 1492 he was, of course, searching for India—the fabled land of spices and peppercorns, which were then as precious as gold in Europe. When he landed in the Americas and found pungent little fruits, he called them red peppers. He also called the natives Indians, even though he was thousands of miles from India.

In South India, coriander leaves garnish spicy omelets that are made from eggs beaten with coconut milk. Coriander is sold in little bunches. Choose fresh, unwilted coriander with crisp stems and no yellow leaves. Store the leaves by standing them in a glass of water in the refrigerator with the tops loosely covered with a plastic bag. They are rich in vitamins A, B, and C. They have a cooling effect on the digestive system. This is one reason why hot, spicy foods are garnished with the chopped leaves.

coriander leaf

CURRY LEAVES

curry leaves

Meetha neem or kari patta. These are highly aromatic, small, dark-green, glossy, and pointed leaves of a tree that is native to India. A number of small leaflets that grow closely on a central stem are stripped and tossed into a cooking pot or sizzled in hot oil. Nothing compares to the aroma of fresh curry leaves. They are sold in small plastic bags or on styrofoam trays in the produce section. Buy ones with springy stalks and unbruised, shiny leaves. The leaves have a sweet, nutty, strong currylike fragrance and a slightly bitter, but pleasant taste. They are used to add aroma, but they are not usually eaten. In India people who use somebody for a particular favor and then dump them are likened to a curry dish that discards the curry leaf after it has been flavored. In South India, curry leaves are used liberally in dals, soups, curries, vegetables, breads, and fish dishes. Curry leaves are also ground with coconut and spices to make chutney. The leaves are fried in hot oil to start a recipe and are added to seasoned oils to finish dishes. Dried curry leaves are pulverized and added to some spice blends. Fresh leaves will keep for about two weeks if refrigerated in a sealed baggie. As the leaves dry and become brittle, they are less fragrant, but they can still be used. Curry leaves are an appetite stimulant and digestive. A paste made from the ground leaves helps heal insect bites. The leaves can be boiled in coconut oil and massaged into the scalp to promote hair growth.

DILL

Anithi. A fennel-like herb in the parsley family, this has feathery, green leaves and silky, slender stalks with a sweet, grassy aroma and a fresh, slightly sharp flavor that is reminiscent of caraway. Dill is sold in bunches. Chopped dill is used to scent and flavor fish, meats, egg dishes, dals, and salads. It is delicious cooked with spinach, chickpeas, chopped potatoes, eggplant, and carrots pureed with spices and eaten with bread. Try fresh snips of dill in scrambled eggs or added to kofta meatballs. Dill is lightly cooked or used as a garnish. Dill aids stomach disorders and prevents flatulence.

dill

FENUGREEK LEAF

Methi. These are the small oval, green leaves of the fenugreek plant that also produces the spice seed. In Indian grocery stores, the leaves are sold in two stages of development: the very tender 4- to 5-inch-long stems of young leaves that resemble watercress with a strong, bitter, tangy taste and the slightly larger 6- to 8-inch-long stalks of less-pungent leaves. The stems of both can be tough, so strip off the leaves to use them. The larger leaves are cooked as a leafy, green veg-

etable with potatoes, spinach, or chicken. The tender, raw leaves are minced and mixed into batters, bread doughs, and stuffings for bread, or they are added to salads. Depending on the season, you will find small, young leaves or larger, older leaves tied in bundles. Look for bright, dark green leaves that are not limp or wilted. Either type can be cooked as a vegetable, but avoid overgrown, extralarge leaves—they are tough and have turned bitter. To remove any bitterness in smaller leaves, wash, sprinkle with salt, set aside an hour, squeeze dry, and wash them in several changes of water. Indian grocery stores also sell sun-dried fenugreek leaves called kasoori methi. They are found with the spices, in small

fenugreek leaf

boxes or plastic packets. Crumbled, dried fenugreek leaves are sprinkled over meat and vegetable curries just before serving. Use it sparingly as its powerful flavor can overwhelm a dish. Fenugreek aids digestion. For dried leaves, look for the MDH brand with a peacock logo on the 3.5-ounce yellow box: Look also for the Swad and Nirav brands in 7- or 14-ounce packets.

GINGER

Adrak. Ginger is the rhizome of a tropical herbaceous plant. Fresh ginger is sold in knobby "hands." It has a smooth, beige skin and a creamy, pale yellow interior that is fibrous but easy to slice. Ginger adds a clean, aromatic, and spicy bite to curries, spice pastes, dals, pickles, chutneys, sweets, and tea. Ginger is peeled, chopped, ground, or grated and sizzled in hot oil, usually with garlic and other spices. Ginger is a tenderizer and is widely used in meat dishes and tandoori marinades. Ginger goes especially well with spinach, cauliflower, eggplant, and potatoes. Shredded ginger is sprinkled on top of cooked dishes and salads. Grated ginger is used in milk fudges. A few slices of ginger flavor tea. You may also find young, stem ginger in the spring and summer. This is the early growth of the stems. It is milder and

ginger

fiberless with paper-thin, pink skin and greenish, juicy flesh. Stem ginger is used in cooking, ground to make ginger chutney, or julienned and sprinkled with salt and lime juice to make a delicious relish.

When buying mature ginger, avoid any that looks wrinkled or has discolored moldy ends—it will be tough and overly fibrous. Ginger will keep for several weeks in a paper bag in the refrigerator. To preserve it longer, peel and slice the roots and cover them with rice vinegar or dry sherry in an airtight jar. Ginger stimulates the appetite, aids digestion, and combats nausea. Ginger tea relieves cold symptoms.

HOLY BASIL

Tulsi or sabzah. This is considered sacred and purifying to Hindus, and it is an essential part of worship in homes and temples. The Hindu god Vishnu wears a crown of basil leaves. The herb is often planted around temples or in decorative, sacred pots in homes. There are two types:

Krishna tulsi with reddish purple stems and leaves and tiny, pinkish purple flowers, and Rama tulsi with green leaves and white flowers. The leaves of both are narrow and dark green. Holy basil has an intense, peppery, sweet aroma and tastes like a cross between ginger and mint. In India, basil is worshipped more than it is used in cooking. It is, however, added to strong-flavored fish curries, chili-based sauces, and clear soups. Holy basil is boiled and steeped to make teas. It also goes well with tomatoes and adds an aro-

holy basil

matic accent in salads. Basil leaves aid digestion and are effective against coughs and colds. Basil is a tonic for the heart and clears the mind.

HORSERADISH ROOT

Sahijan. The gnarled, greenish gray roots of a plant in the mustard family are mainly used in the cuisines of Bengal and Orissa. The pungent, hard roots are scrubbed and the skin is peeled off before use. The hard, lumpy, dimpled roots have a woody inner core that should be cut out and discarded. The remaining firm flesh is grated or finely shredded, adding peppery bite to vegetable dishes. Try cooking potatoes, cauliflower, green beans, or yams with a little grated horseradish. Grate it just before using it to retain the pungency. Grated horseradish is also used as a condiment with meats or is blended into yogurt raitas. Store it up to several weeks, refrigerated in a paper or plastic bag. Horseradish stimulates the appetite.

In India, according to ancient custom, a gift is not a gift unless it is given away with a holy-basil leaf. Thus, at Hindu weddings the parents of the bride give her away by presenting the groom with a holy-basil leaf. Wealthy Hindus offer a solid-gold leaf studded with gems, which is later made into jewelry for the bride.

LEMONGRASS

Sera or bhustrina. This is an aromatic tall grass with fibrous roots and narrow, razor-sharp leaf blades. The citronella-scented, bulbous stem is used for its lemony, floral aroma and flavor. Fresh, yellow-green lemongrass is sold stripped of its leaves in long woody stalks or in small bundles. In India, lemongrass is mainly used in tea and light, clear soups. To prepare for cooking, peel away the long leaf blades from the bulb base and bruise the stem with a pestle or mallet. Tie the stem and blades in a loose knot to drop into boiling water or broth. For tea, boil it in water for 2 to 3 minutes, add tea leaves or a teabag, steep it, and add sugar and milk to taste. Hot and sour tamarind broth is flavored with lemongrass, ginger, and holy basil. It is simmered with grated carrots, peas, and green beans to make a light soup. Store it, wrapped in plastic, in the refrigerator for up to three weeks. Lemongrass is a diuretic and stimulant. It promotes digestion and induces perspiration that cools the body.

lemongrass

LIME

Kagzee nimbu. Limes thrive in hot tropical climates, unlike lemons, which do better in cooler conditions. In Indian markets you will find nimbu limes. They are small, about 1- to 2- inches in diameter, with thin, yellow-green, oily skins. Both the skin and the juice are powerfully sour. Nimbu limes taste like a tart cross between a lime and lemon. Choose plump, heavy fruits with firm skins that are free of bruises. Nimbu is cut into wedges and used as a condiment. It is squeezed over dals, soups, salads, curries, and fish. The juice is mixed with water, sugar, salt, and ice to make nimbu pani, a refreshing drink. The finely grated zest is added to some spice blends and curries. Whole limes are preserved in salt. Salted limes add tang to chutneys, and they are chopped and mixed with sliced chilies and onions to make a delicious relish. Limes help counter the heat of hot, spicy foods, improve the appetite, aid digestion, and relieve heartburn and nausea.

MINT

Podina. Several species of mint are available. Mint has small, textured, dark green leaves with uneven edges. The stalks vary from pale green to

dark purple, becoming woody as the plant matures. Fresh mint is sold in small clumps. Select bright, green, crisp leaves and avoid blackened or wilted leaves. Mint has a clean, fresh aroma and a tangy, cool-sweet taste that goes well in both savory and sweet dishes. Its most common use is in mint chutney, a simple mixture of fresh mint

mint

pureed with yogurt, green chilies, salt, and sugar that is served with samosas, steamed cakes, chaats, fried breads, and countless other snacks.

Mint was probably introduced to India by the Muslim rulers of Delhi, who used mint to flavor and perfume their meats. Mint still embellishes rich chicken and lamb curries, and it is added to vegetable dishes, dals, pulaos, sauces, bread stuffings, teas, and cooling drinks. Sprigs of mint garnish meat dishes, drinks, and salads. Store it by standing it in a glass of water in the refrigerator with its top loosely covered with a plastic bag. Less flavorful dried mint is also available in small plastic packets or boxes, in the spice aisle. It is used sprinkled over meats, curries, and dals, or it is steeped to make tea. Look for the Laxmi and Swad brands. Mint aids stomach disorders and is a kidney tonic. Mint tea treats nausea, flatulence, and vomiting.

NEEM LEAF

Meliaceae. Also known as vapu, this leaf comes from the margosa tree, a tropical tree in the mahogany family. The trunk exudes a gum, and the bitter, black bark is used in herbal tonics. The fruit and seeds yield a medicinal aromatic oil. It grows in the arid climate of Punjab and Rajasthan. The people there use the wood as fuel, the twigs as toothbrushes, and the leaves and flowers as bitter seasonings. Neem leaves look like large curry leaves. They are added to vegetable stews, curries, and dals to impart a pungent aroma and an aspirin-astringent, bitter taste.

neem leaves

In Bengal neem leaves are fried with cubes of eggplant to make neembegun. You can substitute dry-roasted fenugreek seeds, which impart a similar bitter, curry flavor. Neem leaves stimulate the appetite, clear intestinal worms, and ease headaches. Neem oils are used in toothpaste. Neem oil or soap is used as a bug repellent and is a natural insecticide. Neem leaves are almost never found fresh, but they are available frozen in some Asian groceries. Sawed-off bundles of leafy twigs with tiny clusters of pale, yellowish flowers are sold in sealed plastic bags. Look for the Eastland Thai brand's margosa leaves in 8-ounce bags.

SALAM LEAF

Also known as Indonesian bay leaf, this large, slender 3- to 4-inch-long, dark green leaf is from a tree in the cassia family. It is sometimes available fresh and may also be sold dried in plastic packets. Salam leaves are added whole, like bay leaves to curries, soups, stews, and rice dishes. The leaves release a spicy aroma when cooked and add a unique, sweet, earthy taste. The flavor stands out in mild dishes and rounds out the flavors in hot ones. If you can't find them, substitute curry leaves. Do not use bay leaves because they have a much different flavor.

Aromatic plants, leaves, and roots have been used in Indian cooking for thousands of years for medicinal and gastronomical purposes. A small amount adds maximum flavor and aroma. Fresh herbs, chilies, and rhizomes are well worth seeking out to add zest, depth, and aroma to many dishes. Herbs and aromatics meld and marry with other ingredients, altering even the simplest dish into something fragrant and deeply delicious.

Stocking Up

Basic aromatics and herbs to keep in stock are fresh chilies, coriander leaves, and ginger root. Curry leaves—the fresher the better—are essential for Indian cuisine. Nothing can match the unique aroma that they add to curries, dals, soups, and seasoning oils. Toss a few limes into your cart to squeeze over foods for a touch of tartness. Dried fenugreek keeps well and is good for sprinkling over meat dishes, dals, and curries.

7

Vegetables

वेजिरेबलस

Hindi word for "vegetables"

In India the words "subji," "shak," "tarkari," and "bhaji" all mean, "cooked vegetables." Indians love to cook and eat their vegetables. They show great respect for each one's integrity and flavor. Millions of Indians are vegetarians, so they have perfected the art of vegetable cooking and have created hundreds of succulent vegetable dishes. Vegetables are one of the most important ingredients in Indian cuisine, appearing in several dishes at every meal or as the meal itself. The versatile vegetable sparkles in vegetarian dishes and complements other ingredients in complex flavor combinations. Spices, seasonings, chilies, nuts, coconut, garlic, ginger, and yogurt add flavor, texture, and variety. Indian vegetables are never dull or plain. They are generally cooked "dry" (sukhi subji) either sautéed or braised, or "wet" (tari subji) in a flavorful sauce. Vegetables can be cooked until just tender and crisp or simmered until buttery, soft, and melting. Vegetables are stuffed, deep-fried, roasted, baked, made into koftas and patties, or shallow-fried in ghee with spices. They can be cooked whole, sliced, or pureed. Fresh, properly cooked vegetables are the basis of good eating in India and anywhere in the world, including your kitchen.

Start by selecting a variety of vegetables from different groups such as leafy greens, roots, gourds, squash, beans, and eggplant. The produce bins of large Indian grocery stores will be brimming with fresh, seasonal vegetables. Many, such as cauliflower, potatoes, and okra, are familiar. Others like snake gourd, tinda, and drumsticks, you may never have seen before. You will find out what they are and how to cook them in the next few pages. Choose firm, unbruised vegetables and crisp, leafy greens. Also keep in mind that on the whole, small produce has more flavor than the oversized giants. Sturdy roots and tubers can be stored for several weeks if kept free of moisture in paper bags or in hanging wire baskets in a dark, cool place. Fruit-type vegetables are best if used within a week. They should be refrigerated and stored in open paper or plastic bags to allow them to breathe. Leafy greens should be kept dry and unwashed in plastic bags and used within three to four days. For the best selection of vegetables, you have to visit a large Indian grocery store. Small shops mainly have dried goods and only a few basic vegetables.

Root Vegetables

LOTUS ROOT

Nedar, kamal, or bhen. These are the rhizomes of the lotus flowers that grow in the lakes of Kashmir. Tourists admire the large, pink blossoms from beautifully upholstered gondolas. Locals relish both the roots and the tea that is made from the stamens of the flowers. The

grayish beige roots resemble linked sausages. The off-white flesh has a crunchy texture with a mild, sweet taste reminiscent of artichokes. To use it, peel it and cut crosswise to reveal a lacy pattern of airholes that run the length of the root. When cooked, they never become soft, just tender and crisp. They are cooked with fish, tender young greens, or lamb. When mashed and mixed with chickpea flour, they are shaped into balls and fried, then simmered in spiced yogurt to make yakhni. When sliced and dipped in a rice flour batter and fried in mustard oil, they become crunchy chips called nedrchurm. Buy crisp, firm roots free of brown bruises. They will keep, uncut and refrigerated for two to three weeks.

lotus root

LOTUS STEMS

Kamal kakri. The slender, pale stems of the lotus flower are found in some stores. When they are cut, you will see a lacy network of tiny holes, like the Swiss-cheese pattern of the sliced root. To clean them, scrape off any mud with the blunt end of a knife, soak them in water for half an hour, rub them to loosen any lingering mud, wash them in several changes of water, and wipe them dry with a cloth. Cut them slantwise into 2- to 3-inch pieces and remove any remaining mud from the crevices with a toothpick.

In Kashmir the pieces are pounded until flat, salted, dipped in a spiced, besan flour batter, and deep-fried to make nadru pakoras. A Sindhi dish features lotus stems cooked in an earthenware pot. The pieces are partially boiled, wrapped in cloth, and slow-cooked in a clay pot sealed with soft dough for about 30 minutes. The unwrapped stems are pressed flat and smothered with tangy, green-chili-tamarind chutney. Lotus stems are sold in loose bundles, have a celerylike taste, and a crispy texture. They are good when used raw in salads. They become slightly mealy after cooking. Store them loosely wrapped and refrigerated for up to three days.

MOOLI

Giant white radish or daikon. These are large, smooth-skinned white-radish roots that resemble giant albino carrots. Some can weigh up to 30 pounds or more, but most are about 1 to 3 feet long and are less hefty. The greens can be eaten too, but in most stores they have been lopped off. Mooli has a sweet, mild, peppery flavor and a crisp texture. It becomes very soft when cooked, soaks up other flavors, and blends well with rich or spicy ingredients. Raw, grated mooli is used in sal-

ads to accompany fried foods or grilled meat. Shredded mooli is added to bread dough or stuffings and cooked with mung beans in dal. Slices or chunks are cooked with spinach, ginger, chilies, and spices, then are added to vegetable curries and stews. In Kashmir, mooli is cooked with fish and made into chutney. White radish is also pickled and added to yogurt salads. The thin skin should be scrubbed before using it. Select rock-hard roots that feel heavy. Store wrapped in plastic for up to two weeks in a refrigerator. White radish improves digestion, flushes toxins from the liver, and helps to relieve gas.

mooli

POTATO

Aloo. The humble spud, grown worldwide, originated in the Andes of South America. In India it is a very important vegetable. It is cooked with spices and served in curry or as a dry, spicy dish to accompany chapatis. It is also used extensively in snacks, acting as a bland, neutral carrier for hot, salty, tangy, spicy flavors. White or red, slightly waxy potatoes work best in Indian recipes. Potatoes are boiled, baked, stuffed, steamed, and mashed. They can be cooked with tamarind, onions, herbs, eggs, paneer cheese, peas, spinach, cauliflower, or meat. They are added to layered rice biryanis and cooked with ghee and spices. In North India, khatte aloo, or sour potato curry, is popular. Cubes of boiled potatoes are simmered in a buttermilk sauce seasoned with turmeric, cayenne, and cumin, then garnished with mint leaves. Mashed, spiced potatoes are used in bread, dosa, and samosa fillings, blended into bread doughs, or made into croquettes and koftas. Potatoes are grated and deep-fried to make latche, similar to french fries. Alluwa is a fudge made of mashed potatoes, sweetened condensed milk, butter, sugar and finely chopped cashews. Choose firm potatoes with no green spots or sprouting "eyes." Store them in a dry, cool place. Potatoes are used to make aloo chaat (see the recipe on page 239).

SAKRIYA

sakriya

Jamikand or suran. These are small yams with thin, reddish brown skin and pale orange flesh. They grow as a vine and often have a twisted, trailing stem still attached to one end of the oval, uneven-shaped tuber. To use them, scrub, peel, and cook them in chunks. They have a slightly sweet, bland taste, and they absorb flavors. Sakriya are used in curries and added to chickpea, vegetable, or meat stews. They are mashed with ground nuts, spices, and a little chickpea flour, shaped into patties, dipped in rice flour, and pan-fried. Yams are also grated and deep-fried, then combined with roasted nuts, raisins, and spices to make tasty snack mixes. Yams are best stored in a dark, cool place. A poultice of yam reduces swelling.

SWEET POTATO

Shakarkand. The only edible tuber of hundreds of morning glory varieties. Sweet potatoes have thin, patchy, dark orange skins and a deep orange flesh with a rich, sweet taste. They are used in curries, layered biryanis, and meat stews. Mashed sweet potatoes are blended into bread dough to make delicious puffed puris. They are also pureed with ghee and spices. They are boiled, cubed, and blended into yogurt with chopped dates, cumin, and orange zest to make a yogurt salad. They are grated and deep-fried for snack mixes. Sweet potatoes should be scrubbed and cooked whole or cut into chunks. They can be peeled before or after cooking (after is easier, they just slip off). Choose even-shaped, unblemished tubers and store them in a dark, cool place.

> Maan kachu is the undisputed king of taros. The name means "prestige" or "of good repute" in Bengali. This gigantic tuber weighs up to 30 or more pounds, and it is treated with well-deserved respect. Its Ayurvedic properties purify the blood and clear the skin. Due to its size it is usually sold in pieces. Chunks are boiled and mashed with mustard oil and salt, or they are grated raw into a marshmallow-like paste and mixed with shredded coconut, salt, sizzled mustard seeds, and minced green chilies to make an enjoyable side dish.

TARO

Arvi or patra. Called kachu in Bengali, this tuber ranges in size from a small potato to a fat yam. It has dark, shaggy, brown skin and pale, speckled, or purplish streaked bland flesh. It can be baked, braised, boiled, stewed, or pan-fried in ghee and spices. It can also be thinly sliced and deep-fried into chips. Sindhis boil small ones, peel and slit them, stuff them with a spice mixture, crush them between the palms of the hands, roll the

taro

flattened result in crumbs, and shallow-fry them. Taro becomes somewhat slimy or gummy when cooked. It must be peeled before using it. The sticky juice that oozes out can irritate the skin, so be careful or wear rubber gloves. Immerse the peeled tubers in water immediately until you are ready to cook. To keep the texture from getting too gluey, boil, drain, and dry them, then pan-fry them. It is best when cooked with assertive flavors: garlic, ginger, cumin, and black pepper. Choose firm ones—press the skin to make sure that the root is not soft or dried up. Store them in a cool, dry place in a paper bag. Just use them within a week. Taro expels mucous and helps dry coughs.

Leafy Green Vegetables

AMARANTH

Marsa, tamri bhaji, or lol cholai. This is a weedy plant with pointed, textured leaves and tiny clusters of flowers, from which the seed grain is obtained. There are two types that you may find. One is green and similar to spinach, but has broader leaves and thicker, light green stems. The other variety has dark red stems and green leaves with reddish purple streaks in the center. Both have an earthy, cresslike, slightly peppery flavor. It cooks quickly and is more nutritious than spinach. Amaranth leaves are cooked with grated coconut and spices, added to curries and soups, and stir-fried with garlic and spices. The leaves are especially good when cooked in coconut milk with spices and red lentils and spooned over rice. The strong flavor of the leaves stands up to pungent spices and chilies. Amaranth should look fresh with no wilted leaves. It is best if used within a day or two. To use it, discard the roots and tough lower stems and wash it thoroughly to get rid of any sand.

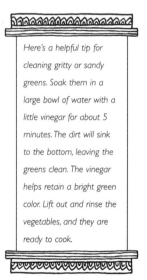

Here's a helpful tip for cleaning gritty or sandy greens. Soak them in a large bowl of water with a little vinegar for about 5 minutes. The dirt will sink to the bottom, leaving the greens clean. The vinegar helps retain a bright green color. Lift out and rinse the vegetables, and they are ready to cook.

GONGURA

gongura

This is a type of hibiscus leaf. Also called nalida, ambadi, kenaf, and mesta, it has dark red, gritty stems and flat, green, grooved, pointed leaves. It is sold in large bunches. To use it, pull off the leaves and discard the tough stems. Boil it for about 5 minutes in a little salted water. Drain and grind it into a coarse puree in a blender. Fry chopped onions and spices in oil and add sliced meat (beef, lamb, or chicken) or potatoes and cook everything until tender. Then stir in the gongura-leaf puree. The leaves are also used to make a sour, spicy chutney. Make sure that there are no slimy, black leaves near the base of the bunch. Store it in an open bag in a refrigerator. Use it within a day or two.

PATRA LEAVES

Arbi ki patra. Also known as colocasia leaves, these are the huge, heart-shaped, dark green "elephant ears" of the taro tuber. They must be carefully cooked to destroy the tiny crystals of calcium oxalate in the leaves. If they are undercooked, your mouth, tongue, and throat will tingle with the sensation of being pricked by thousands of tiny needles. By cooking or steaming them at least 45 minutes, all danger is eliminated. Patra leaves have a strong chard flavor and a soft texture after cooking. Use them chopped and simmered in curries, soups, and stews. The can also be boiled, drained, chopped, and cooked with coconut milk and spices. Patra leaves are also used whole as wrappers. After cutting away the thick center spine, the

patra leaf

leaves are steamed and rolled up with a paste made of chickpea flour, lemon juice, chopped chilies, ginger, and turmeric. Then they are cut into uniform pieces. These are then deep-fried until dark brown and crispy. Choose large, unwilted leaves. Store them refrigerated in a plastic bag. They are best when used within two to three days.

> Bengalis are crazy for the wild, leafy greens that spring up in the wet lushness of the monsoon season. Succulent stems (shak) are relished. These long, hollow stems, a type of taro with a faintly asparagus taste and unctous texture, are considered a delicacy. A delicious dish is made by seasoning boiled stems with ground cumin, turmeric, chili, coconut, and ghee. Cooked, small, dark, chickpeas are added. The stems can also be cooked with shrimp or large fish heads (muro).

POOI

Also called Malabar nightshade, puin, puishak, or climbing spinach. This is a spinachlike plant in the mallow family. It has rounded, heart-shaped, dark green leaves and thick stems. The leaves are large at the base of the spiraling stem, growing smaller and smaller toward the tiny leaves at the top. Each stem and branching tendril is crowned in a cluster of tiny, round, pale green, grapelike balls. Pooi tastes like slightly astringent spinach, but it has thicker leaves with a slippery texture when cooked. It is sold in loose bunches, chopped into large pieces, or with the roots trimmed off. It just needs to be washed. It cooks very quickly. It is cut into segments and added

pooi

to curries, or it is stir-fried with grated coconut and spices, or with mustard seeds and garlic. It is also good in coconut milk soups. The greens are delicious when stirred into dals near the end of cooking. Lightly steamed and chopped, it can be added to salads or blended into yogurt with toasted cumin seeds, salt, and chili powder. Buy fresh, unwilted greens. Store pooi loosely wrapped in the crisper bin of your fridge, and use it within a day or two. Like spinach, it is rich in vitamin A, iron, and calcium.

RED SAAG

Often called red spinach, this is similar to amaranth, but it has dark red leaves and light-red stems. It has an earthy, spinach flavor. Red saag curries are mixed into plain rice, turning it a lovely pink color. To cook it, cut off the lower tough stems, then wash and chop it coarsely. It can also be cooked, pureed with spices, or stewed with chicken, fish, or cubes of paneer cheese. Tambli bhaji is red saag cooked with coconut milk, spices, and tamarind. Store it the same way as amaranth.

Fruit Vegetables

ASH GOURD

Petha kaddu. Also known as winter melon, this pumpkin-shaped vegetable has frosted white, pale green skin. It can range from a few pounds to up to 100 pounds! You will often find it cut in wedges, wrapped in plastic, and sold by weight. The interior flesh is white with pale yellow seeds. If buying it by the wedge, check to make sure that it hasn't dried up or turned yellow. The flesh is soft with a sweet, mild flavor. It turns translucent when cooked. It is popular in soups or when simmered in gently spiced coconut milk until tender. Olan is a South Indian specialty made of little cubes of ash gourd poached with lentils and yogurt. Chunks are crystallized to make the sweet called angoori petha. Whole ash gourds will keep for two to three months in a cool, dry place. Plastic-wrapped wedges will keep for about one week.

BANANA BLOSSOM

Kere kafool. Called mocha in Bengali, this is a large, reddish purple, teardrop-shaped flower. It is cut off the banana plant's long central stem, from which it dangles. At the base of the blossom are neat rows of pale yellow buds encased in dark-magenta bracts. In India, banana blossoms are used as a vegetable in spicy curries and salads. The taste is similar to artichokes or heart of palm. To prepare it for cooking, remove and discard the outer bracts and the furled, red, ridged

banana blossom

petals until the inner portion is revealed. There are more tiny bud bracts under each layer of petal as you peel them off. Simmer the hearts in lightly salted water for about 20 minutes. Sprinkle them with lemon juice to prevent discoloring. Cool them, then cut them in slices. It is delicious mixed with salt, chili powder, oil, and sliced onions. It is served on salad greens or simmered in thick coconut milk with spices. Banana blossoms are sold wrapped in plastic to keep them from drying out in the produce section or in the refrigerator case. They are best when used within two to three days.

BITTER GOURD

Karela, bitter melon, or balsam pear. It resembles a light-green cucumber with warty bumps and ridges. It has pale, firm flesh. The bitter taste is due to the presence of quinine. The brighter green and younger they are, the better. Older, yellowish ones are tough with fibrous cores. When young, the whole gourd is eaten, including the pith and seeds. In older ones, scrape the seeds out. It is eaten raw, thinly sliced in salads, or added to rich, spicy curries to mellow its bitterness. Bitter gourd is stir-fried with spices and lime juice or deep-fried into crunchy chips.

bitter gourd

Bengalis add it to vegetable soups and stews, while Punjabis slit and stuff them with spicy, mashed potatoes or ground almonds and pan-fry them. The gourds are also pickled with garlic and tamarind. Cooks often salt or blanch them to reduce the bitterness before cooking. Look for small, firm, shiny bitter gourds. Avoid overripe ones that are soft and yellowish. You may also find spiny bitter gourds that look like small, prickly, yellowish green pickling cucumbers with long, pointy stems. They are kantola (or kakrol) and are a slightly less bitter cousin of bitter gourds. They are used in the same way. Try them sliced crosswise, rubbed with salt and turmeric, and fried until golden. Either type will keep for two to three days if refrigerated. The gourds continue to ripen if kept longer, and they develop a hard center. Cooked bitter gourd cleanses the liver, stimulates the appetite, and purifies the blood.

BOTTLE GOURD

bottle gourd

Doodhi, ghiya, lau, or louki. This is a pale green, smooth-skinned gourd that tastes like a cross between summer squash and cucumber. Bottle gourds resemble small baseball bats. They have narrow stems and broad bases. It is best to buy small, slightly immature ones, about 8 to 12 inches in length. The skin will be paper-thin and seeds will be underdeveloped. Older, larger ones must be peeled and the seeds scooped out. When it is cooked the flesh is tender and slightly sweet. When fully mature it develops a hard, woody shell that is used to make bottles, bowls, and musical instruments. Chunks of the gourd are added to dals, curries, and soups. Slices are dipped in batter and deep-fried. It is shredded, mixed with chickpea flour and spices, rolled into balls, deep-fried, and served in a dish of yogurt. In Bengal, lau chingri is a dish made from steamed gourd chunks cooked in seasoned oil with shrimp. It is also made into a dessert with evaporated milk, sugar, and ghee. Look for small, firm gourds. Store them refrigerated for up to two weeks. Thin slices are added to tomato broth to ease indigestion.

CAULIFLOWER

Gohbi. This is a very popular vegetable in India that stands up well to hot, spicy flavors. Select firm, compact heads with pale green stem leaves attached. Depending on how it is cooked, the texture can be buttery and soft or crispy and crunchy. To use it, wash and cut apart the florets, then discard the tough stem. Cauliflower is steamed and served in delicately spiced cream sauces, added to curries, or simmered with other vegetables in thin, spicy sauces. Aloo gohbi is spicy, stir-fried potato and cauliflower. Florets are browned in ghee with spices and blended into yogurt. The mixture is then added to rice and steamed with a cinnamon stick and a few cardamom pods to make a delicious pulao. Whole heads are stuffed with spices between the florets, steamed upside down, and served upright with a rich saffron sauce poured over it. Cauliflower heads will keep for about one week if loosely wrapped in plastic and refrigerated.

DRUMSTICKS

Sahjan, saragova, setka ni sing or muruggai. These are the long, slender bean pods of an Indian tree, that is known as the horseradish tree because the roots have a similar pungent taste. Both the half-ripe pods and the small, tender, oval leaflets are eaten. The bean pods are as stiff and hard as drumsticks, thus the name. The dark green, ridged pods are about 2 feet long. They taste a little like asparagus. They are cut in finger-sized lengths and simmered for 7 to 8 minutes in salted water. They are eaten plain or added to curries. The tangy leaves are cooked as a vegetable with spices and grated coconut.

Returning from the meditative grounds of Bara Khyang, a Buddhist monastery, I ran into the weekly floating market near the tiny town of Ramu. Flotillas of sampans and wooden dugouts with long, curving sterns clog a sectioned-off area along a muddy embankment. A gourd seller wades ashore as another man unloads bunches of long white radishes, snowy heads of cauliflower, bundles of greens, and lavender eggplants. Plump turnips and bumpy bitter gourds pass overhead in a basket. Downstream a bamboo market booms, the lashed rafts headed for the Chittagong pulp mills.

While they are delicious, the pods are tricky to eat unless you know what you are doing. The only part consumed is the soft, jellylike interior pulp in which tender, crunchy seeds are imbedded. Split the small sections open with a spoon and use the spoon to scrape out the pulp. A less formal method is to pick up a piece and scrape away the soft pulp with your teeth, then discard the skin to the side of your plate. It takes a lot of effort, but the gelatinous pulp is a real delicacy. When purchasing drumsticks, look for green, rather than brownish, pods. Avoid bumpy ones—they are bitter and have big, hard seeds. To prepare them for cooking, lightly scrape the skin with a vegetable peeler to remove some of the ridges and any dark patches. Drumsticks will keep a few days if wrapped in plastic and refrigerated, but they are best when eaten right away. Some markets such as the Rajas'—who have a tree right outside the store—sell bundles of the twigs and leaves. To use these, pull off the round, oval leaves and fry them in hot oil with spices. Fresh leaves are used to stop cuts from bleeding and to heal wounds. A paste of roasted, ground pod seeds is applied to painful joints.

drumstick

EGGPLANT

Brinjal or baingun. Native to Asia, the eggplant is a member of the nightshade family, along with tomatoes, potatoes, and chilies. Eggplants are the most popular and widely used vegetable in India. You will find slim and long or plump and stubby eggplants with pale lavender to dark purple skins and a black stem. They have a delicate, mild flavor, and an absorbent meaty texture. Eggplant blends well with other ingredients. It is free of the tiny seeds that make Western eggplants bitter, and does not require peeling, salting, or rinsing. Eggplant chunks are added to mung-bean dal, curries, and vegetable stews. It is diced, fried, split and stuffed with spices, and

braised, roasted, broiled, baked, or mashed with spices and yogurt. Eggplant is grated and mixed with batter to make fritters. It is also simmered with ginger, chickpeas, and spinach, or is curried with chunks of potato. Slices are dipped in batter and poppy seeds, then deep-fried. A specialty of Bengal is sweet-sour eggplant. Slices are fried, coated in a spicy glaze made from melted palm sugar and lemon juice, then broiled

eggplant until warm and bubbly. Eggplant is also pickled. Look for firm ones with taut, unwrinkled skins. They can be stored for one week if refrigerated in plastic bags. Eggplant helps prevent hardening of the arteries and blood clotting. A recipe for mashed, curried eggplant is on page 247.

GREEN BEANS

The general term for green beans in India is seema, but there are several different varieties. Snap or French beans are known as semma avara or barbatti. Tuvar or gwarsing beans are short, plump, green pods filled with several tender peas (the mature, dried peas are sold as toovar dal). Guar phali, also called cluster beans, are slim, bright green, pointy-ended beans. Valor, or sem, is also called papri in Gujarat. They are a type of Indian broad bean and have light-green, flattish, furry-edged, slightly curved pods with bulges where the small seeds are (when mature and dried, the seeds are sold as val dal). A variety that resembles plump pole beans is sold as round valor. In

guar phali

the same family is bada-sem, which is a large, flat pod also known as jackbean or sword bean. Lastly, you may find papdi liva, or Indian seed beans. These are plump, broad, curved pods filled with pale yellow-green seedlike beans. They closely resemble valor, but they are smoother and a brighter green. They are sometimes called double beans.

All types of green beans should be topped and tailed before cooking, either whole or chopped in pieces. Green beans are added to yellow-lentil dals, curries, rice, and potato dishes. They are also stir-fried with mustard seeds, chilies, turmeric, and grated coconut to make thoren, a South Indian side dish. Cooked, chopped green beans are folded into yogurt and sprinkled with toasted

bada-sem

poppy seeds. Guvar beans are made into koftas, boiled and ground into a paste with besan flour and spices, formed into balls, deep-fried, and served with chutney. The delicate beans from papdi liva pods are cooked like peas and added to curries and pulaos, or they are steamed and drizzled with seasoned oil. Choose firm, crisp pods without any brown spots. Store them refrigerated in a loose paper or plastic bag, and use them within a few days. Green beans are used in the thoren

valor

recipe on page 248.

CHOLIYA

These are unripe chickpeas. They are not really a vegetable but are sold in spring and early summer in the produce section. The pale, bright green legumes are encased in oval, paper-thin, light-green sacs. They are best when enjoyed zapped in a microwave or dropped into boiled water for 1 minute, popped out of their shells, and sprinkled with salt. They have a fresh, bean flavor. They are crisp but slightly mealy. They are good added to curries, stir-fries, and rice dishes. Store them in plastic or paper bags in the refrigerator for three to four days.

choliya

RIDGED GOURD

Toray, sinqua, or ghisoda. Also known as angled luffa and silk squash, this popular vegetable is a member of the cucumber family. Anywhere

from 8 to 12 inches long, the dark green, cylindrical gourd has long, spiny ridges that run along its entire length. Peel off the ridges and slice it crosswise. If the gourd is small and very young, leave on some of the skin. If it is older, peel away all the skin as it can be bitter. The buttery, off-white flesh is mild and tastes like a cross between zucchini and cucumber. When it is cooked, it becomes soft and spongy, absorbing the flavors with which it is cooked. Slices are added to vegetable stews and curries. It goes well with green peppers, peas, and tomatoes. It is good fried like an omelet or thinly sliced, deep-fried into crisps, and served with a spicy dip. Look for a firm, small-sized

ridged gourd

gourd without dark spots. Refrigerate it in paper or plastic bags. Use it within two to three days as it will toughen if left longer.

SNAKE GOURD

Chichinda or padwal. This is a long, slender gourd that can grow up to 6 feet long. Rocks are often tied to their ends so that they won't curl up. They are grown on wood frames, and they resemble pale icicles dangling from a canopy of leaves. Some are pale, frosty green and others are dark green with pale stripes that run the length of the gourd. Most of them are about 1 to 2 feet long and are slightly curled at one end. Snake gourd is a very mild, quick-

snake gourd

cooking, absorbent vegetable. It should be peeled, split open, seeded, and cut into chunks before using it. In North India it is cooked in dals, while in South India it goes into hot, spicy soups and lentil stews. It is also stuffed with spicy, minced meat and baked or simmered in coconut milk with spices. Look for firm, hard ones and store them for up to four days in the refrigerator.

SPONGE GOURD

Meetha-toray or galka. Also known as dishwash gourd, this is the vegetable that produces the loofah sponge. When it is fully ripe, the skin and flesh are removed, leaving a stiff, meshlike skeleton that is used as a scrubber. The smaller, immature gourds are eaten throughout India and Asia. They are long, slender, and light green. They have a faintly mottled skin and have small ridges running the length of the slightly curved gourd. The cooked flesh is tender with a mild, zucchini taste. To use it, peel off the skin and slice the gourd crosswise into rounds. It is added

sponge gourd

to soups, stir-fried with spices and shrimp, and boiled and served in a hot sauce. Choose small gourds without soft spots and refrigerate them for up to three days.

OKRA

Bhindi or "ladies fingers." The slender, tapering, bright green pods are about 3 to 4 inches long. They contain small, round, white seeds. The exterior is slightly fuzzy with ridges that run from stem to tip. Never wash okra in water. Just wipe it with a wet cloth, then dry it to keep it crisp. When it is cooked whole in dry curries, it will not get slimy or gummy, which it does when cut and cooked in water. Okra is slit, stuffed with spice pastes, and deep-fried. It is also pickled in oil and spices, simmered in coconut-milk curries, or stir-fried in curries. It can also be used in salads, lightly steamed, mixed into a vinegar-pepper dressing, and topped with fried garlic. Sliced rounds of fried okra are blended into spiced yogurt or fried with grated coconut and spices. Select small, slim, crisp pods. Large, thick ones tend to be fibrous and stringy. Refrigerate in a plastic bag for up to four days. Okra boiled in salted water relieves heartburn.

okra

PARVAL

Parwal or patol. Also called pointed gourd, these small, oval gourds are about 4 to 5 inches long, plump in the middle, taper at each end, and have dark and pale green stripes that run the gourd's length. The flesh is creamy and firm. They have small seeds and a mild, summer-squash taste. Riper, larger parval have harder seeds, which Bengalis consider a delicacy. They are good fried whole, whether unpeeled or peeled. They are cut into chunks and added to soups, stews, and curries. They are also cooked in a spicy yogurt sauce to make dahi parval. They can also be hollowed out and stuffed with a mixture of meat or fish, or they can be steamed or sautéed. Look for firm gourds and refrigerate them in a bag for up to five days.

PLANTAIN

Kacha kela. These are green, unripe cooking bananas. They are about 9 to 12 inches long with thick, green skins. Plantains are

After helping push the bus to get the engine going, we lurch off through more miles of humid wetness and soft rain, nearing Aurangabad in late afternoon. A mobile bazaar is set up on the outskirts of town in a clearing under tamarind trees, surrounded by brightly painted caravans. Glass-bangle sellers vie with spice, betel, and saree-fabric sellers. Eggplants that range from purple and orange oblongs to creamy globes, okra, various green beans, taro leaves, twisted snake gourds, tomatoes, and sweet potatoes are laid out on straw mats in color-coded piles.

used as a starchy vegetable and have a bland, slightly sweet taste. The flesh is firm and pale yellowish. They are cooked in several ways, most commonly peeled, shredded, or thinly sliced and fried until golden brown and crispy. Bengalis add them to simmered vegetable stews and curries, while South Indians bake them with coconut. Plantains are also sliced, rubbed with turmeric and salt, and pan-fried. Choose firm, green ones and store them in a dry, cool place up to a week. After peeling them, pull off any long fibers on the outer layer of flesh. You may want to oil your hands first to protect yourself against sticky sap. They develop dark spots and begin to turn yellow as they ripen, but they will never become sweet. It is fine to use spotted ones.

plantain

SNAKE BEAN

Payaru or lobhia. Also called yard-long bean because it grows up to 3 feet long, it is often sold in looped coils or loose knots. These slender ropelike beans are the immature pods of a seed, taste like a cross between navy beans and asparagus, and resemble black-eyed peas. They are drier, denser, and crunchier in texture than regular green beans. Chop them into short, equal-sized pieces to use them. The bean's mild flavor blends well with hot, spicy seasonings. The texture holds up to long cooking in dals, stews, and curries. They can be blanched or used raw in salads, or they can be deep-fried and mixed with tamarind or coconut chutney as a snack. Look for fresh, flexible bean pods without dark spots. Store them in the refrigerator in an open plastic bag, and use them within three to four days.

snake bean

TINDA

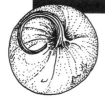

Punjabi tinda or melon squash. This is a plump, round, tomato-sized squash with smooth, creamy, yellowish green skin and the firm texture of cucumbers. The taste is mild and similar to summer squash. Peel tinda, split it open, and scoop out the seeds. It is often used whole, hollowed, and stuffed with a spicy meat or paneer-cheese filling. It is then baked

tinda

or simmered in a covered pan until tender. The squash is chopped and added to dals and curries or used in any squash recipe. It is grown in the Punjab region. Choose firm ones without bruises. Refrigerate it for up to a week.

TINDORA

Indian cucumber or gherkin. This small, stubby, 2- to 3-inch long, bright green squash has pale green, vertical stripes. It looks like a mini-pickling cucumber and has a smooth, shiny skin. The flesh is pale green and firm. It has a mild, zucchini-cucumber flavor. To

tindora

cook it, cut it into julienne strips and stir-fry it in spices, turmeric, chilies, and salt. Tindora slices are also added to spicy soups and curries, pan-fried in ghee and spices, steamed, sliced and added to salads, folded into spiced yogurt, and pickled in oil and spices. Choose small, firm, unwrinkled ones and refrigerate them in paper or plastic bags for up to four days.

OTHERS

You will also find cucumbers, beets, carrots, cabbage, onions, turnips, tomatoes, spinach, and pumpkins in most Indian grocery stores. Adding healthy and nutritious vegetables to your diet is easy and delicious when you cook Indian-inspired dishes. Indian meals revolve around the vegetable kingdom and imaginatively spiced and varied preparations. With a good stock of veggies, you need only a pot of rice or a stack of chapatis and small amounts of meat, seafood, yogurt, or dal to round out a meal. If you think vegetables are boring, you are in for a discovery!

Stocking Up

Load up on the versatile potato, yam, or sweet potato. Get some eggplant and cauliflower. Then pick out a leafy green and add some green beans and okra. Select a squash or gourd. On each visit try something new. Maybe try some bitter gourds, plantains, or drumsticks to broaden your vegetable palette.

8

Fruit

Hindi word for "fruit"

In Indian culture, fruits are as rich in symbology as they are abundant. Fruits are essential in temple services and as offerings. Statues of deities are bathed with ghee, coconut juice, milk, honey, sugar cane juice, and fruit mixtures. Sweet rice, coconuts, and bananas are placed on betel leaves at the statues' feet. The last evening of Diwali, the festival of lights, is Laxmi Puja. This involves worshiping the goddess of prosperity with offerings of fruit and sweets in hope that the following year will be fruitful. According to Indian legend the banana tree was a gift from the gods, which explains why it is called the "fruit of paradise." Banana leaves and sugar cane stalks festoon the entranceways of Indian temples when a wedding is celebrated. Gifts of mangoes are exchanged as a symbol of friendship.

Ripe, luscious fruit is the favorite dessert of India. It is peeled, sliced, and heaped on platters. Fruit is plentiful and makes a cool, soothing end to a hot or spicy meal. Fruit grows throughout India, especially in the tropical south. Fruit is eaten fresh, made into cooling drinks, pureed with yogurt, and preserved in jams and chutneys. Some unripe, sour fruits are cooked as a vegetable, grated for salads, or pickled. While a juicy mango might taste best after a dip in the Arabian Sea along a Goan beach, many exotic, delicious Indian fruits are imported. Some come from the orchards of California and Florida. For a taste of sultry India in a bite of fruit, head to the fruit crates near the front of several aisles of the Rajas' grocery store. What is available depends mainly on what fruits are in season. Some will be familiar, others a new taste sensation to discover. Most can just be peeled and eaten.

AMBERELLA

Jungli amba or hog plum. These plum-shaped, yellowish-orange fruits with a sweet and sour flavor taste somewhat like pineapple. The soft flesh cushions a large, spiny seed that should be carefully nibbled around to avoid piercing your lip. If it is unripe, the green skin is peeled, and the firm, pale flesh is cut into slices, dipped in chili powder and salt as a snack, or cooked in chutneys. Ripe amberellas are simmered in curries and made into cinnamon-spiked conserves. Half-ripe ones are used in sweet-tart chutney with raisins, garlic, ginger, and spices. Choose hard, greenish yellow fruit if you want to make chutney. Look for yellowing, nearly ripe fruit if you want to eat them. Since they are a hard fruit, they will keep well until fully ripe.

The origin of the banana leaf's center stem is a charming tale, which is told in the epic Ramayana poem. When Sita, Rama's wife, was abducted, Rama set aside a portion for Sita at each meal. He took a banana leaf and drew a line down the center. From that day onward the banana leaf has had a center stem. Since nothing is wasted in India, when temples serve mass vegetarian meals to pilgrims, herds of cows are let into the eating area to munch up all the banana leaves on the floor.

BANANAS

Kela. Over a dozen different types of bananas are grown in India, from plump, red ones to yellow, dwarf "ladies fingers." There are large kela raja, or king bananas, which are used in desserts or sliced, battered, and deep-fried. Bananas are also added to curries, roasted with coconut, and steamed with spices. They are also sliced, sprinkled with lime juice, and added to spiced yogurt. Some varieties are

dried and ground into an easily digested flour. Banana leaves are used both as wrappers for steaming and grilling foods and as disposable plates. There are restaurants in South India known as "banana-leaf shops" where you can get an all-you-can-eat vegetarian meal for about a dollar and a half. You have to beg the servers to stop filling your "plate" by folding the leaf over. In most Indian grocery stores you can choose

bananas

from two to three types of bananas. Frozen sheets of banana leaves good for steaming fish in, are in the freezer case. Bananas help heal ulcers, relieve constipation and ease muscle cramps.

BILIMBI

Bilimbikai or belimbing. This waxy-skinned, light, yellowish green fruit has a crisp, watery flesh, flat seeds, and a sharp, acidic taste. It looks like a miniature cucumber and grows in clusters on a tree. The fruit is closely related to star fruit, but it has smaller ribs. Bilimbi are too sour to eat. They are used in curries to add acid flavor or are made into jams and chutney. They are salted and dried for use as a souring agent. The fruits are pricked all over with a fork, liberally salted, and sun-dried until brown and leathery.

CHICKOO

chickoo

Sapodilla or naseberry. These are the fruits of a tall ever-green tree. Chickoo are about the size and shape of a kiwi. They have rough, grayish brown skin that peels off easily. The flesh is translucent honey brown to reddish yellow with a slightly granular texture. Juicy and fra-grant, the sweet honey-pear flesh melts in your mouth. The core contains flat, dark brown seeds. Chickoo get their name from the white latex sap called chicle that oozes from the bark and is used in chewing gum. They should be eaten when soft, fragrant, and very ripe. If you eat one that leaves your mouth and lips sticky, dissolve some chocolate in your mouth to neutralize the chicle. The fruit is peeled and sliced or halved, while the flesh is scooped out with a spoon. Slices can be mixed into a thick cream or rice pudding. In India, chickoo are known as the fruit that Krishna favored.

CUSTARD APPLE

Sitaphol, sharifa, srikaya, sugar apple or cherimoya. This plump, heart-shaped fruit is made of olive-black and light-green nodules that resemble a small hand grenade. The scaly, bumpy skin contains creamy, white, slightly granular, sweet flesh that is divided into seg-

custard apple

ments, each one embedded with a large, black seed. When it is ripe, the area around the stem turns blackish, and the fragrant fruit seems swollen and about to burst. It tastes a bit like a piña colada. To eat it, break it into pieces or scoop it out of the shell with a spoon. The seeds are large enough to separate from the pulp in your mouth. You can also sieve the flesh and whirl it with yogurt or vanilla ice cream in milk shakes. Buy firm fruit and ripen it at room temperature. When overripe, the flesh becomes unpleasant tasting and mushy. Once ripe, it will keep for two days if refrigerated. It is in season during mid-to-late spring.

GUAVA

Amrood. Guavas vary in shape from round or oval to pear shaped. They range in size from a chicken egg to a baseball. The thin, edible skin ranges in color from yellowish green or golden yellow to green,

guava

and it sometimes has tiny black or pink spots. The color of the flesh may be white, salmon pink, or watermelon red. They have a central core of tiny, hard seeds. The pulp in the middle of the seeds is sweet and soft compared to the crisp, slightly granular flesh around the seeds. Guavas permeate a room with their distinctive, floral fragrance. They have a tart, sweet taste. Underripe, firm, sour slices are enjoyed dipped in chili powder and salt. Ripe guava, besides being eaten, is made into jellies, jams, and thick, sweet pastes. They are in season between July and January. Guavas are good for the bones and lymphatic system.

JACKFRUIT

Kathal or chakka. This monster is a close relative of breadfruit. It tops the chart as the world's largest fruit—growing up to 100 pounds! Most of them weigh between 15 and 30 pounds and vary between 1 and 3 feet in length. The rind is light-green, thick, and covered in tiny, knobby spines that deepen to golden yellow as it ripens. It has the leathery texture of a basketball. Inside, the fruit is divided into numerous segments encased in stringy, white tissue. Each segment contains shiny, white seeds. Ripe jackfruit has yellow-orange flesh and gives off a fermented pineapple smell. It tastes like a mix of banana, mango, and pineapple.

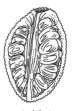

jackfruit

Because of its size, jackfruit is usually sold cut into pieces or in segments on Styrofoam trays that are wrapped in plastic. The flesh is firm and crisp or soft and stringy, depending on the variety. Eat the segments by themselves or slice and add them to fruit salad. The seeds are eaten as a snack, boiled, or roasted and added to curries. They have a soft, mealy texture and have to be removed from their plasticlike seed case before eating. They have a chestnutlike flavor. The seeds are also dried, ground into flour, and used to make chapatis and papaddams. You may also find canned jackfruit in syrup.

LONGAN

Native to India and closely related to the lychee, these are clusters of large, grape-sized fruits with thin, brownish yellow, brittle shells. Inside, the translucent, white flesh is syrupy and sweet with a hint of fresh fig. The flesh encases a large, smooth, brown seed that is visible

longan

through the pulp. This is the reason why it is also called "dragons-eye fruit." To eat them, remove their shell by splitting them open at the stem and peeling. You can pit them in advance or as you eat them. Longans are usually sold in bundles of twigs with clusters of fruit attached. Look for uncracked, bright-colored specimens. Store them in the refrigerator. They will keep for two to three weeks. However, they lose flavor rapidly. For maximum flavor, eat them right away.

MANGO

Aam. Native to India, golden pink mangoes are adored and eagerly awaited each summer as they flow into the markets and fill the air with their sweet fragrance. They are an everlasting symbol of desire, love, friendship, and plenty. The paisley mango motif is widely used in Indian textiles, jewelry, paintings, and decorative henna tattoos. The name is an adaptation of "man-gay," the

mango

Tamil word for mango. A relative of the cashew, mangoes vary in size, color, and taste. Some are round while others are oval or kidney shaped. Skin colors range from yellowish green to reddish orange. The two most prized Indian mangoes are the Alphonso, or Aapoos, and the Dussheri. The Alphonso, from the Konkan coast of the Maharashtra state, are large, plump, yellow-skinned mangoes tinted in a red blush with buttery, smooth, firm, orange flesh. They taste like a cross between a peach and an apricot with just a hint of pineapple sourness. Lucknow in Utter Pradesh produces the Dussheri mango. These are elongated with golden skins and nectar-sweet, bright orange, soft flesh. Both contain slim, flat, white, oval seeds. Other good types are the Himsagar from West Bengal and the Langra from Benares.

Look for ripe, fragrant mangoes that yield to gentle pressure. They are past their prime if they have soft, black spots and pitted skin. To ripen hard ones at home, wrap them in newspaper and store them in a straw basket. Once ripe they can be refrigerated, but let them reach room temperature before eating them. Many people are allergic to the sap that is concentrated at the stem, which causes them to break into a fierce itch like a poison-ivy reaction. Take precaution and slice the stem off before eating a mango. They can be peeled and sliced, or you can leave the skin on and slice off the cheeks on each side of the pit. With the tip of a knife, cut a crosshatch pattern in the flesh without cutting the skin. Turn the skins inside out so that the cubes of flesh pop up. Nibble the cubes off or detach them from the skin with a knife. Mango pulp is pureed with yogurt in drinks or added to puddings and milk fudges. Unripe, green mangoes, called kacha am, are used in curries, salads, chutneys, and

A small image of Ganesh on the side of the Chidambaram temple tells an old story. Shiva set his two sons, Ganesh and Kartikkeya, on a race around the universe. Kartikkeya mounted his swift peacock. Short, pudgy Ganesh was stuck with his tiny mousemount. However, using his brains he rode around his parents. Shiva asked him what he was doing, and clever Ganesh said, "Circling the supreme Lord Shiva and Goddess Parvati who create and contain the universe is tantamount to going around the universe." Happy with his slow-footed but quick-thinking son, Shiva gave the prize, a delicious mango, to Ganesh.

pickles, or they are enjoyed sliced and sprinkled with salt and chili powder. They are also dried and ground into green-mango powder. Mangoes are most abundant in spring through early summer, peaking in June and July. Mangoes are regarded as a system cleanser and a kidney tonic. They are also good for the complexion.

MANGOSTEEN

Manguskai. This is a round fruit that resembles a plump, dark-purple pincushion with four green, petal-like leaves on top. The thick, hard

shell encloses five to six segments of pearly, white, juicy flesh with a sweet, tart, refreshing taste. Some segments contain edible pinkish seeds. To eat this, cut the shell horizontally around the middle of the fruit, being careful not to pierce the flesh. Lift off the top shell and spoon the segments out of the lower shell. Be careful

mangosteen

not to get any sap on your clothes as mangosteen rind contains tannins that can stain—they are used for dyeing in the leather industry. They are at peak ripeness when they are slightly soft. Avoid ones with very hard skins that are overripe. They spoil rapidly, so eat them as soon as possible. They are in season between December and February. They are a refreshing fruit.

PAPAYA

Pappali. Papayas resemble small, oval, or pear-shaped melons with thin skins. They turn from green to yellowish green and yellow-orange when they are ripe. Its perfumed, musky, sweet flesh is orange or red-orange and slightly softer than a melon's flesh. The center contains a mass of round, black seeds with a peppery flavor. These are used as a condiment or garnish. Choose heavy, firm fruits that are just beginning to soften. To eat this, cut it in half, scoop out the seeds, peel it, slice it, and serve it with a squeeze of lime juice. Or just spoon the flesh out. Papaya are rich in the enzyme papain, which breaks down proteins and is used in marinades as a meat tenderizer. Unripe, green papaya is shredded and stir-fried with spices and grated coconut, added to curries or pickled. Papaya aids digestion and is considered a system cleanser and liver detoxifier. It helps keep the eyes bright and the skin clear.

papaya

POMEGRANATE

Anar. The name means "fruit of many seeds." They are a symbol of fertility in Indian mythology. Measuring about 3 inches in diameter, the roundish pomegranate has thick, red or pinkish, leathery skin. Thick white membranes divide the interior into six sections that encase a large number of ruby-red seeds. To eat this, slice the skin into four equal parts and pry it open carefully as the juice can stain. Scoop the seeds out with a spoon and discard the bitter membranes. The small, angular, translucent, pulpy seeds contain a small, white pip. The seeds

have a tart, refreshing flavor. Most people prefer to
eat the pulp and discard the astringent-tasting inner
pips, but they are edible. The seeds can also be added
to fruit salads or green salads or used to garnish curries and soups. The juice is made into the cordial
syrup called grenadine.

Choose large, unblemished, smooth-skinned fruits,
which are heavy for their size. Avoid wrinkled ones or
those with dull or pale skin. Pomegranates will keep at

pomegranate

room temperature for a week or more and up to a month if refrigerated.
Pomegranate promotes the production of red-blood cells and helps treat
anemia, fever, and heart conditions. It is also used to treat nausea, vomiting, rashes, and morning sickness. Fresh juice in each nostril will stop a
nosebleed, and a drop in the eye relieves burning.

QUINCE

Native to Persia, the quince resembles a large, plump pear. It is grown
in Kashmir. The thin skin changes from light green to yellow as the
fruit ripens. Ripe quince gives off a flowery, vanilla, guava, and pineapple aroma that fills any room that it is in. The flesh is pale, firm, and
dry with two crescent cores filled with seeds like those of an apple.
Quince cannot be eaten raw because their high tannin content gives
them a bitter taste that disappears with cooking. They are used in jams
and jellies due to their high pectin content. The word "marmalade"
comes from the Portuguese "marmelo," which means "quince jam."
The flesh turns pink or red when cooked. Quince can be poached in
sugar syrup, wine, or honey. They can be made into a thick, sweet
paste. In Kashmir they are poached and stuffed with a spicy, spinach
mixture and baked. Choose plump, firm, undamaged fruit with partially yellow skin. Allow them to ripen at room temperature. Wrapped
individually and refrigerated, ripe quince will keep for a few weeks.
Once cut, sprinkle with lemon juice to prevent discoloration. Quince
are rich in vitamin C and are good for the gastrointestinal system.

SOURSOP

Seetha or prickly custard apple. This is an elongated, heart-shaped fruit
with deep-green skin dotted in short, hooked nubs. It ranges in size
from 12 ounces to up to 10 pounds. The interior white flesh tastes
sweet and tangy, like a slightly acidic blend of mango and pineapple.

The thick pulp is often fibrous and contains hard, shiny,
black or brown seeds. These should be removed before
eating or pulping the fruit as they are said to be toxic.
Peel and eat it, or pulp it for making juice, custard, ice
cream, or smoothies. The pulp has a creamy consistency when blended with water. Choose heavy fruits
that yield to pressure. Store it at room temperature for
up to two to three days. It can be refrigerated for about

soursop

one week.

STAR APPLE

Jamun. This is a plum-sized, round fruit with smooth, shiny, purple skin that encloses 8 translucent segments of rose-tinged, white pulp, each containing a hard, dark-brown seed. Sliced in half horizontally, the star-shaped pattern of segments reveals how the fruit got its name. The taste is tangy and sweet. Star apples have to be soft and fully ripe to eat or the pulp will be hard and not very sweet. Once it is ripe, eat it right away or refrigerate it for two to three days.

STAR FRUIT

Kamrakh, carambola, and five finger fruit. This is a small, waxy, yellow fruit with an unusual shape. It consists of five prominent ribs that run its length. When the fruit is sliced crosswise, the slices are star shaped. The thin, shiny skin is a translucent, yellowish green color, turning golden yellow when fully ripe.

star fruit

The edible skin encloses translucent, crisp, slightly acid, very juicy flesh. There are flat seeds in some of the ribs. Very ripe star fruits bruise easily and may have brown patches along the ribs, which can be removed with a vegetable peeler. To eat this, slice it and remove the seeds. Star fruit is added raw to salads and added to soups and curries as a souring agent. Star-shaped slices garnish fish and seafood dishes. It can also be made into chutney or jam. Under-ripe, sour star fruit is eaten as a snack when dipped in chili powder and salt. Despite its fragile appearance, it keeps well. It can be left out at room temperature for several days if it is not fully ripe. Refrigerate ripe ones for up to two weeks. Star-fruit juice is claimed to be a cure for hangovers.

A good way to explore the backwater canals of Kerala is by converted rice barge. Thick palm groves and thatch-hut villages float past on tobacco-colored water. Kids splash in shallows and wave at us. Our vessel is well equipped with rattan lounging chairs, a canvas canopy for protection from the elements, and sleeping cushions. Two sinewy skippers navigate by pole and motor, doubling as on-board cooks. They also provide toddy, which we sip between bites of fried karimeen (a type of carp) garnished with slices of sour star fruit. The star fruit is to ward off the effects of the toddy.

TAMARILLO

Tree tomato. Originally from South America, this member of the nightshade family is cultivated in India. Two varieties may be found. One is golden orange with yellow flesh, and the other is reddish purple with orange flesh. They are both oval and egg-sized fruits with satin-smooth skin. The bitter skin covers firm flesh with a tart gooseberry flavor. The golden variety is milder and sweeter. Both contain a ring of dark edible seeds, similar to the ones found in tomatoes. To eat this, peel it with a

tamarillo

knife, or blanch it first for easier removal of the skin. It is good raw, sprinkled with sugar or salt and lime juice. Tamarillo is made into chutney, jam, and pickles. It is also pureed to flavor yogurt and ice cream. Unripe, it is cooked as a vegetable in curries and soups. You can use it in any recipe that uses tomatoes. Choose firm fruits with shiny, unblemished skins that yield slightly to pressure. Once ripe they can be stored in the refrigerator for up to two weeks.

WOODAPPLE

Villati, kaith, or kapittha. Also called elephant apple, this native of India and Sri Lanka is a jungle fruit that is harvested under license as forest produce. According to legend, wild elephants pick up the fruits with their trunks and swallow them whole. Woodapples are round with rough, grayish, hard, woody shells. They are about the size of an apple. The easiest way to break one open is to smash it with a hammer and scoop out the pulp. The pale, firm pulp of unripe woodapples is grated, mixed with chopped onion, and seasoned with salt and lime juice to make a very sour relish. When fully ripe the pulp turns a chocolate-brown color and has a mealy texture with numerous small, round, pale seeds. The taste is sweet and sour. Ripe fruit is pulped, strained, and blended with coconut milk and sugar to make a popular drink, dimbul kiri, or woodapple milk. The pulp is also made into jam, jellies, and milk fudge. To select a ripe one, shake the fruit. If it bumps around loose in the shell, its ripe. The ripe pulp resembles chocolate pudding. It is also sold canned as woodapple cream.

Other

Besides the fruits already mentioned, you may also find oranges, apples, watermelon, sugar cane, plums, cherries, and pineapples. It is worth trying some of the exotic fruits that you might not be familiar with. Also try some unripe fruits in tart, tangy salads or stewed like a vegetable. What you find ultimately depends on what is in season.

9

Canned Goods

केन ड्रुडस्त

Hindi word for "canned goods"

Canning is, of course, the popular method of preserving foods for export, long shelf life, and availability. This is especially true of many Indian vegetables and products that are not grown or processed in the United States.

Moving through the Rajas' grocery, let's take a look at shelf 9. You will see a long row of stacked cans wrapped in colorful labels. Small and medium cans share space with jumbo tins filled with everything from chickoo pulp to violet yams. You will want to stock up on heat-and-serve canned entrees, dals, beans, and curries. There are also strange vegetables, fruit pulps, coconut milk, cooking sauces, cheeseball sweets, and jackfruit-seed curry to check out. In exploring the canned goods, you will find items arranged by content: vegetables, sauces, sweets, fruit pulps, and so on. Find the category you want and select from the different varieties and brands available.

Canned Vegetables

Some of the vegetables are also found fresh in the produce section. But the canned version saves you prep time. There are drumsticks, tuvar, guvar green beans, valor beans, bitter gourds, kantola (spiny bitter gourd), lotus root, Punjab tinda, suran yams, and tindora. Others

rarely make the crossing from India in fresh form. Almost everything listed in this chapter can be used in curries, stews, stir-fries or added to simmering dal. The vegetables are precooked and packed in a salt brine. They just need to be drained, rinsed, and gently heated. Don't overcook them or they will be mushy. Most of them are found under the Ashoka and Nirav brands in 14- to15-ounce cans.

CHOLIYA

These are green, unripe chickpeas. Use them like fresh peas. They are delicious in rice pulaos, curries, and salads. They are also good cooked in ghee with salt and pepper, or mashed with garlic and spices as a dip. Look for the Ashoka brand.

GREEN JACKFRUIT

Green jackfruit is the young, unripe segments of jackfruit canned in brine. It is used as a starchy vegetable. It is added to curries, stews, and South Indian coconut-milk soups. The taste is similar to chayote squash. Since it has been cooked and processed, it is softer than firm, fresh green jackfruit would be. Add it near the end of cooking time so that it won't fall apart. Look for the Swad brand in 2-pound cans.

PAPDI LILVA

These are the small, oval, greenish yellow seeds from the pods of Indian green beans (papdi). Lilva means seed. Cook them like beans or fresh peas. They are good in rice and dal dishes. Look for the Ashoka and Nirav brands.

papdi lilva

PARVAL

These are small, oval, pointed gourds with green-striped skins that taste like zucchini. Use them whole, slice them in half lengthwise, or chop and use them in any squash recipe. They are good in soups and curries or stir-fried with spices. Look for the Swad, Ashoka, and Nirav brands.

parval

PATRAVAL

These are steamed, large taro leaves stuffed with a spice paste and rolled up. They are dry packed. To use them, cut them into pieces and deep-fry them until they are dark brown and crispy. Serve them with chutney, chili sauce, or ketchup. Look for the VAFA brand in 13-ounce cans,

patraval

which have a photo of the rolls on a yellow and red label. Look also for the Nirav brand's curried patra in 12-ounce cans and for the Swad brand's patra leaves in 13-ounce cans.

RATALU

These are chunks of a large, pale orange Indian yam; which are also called elephant yams. A violet-tinted variety is called kandh. Use either like a potato. It has a bland flavor. It is good in spicy stews and curries or mashed and mixed with ghee and spices. Look for the Amrit and Ashoka brands in 14-ounce cans.

SARSON KA SAAG

These are curried, pureed mustard leaves, which are a delicacy of the Punjab region. They have a creamy texture and a peppery, spinach flavor. Heat and serve them with rice and yogurt or season them with melted butter, sizzled mustard seeds, and fried onion bits. They are good cooked with cubes of potato or lamb. Look for the Ashoka, Sohna, and Nirav brands. Look also for the Jyoti brand mustard and spinach with ginger and hot pepper in 15-ounce cans.

SURTI PAPRI

These are valor (Indian broad bean) seeds from Surti, a region in Gujarat. There are also cans of valor beans under the VAFA label.

TOOR LILVA

These are the seeds from yellow-lentil (toovar) pods. They have a slightly nutty, pea taste. Use them in rice dishes and curries, or sauté them with spices and leafy greens in ghee or butter. Look for the Ashoka and Nirav brands.

Ashoka, a popular brand of canned vegetables, was named after the first emperor of India in the 3rd century B.C. A Buddhist, he was tolerant of all religions and infused the concept of dharma (keeping of the world order) with his governing principles. Ashoka's edicts were inscribed on enormous stone pillars throughout the land. Ashoka's lion capital at Sarnath (where Buddha first achieved enlightenment) was chosen in 1947 as the emblem of independent India. The emblem shows four lions crowning a 24-spoked wheel of law on a lotus base.

Canned, Ready-to-Eat Entrees

Authentic Indian meals are a can opener away when you have heat-and-serve canned foods in stock. Most are in the traditional moghul style, which involves richly spiced dishes. Makhani dishes have a butter-cream sauce. Many of them are mild rather than searingly hot, and all of them are vegetarian. Canned food is never the same as food cooked from scratch, but you can doctor the contents. Sizzle some garlic, onions, and bell peppers or chilies in a little oil, then slip them in with the canned product. Garnish them with a sprinkle of garam masala, fresh herbs, or fried onions. Add fresh vegetables, meat, chicken, or seafood for heartier fare. Most of them are found in 15- to 16-ounce cans. Look for the Ashoka, Maya "Veggie," Nirav, and Jyoti brands.

In India inviting a guest to dinner means taking into consideration the phase of the moon (new and full moons are fasting or vegetarian days), dietary restrictions or taboos (Hindus eat no beef, Muslims eat no pork), the time of year (summer for "cooling" foods, winter for "heating" ones), and even what day it is, as personal deities are worshiped on a particular day of the week. The planets also have corresponding days of the week. If a person has, for example, bad luck indicated in Saturn in their horoscope, they would be advised to abstain from certain foods on Saturday.

DAL

This is a Gujarati home-style dal made with small black lentils (urad dal), red kidney beans, ghee, onions, and spices. It is thick, flavorful, and hearty.

DAL MAKHANI

These are curried black lentils (urad dal) in a medium-hot, buttery, creamy, spiced sauce.

DAL MUGHALI

This richly spiced, North Indian-style, mixed-lentil dal is made from chickpeas, yellow lentils, and urad dal (black lentils) cooked with tomatoes and spices. It is delicious with cooked chicken pieces added.

CHOLE

These are chickpeas and cubes of potato cooked in a tangy tamarind sauce. It is fragrant with spices and hot with ginger and chilies.

FRIED JACKSEED CURRY

This is a Sri Lankan curry made of the large, boiled, and fried seeds from giant jackfruit. They are cooked in a spicy sauce. The seeds have a mealy texture and a mild, chestnutlike flavor. Look for the Larich brand in 21-ounce cans.

KALA CHANNA

These are small, dark, blackish brown chickpeas with a nutty flavor in a water-salt brine. Drain and use them in any number of dishes. Cook them with vegetables, chicken, green peppers, onions, and spices. Or puree them and make creamy soups or dips. Add them to salads and soups or steam them with rice.

kala channa

KASHMIR DUM ALOO

This is potato curry made of small, boiled, deep-fried potatoes in a medium-hot, rich, North Indian-style, tomato-yogurt sauce. Heat and garnish it with a sprinkle of garam masala and chopped coriander leaves. Serve it with naan.

KARHI

Also known as Punjabi kadhi. These are buttermilk- or yogurt-based, mild, tangy, cooling curry soups with chickpea flour and potato dumplings (also called pakoras). Serve them as a main dish with rice and a salad. They can also be a starter or side dish. Look for the Jyoti brand's karhi and for the Ashoka, Maya "Veggie," or Nirav brands' Punjabi kadhi.

MATAR MUSHROOM JAHANGIRI

These are curried green peas and button mushrooms in a mild sauce. Add cooked chicken pieces if you want. It is good with bread.

MATAR PANEER

These are curried green peas (also known as mutter) and cubes of paneer curd cheese in a medium-hot sauce. They are especially good with chapatis.

NAVRATAN KORMA

The name means "nine jewels" and refers to the number of vegetables in the dish. It was named for the moghul emperor Akbar's nine courtiers. These are Punjabi-style mixed vegetables in a mildly spiced, slightly sweet, cinnamon-infused, creamy korma sauce.

PALAK PANEER

This is mildly spiced, thick, creamed spinach with cubes of paneer curd cheese. Serve it over rice or scoop it up with chapati. This popular dish is also known as saag paneer and is a staple of North India where milk products are a common cooking ingredient. It is a staple of all Indian restaurant menus.

palak paneer

PANEER MAKHANI

These are cubes of paneer curd cheese in a mildly spicy, North Indian-style, thick, tomato-butter-cream sauce. Makhani (also spelled makhni) is a classic Northern style creamy-tomato saffron sauce; the name refers to the Hindi word makhan which means butter. It is almost always eaten with tandoori-style chicken and tandoori bread.

paneer makhani

PAV BHAJI

This is bread with vegetables. The can contains the bhaji, mashed potatoes, mixed vegetables, and onions cooked in a rich, spicy sauce.

This thick, pastelike dish is traditionally eaten with small bread called paav (or pao), which are split and fried on a tava in melted butter. The bhaji is scooped up with the bread.

POLOS CURRY

This is a Sri Lankan curry made with chunks of green jackfruit, onions, coconut milk, garlic, spices, and palm oil. It is delicious spooned over rice, and it has an unusual flavor. Look for the Larich brand in 21-ounce cans.

PUNJABI CHATPATE CHOLEY

These are punjabi-style, white chickpeas in a rich, spicy, slightly tart sauce. Heat and garnish them with chopped chilies, fresh ginger, onions, tomatoes, coriander leaves, and lemon wedges. As the name suggests, eat them with chapatis.

SAMBHAR

This is a spicy, South Indian-style, yellow-lentil stew with eggplant, green peppers, onions, and carrots. Heat and serve it with rice, or thin it with water or broth as a soup. You can add boiled, cubed potatoes, crushed tomatoes, and chunks of chicken for a heartier dish.

SHAHI RAJMA

The word "shahi" means "royal." This is a rich, North Indian-style kidney-bean curry in a thick, spicy sauce. Add chunks of lamb or other meat for a more substantial dish. It goes great with the wheaty flavor of chapati.

shahi rajma

SURTI UNDHIYU

A specialty of Gujarat, this is usually served with puri breads at weddings and banquets. It is made of mixed vegetables and red lentils seasoned with spices, grated coconut, and palm sugar in a mild sauce. Garnish it with chopped peanuts and toasted, grated coconut, then serve it with rice.

Coconut Milk

This is the unsweetened, processed liquid made from the grated flesh of coconuts. It is essential in many South Indian curries, soups, and sweets. Canned coconut milk has a thick layer of cream at the top. Under this is a clearish liquid, the coconut water. Both parts are added in soups but some curries, sauces, and desserts just use the layer of cream. If you want just the cream, open a can without shaking it up and skim off the thick cream. You can also refrigerate the can for a few hours and spoon the hardened cream off the top. Look for the Swad brand in 14-ounce cans. There are also several superb Thai brands, including Chao Kroong, Mae Ploy, and Chefs Choice in 13- or 14-ounce cans. Coconut milk is used in a fish curry recipe on page 250.

Cooking Sauces

These are thick, spicy sauces ready to be combined with fresh veggies, meats, chicken, or seafoods of your choice. Basic sauces help you whip up an assortment of authentic Indian dishes at a moment's notice. Most include recipes on the label to start you off.

CLASSIC MASALA SAUCE

Use this to make homemade curries without roasting and grinding spices. It is a versatile sauce made from pureed fried onions, crushed tomatoes, ginger, and spices. It is good simmered with potatoes, mushrooms, peas, or chicken. Look for the Jyoti brand in 16-ounce cans.

CREAMY COCONUT KORMA

This is a classic, North Indian-style, korma cooking sauce. This is a rich, creamy coconut-milk and yogurt-based sauce infused with aromatic spices, ginger, and garlic. Brown chicken and cook it until tender, add the korma sauce, and simmer it until it is heated through. It is also good with vegetables. Look for the Pataks brand's medium-hot korma sauce in 10-ounce cans.

coconut milk

ROGAN JOSH SAUCE

This robust, tangy, North Indian-style cooking sauce is made from buttermilk, tomato paste, onions, ginger, and garlic. It compliments lamb, potatoes, cauliflower, and beans. Look for the Jyoti brand in 16-ounce cans and for the Pataks brand in 10-ounce tins.

SAFFRON CREAM SAUCE

This rich, mild, creamy, yellow cooking sauce is made with sour cream, tomatoes, cream, onions, spices, and saffron. Use it to make seafood curries or as a sauce for koftas (meatballs or vegetable patties). Look for the Jyoti brand in 16-ounce cans.

OTHERS

Besides these, you may also find Madras' hot cooking sauce, tikka masala for grilled chicken or curries, and hot vindaloo sauce. The Pataks brand offers all of these in 10-ounce tins.

Fruit Pulps

Thick, sweet fruit pulps are used in desserts and sweets, blended with yogurt, or mixed with coconut milk to make drinks. They are made by simmering mashed fruit pulp in a sugar syrup until thick.

CHICKOO PULP

This is a brown, fruit paste made from chickoo (sapodilla) fruit with a brown sugar, pear flavor. It is used as a spread and in puddings, ice cream, pastries, or in creamy drinks. Look for the Nirav, Priya, and Swad brands in 2-pound tins. It is also sold sliced and packed in syrup.

MANGO PULP

This is a thick, golden, sweet, pulp made from mangoes. It is delicious warmed and poured over ice cream or blended into rice pudding, yogurt, or thick cream. It is also used in milk-fudge and yogurt drinks. Look for the Kanaiya, Swad, and Nirav brands' Kesar mango pulp and for the Ratna and Nirav brands' Alphonso mango pulp in large tins.

mango pulp

WOODAPPLE CREAM

This is a thick, chocolatey-brown paste made from woodapple pulp and sugar. This is much sweeter than the tart fruit. It is used as a spread, put in desserts and milk fudge, or blended with coconut milk and crushed ice as a drink. Look for the Larich brand in large tins.

Canned Sweets

These are tinned versions of some of the most popular Indian sweets, which are generally made from milk powder or chenna-curd-cheese packed in sugar syrup. There are vacuum-sealed cans of sweets from Pakistan and mung-bean halwa. The soft, syrup sweets are made by Halidrams in 2-pound cans, with about 20 pieces to a can. Other brands to look for are GC, Ghasitaram, and Swad, also in 2-pound tins.

ANGOORI PETHA

These are pale, crystallized, syrupy ash-gourd chunks with the firm texture of a glace, but it melts in your mouth. It is a specialty in Agra.

CHOM-CHOM

These are oval, squishy, chenna cheesecake patties boiled in sugar syrup. Also spelled cham-cham. These favorite milk-cheese fritters are flattened after frying and soaked in rose-scented syrup. Some are tinted yellow or pink and all can be drained and served dipped in grated coconut.

GULAB JAMUN

These are spongy, fried, milky doughballs in a rose-scented syrup. They are also made by Amul and found in 17-ounce tins in the refrigerator case. These decadent fritter balls are served in every Indian restaurant and their name literally means "rose berries." Gulab jul is the Hindi name for rose water and these soft, aromatic balls are served in a bowl with warm rose syrup.

GUL BAHAR

These are spongy, sweet, milk powder balls in sugar syrup. This is similar to gulab jamun except the boiled down solid milk is replaced with a mixture of non-fat dry milk and heavy cream that is formed into smooth dough balls, fried, and soaked in a scented syrup.

MOONG DAL HALWA

This is a sweet, thick puree of cooked, ground mung beans flavored with ghee, spices, and nuts. This dryish, dark yellow paste can be pushed out of the can (remove bottom and top ends) and sliced, but it is easier to just spoon a portion out. It is eaten as is or used to stuff breads and pancakes. It can also be rolled into balls or decorated with nuts.

RAJBHOG

These are large (twice the size of rosogollas) chenna cheeseballs flavored with saffron and pistachios, soaked in rose syrup.

ROSOGOLLAS

rosogollas

These are soft, juicy chenna cheeseballs soaked in flavored syrups, including mango, orange blossom, pineapple, and strawberry. This favorite was invented in 1868 in a small sweet shop at Baghbazar in north Calcutta. The desperate creator, Nobin Chandra Das, was competing against the wildly popular sandesh, a dry, fudgy, chenna cheese sweet, so he came up with a soft, succulent, syrupy sweet. It was not an instant hit but soon became so popular that it was sold canned the world over.

CANNED HALWA

These are sugary, nut-loaded, hard or chewy sweets packed in 10-ounce tins with colorful paper wrappers. They are made by the Ahmed company in Pakistan. There is habashi, which are brown, whole-wheat, milk-fudge balls with nuts, karachi, which are chewy, gelatinous sweet

canned halwa

slabs studded with nuts, and sohan, which is a hard toffee with almonds and pistachios that comes in three thick, round, cellophane-wrapped pieces. The plastic cans, about 3-inches wide, are difficult to open with a normal can opener—I had better luck breaking the plastic bottom with a hammer.

Stocking Up

An Indian-food fan would stock up on basic cooking sauces, some dal and bean curries, spinach or mustard saag, coconut milk, mango pulp, and gulab jamun.

10

Ghee & Oils

Hindi word for "cooking oil"

Are you wondering what you will use to sizzle your spices, to deep-fry your samosas, to season your dals with, or to smear on your chapatis? Head to shelf 10 in the Rajas' grocery store to pick from a variety of cooking oils. Oils are made from seeds and nuts. Each oil has a distinctive flavor and heating temperature. Ghee, made from clarified butter, is not a true oil, but it is the favored cooking medium of India. It is also used in making sweets and as a spread. Different regions prefer certain oils that define the flavors of the cuisine. Oils should be stored in a cool, dry place away from direct sunlight. They will keep for a long time. The following oils are organized from most to least used. Some oils are used for hair or body massage. These will say "for massage only" on the bottle.

GHEE

ghee

This clarified butter is also called toop. Since ancient times ghee has been a symbol of wealth in India. A person who had a large supply was said to possess liquid gold. Ghee is the purest form of butterfat. It is made from unsalted, melted butter. It is simmered until the dark sediment settles to the bottom of the pan and separates from the clear, golden ghee. Ghee solidifies when cool, but it is still soft and creamy. Clarifying butter keeps it from going rancid and allows it to be heated to high temperatures. Ghee has a sweet, nutty taste. When it is heated it has a caramel-like aroma. Ghee is heated with spices and seasonings. It is used to pep up plain, steamed vegetables, stirred into dals, or used for sautéing and frying.

Indian grocery stores stock both ulsi ghee (pure) and a cheaper vegetable ghee, which is made from hydrogenated vegetable oils. The highest-quality commercial ghee is from Holland. It is bought in bulk by wholesalers and repackaged under store or brand names. Ghee will keep for several weeks at room temperature and for up to six months if refrigerated. Ghee is sold in tins and glass jars on the shelf or in the refrigerator case. Look for the Kanaiya, Nirav, Royal Cuisine, Sugam, Swad, and Virindavan brands in 8- or 16-ounce jars, for the Khanum brand in 2-pound jars, and for the California Fields brand in 12-ounce jars. Vegetable ghee is sold by the Dalda, Krishna, and Phalkha companies in tins.

PEANUT OIL

Moongfalli ka tel or groundnut oil. This is the most widely used cooking oil in central and northern India. It is cold-pressed, which gives it an intense peanut flavor, or refined. Refined peanut oil has a light flavor, and it is the best choice for deep-frying because it heats to extremely high temperatures without burning. It is the best all-around cooking oil. It is almost colorless and odorless. Look for the Golden Collection brand in 16- and 32-ounce bottles. Look also for the Penola and Nirav brands in 1-gallon containers.

SESAME OIL

Til ka tel or gingelly oil. This Indian sesame oil is pressed from tiny, oil-rich, raw sesame seeds. Do not use the dark, Chinese type that is made from roasted seeds. Sesame oil has a light, sweet, nutty flavor. It is the preferred cooking oil in southwest India and Tamil Nadu, where it is called "sweet oil." It is almost clear and has a very high smoking point. It is suitable for most Indian recipes. Sesame oil

sesame oil

is also used as a massage oil. Brands to look for include Deep, Golden Collection, Laxmi, Maya, Royal Cuisine, Priya, Piriyam, and Swad in bottles ranging from 11 to 24 ounces.

MUSTARD OIL

Sarson ka tel. A pungent, dark amber, thick oil pressed from brown mustard seeds, this is used in cooking and pickling. Unlike other oils, mustard oil is always brought to its smoking point before using it. This can be done just before cooking, or it can be done in advance and cooled. It tones down harsh flavors and makes it easier to digest. Mustard oil is widely used in the Bengal and Punjab regions of India and in Bangladesh. It is used to

mustard oil

deep-fry pappadams and sago chips and to flavor fish and vegetable dishes. Mustard oil is a preservative and is used in pickling. Raw mustard oil is used as a massage oil for relief from arthritis, and it is rubbed into the scalp to promote hair growth. Brands to look for include Ace, LATA, Maya, Swad, KTC, and Tez in bottles ranging from 7 to 32 ounces. Also Palace brand in 16-ounce bottles

Mustard oil contains erucic acid (the FDA has found it to pose a health risk) and many brands have started to issue warnings on their bottles of mustard oil. Since the oil is heated before it is eaten, Indians believe that the erucic acid is burned off. This oil has been consumed for thousands of years, with seemingly no ill effects. Scientists are now working to breed the acid out of mustard seeds.

SAFFLOWER OIL

Kardi or kusuma. This is a mild, nearly clear oil pressed from the seeds of the flowering saffron thistle, or safflower plant. The name comes from the flower's red-orange hue. It is also used as a dye like saffron.

After a swim and lolling on Kovalam beach, near Trivandrum in South India, I succumbed to an herbal-sesame-oil massage at the nearby Ayurvedic center across the road from my guest house. The nimble fingers of Mrs. Lalitha worked magic, kneading the aches of travel out of every muscle.

Safflower oil is low in saturated fats, has a mild flavor, and has a very high smoking point. It is used as a cooking and salad oil. Some cooks blend ghee with safflower oil for an economical deep-frying medium. Look for the Golden Collection brand in 16- or 32-ounce bottles.

COCONUT OIL

Nariyal ka tel. Extracted from the dried meat, or copra, of coconuts, this is a creamy, white fat that is hard at room temperature and clear when heated. It is used extensively in South Indian cooking where the strong coconut-oil smell complements coconut-based fish and vegetable curries. Coconut oil is poured over dals and other cooked dishes for additional flavor. Because of its high heating temperature, it is often used for deep-frying. This adds a distinct coconut flavor—and fat to foods. It is very high in saturated fats and can be hard to digest. Indians also use coconut oil for massaging and oiling their hair to encourage growth and to add a lustrous sheen. Look for the Golden Collection, KTC, and Swad brands in 16-ounce jars.

PALM OIL

There are two types: unrefined, yellow-orange oil pressed from the fibrous layer just under the skin of palm kernels, and pale, refined oil pressed from the kernel of the seed inside the palm fruit. Both are high in saturated fats and have a mildly rich flavor. The orange, unrefined type contains vitamin E and beta carotene. Palm oil has a high smoking point. It is used to deep-fry snacks at many roadside stalls in India, adding a rich aroma—and calories. The pale type is used for cooking and is made into products as diverse as margarine, soap, and cosmetics. Look for the KTC brand's unrefined palm oil in 16-ounce bottles.

ALMOND OIL

Badam ke tel. A clear, sweet oil pressed from almonds, this is used sparingly due to its higher cost. It is not a cooking oil at all. Almond oil flavors sweets, lubricates sweet molds, and is brushed on hot flatbreads. As it easily turns rancid, store it in the refrigerator. It is also used in fragrant massage oils and skin products. Look for the Laxmi brand in 8-ounce bottles, the Golden Collection brand, the Maya and Swad brands in 16-ounce bottles, and the KTC brand in 7- or 10-ounce bottles.

almond oil

OTHER LIGHT OILS

Oil made from corn, soybean, sunflower, cottonseed, and rapeseed (canola) may also be found. They are all light in color and taste and can be used in most cooking. But they tend to smoke quickly (except for corn, which has a high heating temperature and can be used for deep-frying). Corn oil can also be reheated without its flavor being altered. Look for the Nirav brand's corn, sunflower, and canola oil. Look also for Golden Collection sunflower and soybean oil in 16- and 32-ounce bottles.

Stocking Up

A versatile cook will keep two or three different oils in stock, including ghee. More than anything else, oils with spices give Indian food its flavor. Ghee adds a rich feel and a layered texture to breads, pastries, and sweets. Invest in a high-quality ghee if you plan on doing a lot of Indian cooking. Then add a light, all-purpose cooking oil such as peanut or sesame. Get mustard oil for seasoning foods and making pickles.

11

Dairy Products: The Milky Way

Hindi word for "milk"

In India, milk is considered a perfect food. To own a cow is to possess wealth. Krishna is often portrayed in pictures in the company of cows and milkmaids. Cows lumber through streets or doze in the middle of roads, causing traffic jams. No one disturbs them. In addition to being sacred symbols in Indian culture, cows provide a supply of fresh milk, which is welcomed in a land of little refrigeration. They are, it seems, great lumbering, portable refrigerators! Hindus often touch the forehead of wandering cows and say a prayer as a gesture of respect and devotion. Cows are associated with Mother Earth as both are sources of food, fuel, and fertilizer. Cows are believed to be the embodiment of the kindness of the gods. The cows' five products (pancagavya)—milk, yogurt, ghee, urine, and dung—are thought to have purifying properties.

Milk (dhoodi) and milk products play an important role in the Indian diet, providing protein and nourishment in the mostly vegetarian regime. Cream is churned into butter (makhan) to make ghee and boiled until thick for sweets. Buttermilk adds tang to soups, sauces, and cooling drinks. Milk is made into yogurt, curd cheeses, milk fudge, puddings, and kulfi (Indian ice cream). Yogurt appears at almost every meal to cool the fire of hot, spicy foods. Indian grocery stores stock many dairy products, including paneer cheese, butter, milk powder, milk drinks, and mixes for making milky desserts. Large tubs of plain yogurt are usually in the grocery stores. You will find tubs of pastel kulfi in the freezer case.

BUTTER

Makhan. In India, milk is left overnight to form curds. These are diluted and churned into buttermilk (chaas or morul) and butter. Besides being melted down to make ghee, butter is served with roti and masala dosa or melted for griddle-fried breads. Commercial butter is made from the cream that is skimmed off milk. It is fermented with a pure culture to give it a richer flavor before churning. The Amul company's butter is imported from a cooperative in India. This brand is found in the refrigerator case in 1-pound, yellow, wax boxes that have a logo of a cartoon girl holding a slice of bread.

YOGURT

Dahi or doi. Indispensable to Indian cooking, whole milk yogurt is often made at home. Milk is boiled, cooled, and mixed with a live bacteria starter, usually a spoonful of yogurt from another batch. It sets in about 6 hours and is then refrigerated. Commercial whole-milk yogurt is fine to use. Yogurt is used in dishes from raita salads to whipped-yogurt drinks called lassi (pronounced lacchi). Yogurt enrichens and thickens sauces, acts as a tenderizer in marinades, is used in creamy dips, or is folded into cooked rice.

In west Bengal when a bride arrives at her husband's house, her first step over the threshold is synchronized with the boiling over of a pot of milk in the kitchen, which symbolizes abundance for the newlyweds. And according to folklore, sipping milk at the beginning of monsoon season provides immunity from snakebites, which are a real concern in rural Bengal where the fields lurk with cobras and other vipers.

Dehin is a thick yogurt cheese made by straining off the whey in a cloth-lined colander in the refrigerator overnight. This is used to make shirkhand, a dessert that is blended with sugar, saffron, and rose essence and sprinkled with chopped nuts. Similar to sour cream, dehin can be flavored with spices as a dip. Kharis are smooth, yogurt-based sauces and soups. Pachadi are yogurt salads that are similar to raita but have grated coconut added. Mishti doi is the Bengali delicacy of sweetened yogurt set in clay pots and served at the end of a meal. Look in the refrigerator case for the Amul brand's cardamom or mango shirkhand in 16-ounce plastic tubs, for the Bombay Breeze brand's spicy, rose or mango lassi which is rather sour and watery, in 10-ounce bottles and for the Swad brand's 1-ounce containers of raita-yogurt dressing. Yogurt is used in the cucumber raita recipe on page 251 and in the vegetable biryani recipe on page 246.

PANEER CHEESE

Paneer is a soft, fresh whey cheese made from boiled whole milk that is coagulated with an acidic agent such as lemon juice or yogurt. The curds are then hung in a muslin bag to drain off the whey or weighted in a colander to press out the moisture. For even firmer paneer, the curds are pressed between two plates, cut into cubes,

muslin bag

and deep-fried until light golden. Paneer has a mild flavor, creamy texture, and looks like tofu. Soft paneer is used in koftas (cheese

paneer cheese

balls) and sweets. Fried cubes are added to rice, grain, or vegetable dishes, salads, dals, and stir-fries. Palak paneer is creamed spinach with cheese cubes. Try making your own paneer, or look for the Deep brand's paneer cubes or solid blocks in 8-ounce bags in the freezer case. Look also for the Amul brand's paneer in 14-ounce cans.

Long before churned ice cream was first manufactured, 15th century moghul emperors in Delhi cooled off from the sultry heat in their marble palaces with the frozen dessert called kulfi. A mixture of khoa, pistachios, and saffron was frozen in pyramid-shaped metal molds and sealed with dough. The ice for freezing the mixture was brought from the lofty peaks of the Himalayas. Then it was stored in insulated earth pits. Another source, closer to Delhi, was the snow-capped mountain called Choori Chandni-Ki-Char.

MILK POWDER

Mava or Khoa. Unsweetened, powdered, evaporated milk is used to make Indian confections. Pedha, or powdered milk fudge, is made by boiling butter, milk, cream, sugar, and flavorings until thickened, then stirring in milk powder. The thick, stiff paste is rolled into balls and flattened into patties. Cheese fudge and gulab jamun can also be made with milk powder. Danedhan are flat, hard cakes of baked milk

milk powder

powder grated over sweets. Look for the Deep brand's mava powder in 14-ounce plastic bags and for the Shamiana Sweets brand in 12-ounce bags.

KULFI

This is Indian ice cream made without eggs. Milk and cream are boiled down, sweetened, and flavored. It is traditionally frozen in 3-inch-high, conical, metal molds with a lid, then pried out with a knife after immersing the mold in hot water. The texture is between ice cream and sorbet. Kulfi in Indian grocery stores is made in delicious and unusual flavors. It is sold in various-sized plastic tubs

kulfi

in the freezer case. Look for the Joy and Reevas brands in pint, quart, and half-gallon tubs. Flavors include saffron-pistachio, falooda (milky rose), malai (condensed cream), cashew-raisin, thandai (spicy almond), lychee, rose, fig, and coffee. Reevas also has 3-ounce conical tubes, perfect for a one-serving treat.

Milky Dessert Mixes

These are small boxes that contain foil pouches of dry milk solids, starch, sugar, and flavorings, mixed with milk. The mixes may be chilled or frozen. Recipe instructions come on or in the boxes. They are all made by A-1A, Badshan, MDH, National Foods, and Shan in 3.5-ounce boxes unless otherwise noted.

badam feast mix

BADAM FEAST MIX

This blend of skim-milk powder, sugar, and finely ground almonds (badam) is flavored with ground cardamom and saffron. Use it to make hot and cold drinks, ice cream, and puddings, or boil it with milk powder, milk, and ghee to make almond halwa. Look for the MTR brand in 7-ounce pouches.

BASUNDI MIX

This creamy-milk, slivered-nut dessert is made by stirring the instant powder into boiling milk and chilling it. The flavor is rich and scented with saffron. Basundi is customarily made on Akshay Triteeya, the 3rd lunar day of the 1st half of the Hindu month Vaishakha. It is believed that the consequences of virtuous actions that are performed on this day are permanent. The thick, rich, reduced-milk dessert is mixed with spices and eaten with puri breads. Look for the Madhur brand in small boxes.

FALOODA MIX

falooda mix

This is an instant mix for the rose-scented milk drink that is thickened with basil seeds, corn flour, and vermicelli bits. Boil the noodles, dissolve tinted sugar in water, mix it with milk and the soft noodles, and serve it over crushed ice. Look for the Mangal brand in 3.5-ounce boxes.

FIRNI KHAS

This creamy, smooth, rice-pudding mix is made of rice powder, ground almonds, and sugar flavored with cardamom, saffron, and khas (screwpine) essence. To use it, simmer it with milk until thick, then chill it.

GULAB JAMUN MIX

This powdered mix is for making deep-fried milk doughballs soaked in rose syrup. Look for the Laziza International brand along with the others.

KALAKAND

This mix is for milk-cheese fudge flavored with cardamom, pistachios, and almonds. Look for the Nestle Milkmaid brand in 5-ounce boxes.

KHEER MIX

This thick, whole-grain, rice-pudding mix is flavored with cardamom and saffron. Cook it with milk and chill it. Add raisins or cashews if you want. Look for the Ahmed brand plus the others.

KULFI MIX

This is Indian ice-cream powder. Flavors include kesar (saffron) and pistachio. Look for the Laziza International and Nestle Milkmaid brands in 5-ounce boxes. To make, add 4½ cups milk to a saucepan and when it's about to boil, pour in mix and stir. Boil over medium heat 15 to 20 minutes until thickened and syrupy (keep stirring). *kulfa mix*
Cool slightly and freeze in metal or plastic molds or a covered bowl.

shahi rabri

SHAHI RABRI

The word "shahi" means "royal." Rabri is a chilled, creamy sweet. This is a mix for a rich pudding dessert flavored with cardamom, saffron, and nut bits. Simmer until thick with milk, then chill until firm. Look for the Nestle Milkmaid brand in 5-ounce boxes.

THANDAI MASALA

This is a mix for a creamy, almond-flavored Punjabi drink made of ground almonds, fennel seeds, poppy seeds, rose petals, black pepper, cloves, and cinnamon. Used to combat heat, it is mixed with milk and served over crushed ice.

RASMALAI DESSERT

This is a mix for making soft-cheese patties in a rich, condensed cream sauce infused with cardamom.

VERMICELLI PAYASAM

This is a mix to make South Indian-style sevian pudding. It contains bits of broken noodle, sugar, ground cashews, cardamom, and saffron. Fry the noodle bits in butter, then boil the powder with milk until it is thick. It is good warm or chilled. Look for the MTR brand in 7-ounce boxes.

Stocking Up

No wonder the cow is sacred in India. It contributes to Indian milk mustaches in all their forms. Yogurt is a must for sauces, salads, marinades, cheese making, and drinks. Pick up some frozen cubes of paneer to boost dal and vegetable dishes, a packet or two of instant dessert mixes, and a tub of kulfi for an icy end to a sizzling meal.

· 12 ·

Pickles & Chutneys

पिकल्स

Hindi word for "pickles"

Pickles are an essential element in Indian meals. They are eaten in small amounts with rice, breads, and curries. Pickles revive a flagging appetite as "palate ticklers." They are very different from Western vinegar-brine pickles. Indian pickles can be oily and salty, fiery hot, sour and hot, or hot and sweet. They are made from a variety of fruits and vegetables. Chutneys, both fresh and cooked, are piquant or sweet, peppery, hot relishes that accent other foods. There are even a few dry, powdered chutneys.

Pickles and chutneys are used as a condiment to liven up foods, much like ketchup or salsa. You can spoon them onto foods, dab them on your plate, dip foods into them, or mix them into your food. They can be blended into sour cream or yogurt as a dip or as a spread for breads, toast, and pappadams. To select from the plethora of pickles and chutneys available, head to shelf 9 in the Rajas' store.

Pickles

In India, seasonal vegetables, fruits, berries, and leaves are preserved in spices, oils, vinegar, lemon juice, or salt. Mustard oil is used for flavor and as a preservative. Properly made pickles will keep for years. Pickling spices include whole, crushed, or powdered mustard seeds, fenugreek, and turmeric. Most Indian pickles look like a thick, oily curry. They are very potent. Vinegar-based ones are thinner and translucent, but they are still pungent. In India a new bride may be asked to demonstrate her culinary skills by making several types of pickles. The only test facing you is which kind to pick from the vast variety available. They are sold in mild, medium, and hot to denote the level of chili heat. Store pickles in a dry jar at room temperature. Never dip a wet spoon into a jar or they will develop mold and spoil.

MANGO PICKLES

Aam achar. By far the most popular Indian pickle, this is made from green, unripe mangoes. Mango pickles have a complex, tart, pungent, salty, and mild or hot taste with a soft, slightly greasy texture when pickled in oil. They run the gamut from tiny, green ones to large chunks or fine shreds. They are preserved in oil, spices, and salt or in vinegar and spices. You will find sweet, jamlike pickles, very hot ones pickled with chilies, and sour, hot types pickled with lemon or lime in oil and spices.

Avakkai and vadu are meltingly soft pickles made from tender, baby mangoes. Gor-keri is a sweet, dark mango pickle made with palm sugar, spices, and mustard oil. Gugara are whole, seeded, baby mango pickles. Tokku is a finely ground type. Chunda are large shreds cooked in a salty, spicy syrup.

Some mango pickles get added punch from garlic and ginger. When choosing mango pickles, decide on the degree of hotness, then whether you fancy a tart, tangy pickle or a sweet, spicy one. Even mild pickles are powerfully flavored and should be used in small dabs. The many types are sold by many brands in jars that range from 8 ounces to several pounds. Brands to look for include Ahmed, Ashoka, Bedekars, Laxmi, Maya, M.M. Poonjiaiji, Nirav, Sahib, Swad, Pataks, and Priya.

LEMON & LIME PICKLES

Nimbu achar. This popular pickle is made from whole, chopped, or ground lemons and limes. Small, sour, thin-skinned citrus is used to make pickles that are pungently hot, sour and hot, or sweet and spicy. The rind softens and the flesh becomes tender. They are always pickled with salt. Oil, pepper, or a mixture of sugar, crushed spices, and lemon juice can be added to the salt. Salt pickles, with or without oil, are musty green and greenish yellow. Ground-citrus pickles look like thick, black paste. Bhara nimbu achar are pungent, hot, whole lemons or limes pickled in spices, lemon juice, and mustard oil. They resemble a thick, ochre curry swimming in orange oil. Some have garlic or chili added. Hyderbadi-style pickles are dark, pungent, chopped lemon pickles preserved in a thick spice paste. There are also milder, sweet, and spicy lemon and lime pickles.

Brands to look for are Ahmed, Ashoka, Bedekars, and Pachranga for mild or hot types. Nirav makes chunky lemon pickles and sweet lemon pickles. Mehran has Hyderbadi lemon and lemon-chili pickles, while Priya has lime pickles in lime juice. Pataks has mild and hot pickles, and Swad offers sweet lime pickles. Most of these are in 10- to 16-ounce jars.

Bengal table mustard, called kasundi, is nothing like the yellow mustard from the ballpark. Kasundi is a nose-tingling pickle made from ground mustard seeds, spices, and mustard oil. This pungent paste is combined with sour green mango, tamarind, or lemon. Most Bengali pickles are made during the scorching heat of mid-April (also known as Bai sakh or pickle season) by drying slices or strips of fruits and vegetables in the sun to preserve them prior to pickling. Making a good kasundi is considered even more challenging than making good pickles, and cooks fiercely guard their recipes.

PICKLED CHILIES

Pungent, hot-to-super-hot, whole, slit, and stuffed green or red chilies. Parboiled chilies are slit lengthwise and sometimes seeded, which diminishes their heat. They are stuffed with a coarsely ground spice paste and pickled in salt, lemon juice, and oil. The heat level intensifies the longer that they pickle. There are also chopped chilies in a spice paste, some with garlic added. There is really no such thing as a mild pickled chili, so choose these if you can handle the fiery-hot, sharp bite that these pack. Look for the Ahmed, Asoka, Bedekar, Sahib, and Swad brands' green chili pickle. The Priya brand has stuffed red and green chilies as well as chopped chili pickles. Pataks offers a hot-chili relish. The Pachranga brand has stuffed red chilies in 2-pound jars. Most of these pickles are in 10- to 16-ounce jars.

GUNDA PICKLE

This is an olivelike, round, Indian fruit that grows in grapelike clusters. It is ready to pickle when ripe and sticky. Gunda have light, olive green skins, a center pit, and a tangy, olive taste. They are pickled whole, seeded (athela), or

gunda pickle

are in chunks (methia) stuffed with spices. They are pickled in a pungent, reddish orange spice paste, salt, and oil. The fruits become meltingly soft, while the skins have a tart bite. They are unusual but delicious. Look for Ashoka methia gunda, Laxmi gunda in oil, Maya premium-pitted, chopped gunda with mango and chili, and Nirav khaman (chopped), pitted, whole gunda pickles. Swad makes whole gunda pickles. Most are in 10- to 14-ounce jars.

CARROT PICKLE

Carrots are cut into thin strips or chunks, then pickled in ground fenugreek seeds, red chilies, turmeric, salt, and mustard oil. The carrots become soft and infused with a pungent heat because of the thick reddish orange paste. Some have chopped chilies added. Look for the Ashoka brand in 10-ounce jars, the Laxmi brand in 9- or 26-ounce jars, and the Mother Made and Swad brands in 9-ounce jars.

carrot pickle

TOMATO PICKLE

This sweet, hot relish is made from firm, ripe, chopped tomatoes pickled in a mixture of chopped onions, ginger, garlic, mango chutney, chili, and spices. Another type is pickled in tamarind, ground chilies, spices, and sesame oil. This thick, dark red, chunky paste has a sweet, tangy, spicy flavor. Both types can be used like salsa, and they are good blended with sour cream as a dip. Look for the MTR, Ruchi's, Pataks, Priya, and Taj brands' tomato pickle in 8- to 11-ounce jars.

BRINJAL PICKLE

This eggplant pickle is made from cubed, quartered, or ground eggplant. It is salted, fried in oil with crushed garlic and grated ginger, and pickled in a ground spice paste made of vinegar, turmeric, mustard seeds, chili powder, salt, and mustard oil. It looks thick and almost black. The eggplant has a creamy texture with a pungent, hot flavor. It is sometimes sweetened with sugar. Look for the Ashoka and Pataks brands in 14-ounce jars and for Maya brand's sweet brinjal in 16-ounce jars.

MIXED PICKLE

mixed pickle

This mix of chopped vegetables, green mango, and lime is pickled in a hot, oily spice paste. It can include carrots, cauliflower, turnips, white radish, and green chilies. The taste is sweet, sour, hot, and spicy. Look for the Ahmed, Bedekars, Gold Seal Indus Valley, Maggi, Priya, Sahib, Sharda, or Swad brands in 10- to 16-ounce jars. Look also for the Ashoka chatpata (exotic hot and sour recipe) mixed pickle in 11-ounce jars.

TAMARIND PICKLE

This South Indian pickle is made from tamarind pulp soaked in vinegar. It is pickled in a paste of ground garlic, ginger, turmeric, cumin, salt, sugar, and vinegar. The paste is fried in oil, then the tamarind is added, and it is simmered until thick. It has a hot, tangy taste. Some have chili added. Use it as a dip, spread, or condiment. Look for the Ahmed brand in 10-ounce jars and the Priya brand in 8.8-ounce jars.

GINGER PICKLE

Peeled slices of ginger root are pickled in salt, turmeric, spices, and lemon juice. They have a sharp, tingly taste. Some have garlic, chilies, or sugar added. Use it as a condiment with meats or curries, or blend it into yogurt as a cooling side dish. Look for the Priya brand in 8.8-ounce jars for the hot or sweet types.

GARLIC PICKLE

Peeled, whole cloves of garlic are pickled in lemon juice, fenugreek seeds, salt, mustard oil, and fried, ground red chili. They have a sharp, hot taste and an oozing, soft texture. Some types are made of chopped garlic, onions, dates, raisins, and chilies with mustard seeds and spices. These have a sweet, hot, mellow flavor. Look for the Pataks brand's sweet relish in 8-ounce jars. The Ashoka, MTR, and Priya brands have whole garlic pickles in 8- to 10-ounce jars.

ONION PICKLE

Small, whole, or sliced onions are pickled in a spice paste made of ground mustard seeds, cayenne, turmeric, sugar, salt, green chilies, garlic, ginger, vinegar, and mustard oil. The onions become soft and translucent. They have a sweet, tart, hot, spicy taste. Look for the Ruchi brand in 10.6-ounce jars.

KERDA PICKLE

These small, olive green fruits from an Indian shrub are about the size of a large caper. The tart, bitter berry is pickled whole in a brine made of salt, citric acid, and water, or in a thick, yellowish spice paste made of crushed mustard seeds and turmeric. Look for the Nirav brand's kerda in brine in 24-ounce jars and for Maya kerda in spices in 16-ounce jars.

TURMERIC PICKLE

Chunks of fresh turmeric root are pickled in salt, ground chili, fenugreek, mustard seeds, turmeric, asafoetida, and peanut oil. This is dark yellow with a slightly bitter, pungent, hot taste. Look for Ashoka in 11-ounce jars.

AMBA-HALDI PICKLE

This pickle is made from chopped white turmeric (amba haldi) pickled with green mango pieces, mustard seeds, spices, and oil. It is hot and pungent with a ginger-mango taste. Look for the Ashoka, Nirav, and Swad brands in 10- to 14-ounce jars.

AMLA PICKLE

Nellikai achar. Sour Indian gooseberries are crushed and the seeds discarded. Then they are simmered until tender with fried, ground red chilies, fenugreek, mustard seeds, salt, turmeric, and oil to make this tangy pickle. Garlic is added to some pickles. The amla pickle is dark brown with a tart, hot taste. Amla murabba is a sweeter version that is cooked in sugar syrup and flavored with saffron. Try both as a dip for fried snacks or as a spread. Look for the Priya brand in 8.8-ounce jars and for the MTR brand in 10.5-ounce jars.

TENDIDA PICKLE

This pickle is made from a tart, sweet, stoneless, green gooseberry (not amla). It is pickled in a spice-oil paste and has a tangy, spicy flavor. Look for the Panchranga brand in 2-pound jars.

GONGURA PICKLE

Gongura-pacchadi. Sour hibiscus leaf is ground and pickled in mustard oil, salt, and spices. Some have garlic or chili added. The thick, dark green paste has a pungent, spicy, tart taste. It is good blended with yogurt as a dip. Look for the Priya brand's plain, garlic, and red chili and for the Sri Ganesh Rams brand in 14-ounce jars.

OLIVE PICKLE

A specialty of Bangladesh, this pungent pickle is made from a type of large, green olive that grows in Sylhet in the northeast. They are pickled whole, with pit in a yellowish orange paste made from salt, mustard seeds, fenugreek, chili powder, and mustard oil. The olives have a soft, dry texture and tart, mildly hot, olive taste. Look for the Ahmed brand in 14-ounce jars.

olive pickle

DRUMSTICK PICKLE

Partially peeled, finely chopped drumsticks (long-tree pods) are pickled in a paste of deep orange tamarind, spices, salt, lime juice, and mustard oil. They are pulpy, piquant, and tangy with small, soft seeds. Look for the Priya brand in 8.8-ounce jars.

BALICHOW PICKLE

A traditional Goan shrimp pickle, this is made from sautéed shrimp, chopped onions, and garlic pickled in a vinegar, salt, and ground-spice paste. The spices are simmered and poured over the shrimp. It has a tart, rich, spicy taste. It is an ideal accompaniment to rice and seafood curries. You can also heat the contents with fresh vegetables and seafood to make a main dish, which is served over rice. Look for the Pataks brand in 8-ounce jars.

HURDA PRESERVES

Haritaki or cherry-plum. This bitter fruit, used as an Ayurvedic medicine, is preserved in sugar syrup. These elongated, hard, ridged, oval fruits are dark brown. They float in a brown syrup. Preserving them in syrup helps counter the bitterness. The molasses-brown syrup has a bitter raisin flavor, and the somewhat hard fruit with a pit tastes like a

cross between an unripe olive and a very bitter date. They are chewed and eaten to stimulate digestion and are believed to flush toxins from the body. They are powerfully astringent. It is not a pickle, but it is found on the pickle shelf. You will see jars of hurda with a picture on the white label of what resembles a wrinkled fig with holly sprig leaves. Look for the Ahmed brand in 14-ounce jars.

hurda preserves

Chutneys

Even the most mediocre meal sparkles with a few spoonfuls of chutney. The hot, spicy relishes and sweet, tangy conserves jazz up and bring out flavors in foods. There are two types of chutney. One is cooked, and the other is a puree of fresh ingredients. The word is derived from the Hindi "chatni," and originally it meant only the fresh-ground type. Confusion arose after the British doctored the mango pickle, cooking it like jam with sugar and adding raisins, candied peel, and dried apricots. This gave birth to the Major-Grey style of chutney. In India, fresh chutneys are made daily. The bottled, cooked ones are reserved for special occasions. The best of both are found in Indian grocery stores. Fresh types are in the refrigerator case. Cooked ones are with pickles on the shelf.

Fresh Chutney

COCONUT CHUTNEY

This is a thick, pale green puree made of grated coconut, green chilies, salt, and lemon juice. It has a tangy aroma and a hot, slightly acidic, coconut flavor. It is served with South Indian snacks such as rice crepes, steamed rice cakes, vada (deep-fried dal-paste fritters) and pappadam. Use it as a spread for breads or blended with yogurt or sour cream as a dip. Look for the Maya and Unique brands in 8-ounce bottles and for Swad in 7-ounce jars.

coconut chutney

CORIANDER CHUTNEY

This dark green sauce is made from coarsely ground, fresh coriander leaves, coconut powder, green chilies, vinegar, cumin powder, salt, and lemon juice. It has a tangy aroma and a snappy, sharp flavor with a chili kick that goes well with fried snacks or blended into yogurt. Use it to perk up salad dressings, toss it with cooked

coriander chutney

pasta, or make it into salsa with chopped tomatoes and onions. Look for the Nirav, Exotic Foods, Swad, and Unique brands in 7-ounce bottles.

In Sanskrit "chatni" means "licking good," an apt description of these palate tinglers. Indian women fancy spicy, sharp, sour flavors, including appetite-stimulating chutneys. No meal or snack is complete without a selection of several chutneys to dip, smother, swirl, or drizzle foods in. Some meals even end with a tart chutney instead of dessert!

MINT CHUTNEY

This is a dark green puree of fresh mint, onion, garlic, ginger, green chilies, garam masala, salt, sugar, and lime juice. It is similar to coriander chutney, but it has a tangy, hot, mint flavor. It is delicious with fried snacks and breads or blended into yogurt. It is also good as a condiment with meats and lamb seekh kebabs. Look for the Sultan, Swad, and Unique brands in 8-ounce bottles.

MANGO CHUTNEY

This is a light, tandoori, orange, pureed mix of mangoes, chilies, vinegar, spices, and salt. It is tangy with a lemony aftertaste and a hot, chili kick. It is good with fried snacks, grilled meats, or fish and as a dip blended with yogurt or sour cream. Look for the Aki's brand in 8.8-ounce jars and for the Sinha brand's hot mango chutney in 20-ounce jars.

LEMON CHUTNEY

This is a deep, rose-colored puree of fresh coriander, green chilies, lemon juice, vinegar, salt, and spices. It has a tart, hot, spicy taste. It goes well with fried foods and creamy curries. It is also good with grilled meats and fish or blended into yogurt as a dip or side dish. Look for the Nirav brand in 7-ounce bottles.

PANI PURI MASALA

This is a spicy, dark green concentrate for making a tangy, cumin-flavored water for small puffs called gol gappa or puchkas. The puffs are stuffed with cubes of boiled potato, chickpeas, and chutney, then filled with the water. The contrast of crisp puff, cold water, and spices is delicious. The concentrate is a puree of fresh coriander, salt, citric acid, cumin, chilies, and spices. It is thinned with water. Look for the Deep brand in 8-ounce jars and for the Poonjiajis brand in 10-ounce jars.

GREEN CHILI CHUTNEY

This bright-green puree is made of green chilies, sugar, and vinegar. It has a very hot, puckery taste. The tongue tingles with a satisfying burn because of this peppy condiment. Mix it into rice and curries, stir it into dal or meat stews, or blend it with yogurt as a dip. Look for the Deep and Aki's brands in 8-ounce jars.

green chili chutney

TAMARIND CHUTNEY

This sweet-sour, dark brown, thin sauce is made from tamarind pulp that is pureed with palm sugar, salt, ginger, green chilies, and spices.

The tangy, hot flavor goes well with deep-fried savory snacks or poured over chaat salads. It is good with grilled meats, shrimp, or chicken. Look for the Deep brand in 8-ounce jars and the Poonjiajis brand in 10-ounce jars. Bhel chutney, a thin, hot, tangy tamarind sauce tossed with puffed rice and savory crunchies is very similar. It is used to make the snack bhel puri. Look for the Maya brand in 8-ounce jars.

CHUTNEY MIX

This thin, mahogany-brown sauce is made from pureed dates, tamarind, fresh coriander, chilies, salt, and spices. It has a sweet-sour, hot, fruity flavor. Use it as a dip for crispy snacks, samosas, grilled meats, and seafood. It is also good with sweet breads and pastries or blended into yogurt. Look for the Deep brand in 8-ounce bottles and for the Nirav brand in 9-ounce jars.

chutney mix

CHATPATI

chatpati

This is a chutney concentrate. It is a mustard-yellow, coarse mixture of ground peanuts, chickpeas, green chilies, vinegar, turmeric, and spices. It has a sour, tart, nutty, hot flavor. Use it thinned with a little water as a dip for fafda, which are deep-fried besan-flour crisps flavored with ajowan seeds. It is also good with pappadam, samosas, fritters, steamed rice cakes, and dosa crepes.

GARLIC CHUTNEY

This is a thick paste made of ground garlic, cayenne, cumin, and coriander seeds. Some types have grated coconut, chopped coriander leaves, tamarind, or chickpea flour added. The pungent paste is used as a condiment in spice blends or in stuffings for vegetables or breads. Look for the Deep and Nirav brands in 8-ounce bottles.

CURRY LEAVES THUVAYAL

This olive green, thick sauce is made from toasted, ground curry leaves, salt, garlic, green chilies, and spices. Fragrant, hot, and delicious, it is used as a dip for dosa (rice crepes) and idli (steamed rice cakes). It also flavors sauces, dips, and dals. Look for the Exotic Foods brand in 8-ounce jars.

Cooked Chutneys

These are made by simmering fruits with sugar, vinegar, and spices into thick jams. At Indian banquets an assortment of tangy, sweet chutneys are served with pappadam crisps between courses as a palate cleanser. You could serve chutney and crisps as an appetizer. Chutneys are also eaten in small dabs with curries and rice.

MANGO CHUTNEY

The most popular cooked chutney, this is made from diced green mango cooked with sugar, spices, garlic, ginger, and vinegar. Some are sweet with cinnamon. Others are pungent and hot, from being infused with ground red chilies, garam masala, and mustard seeds. Katki is chunky. It is made from large pieces of mango. Mango-lime chutney

has chopped bits of lime added. Chhundo is a sweet type made from mango shreds. Major Grey chutney is sweet, tangy, and studded with raisins. Look for the Pataks and Ashoka brands' sweet mango, mango-lime, hot mango, and Major Grey chutneys in 10- to 12-ounce jars. The Ahmed, Bedekars, and Swad brands have sweet, spicy chutneys in 10-ounce jars. Maya has katki in 14-ounce jars. The Sun brand has Major Grey in 10-ounce jars.

mango chutney

MIXED FRUIT CHUTNEY

These are dark-golden combinations of fresh and dried fruits. Some have melon seeds, chopped cashews, walnuts, pistachios, or almonds added. They are piquant, sweet, and spicy. The fruits used include green papaya, mango, pineapple, apricots, apples, plums, and even pumpkin. This chutney is a play of sweet, ripe fruits and sour, green ones. It goes well with rich biryanis, grilled meats, kebabs, and fried snacks. Look for the Pataks brand's tropical-fruit-and-nut-chutney and curried fruit chutney in 10-ounce jars, the Ashoka brand's exotic fruit-and-nut-chutney in 12-ounce jars, and the Navratan or Maya brands' fruit-nut chutney in 10- and 16-ounce jars.

mixed fruit chutney

Chutney Powder

COCONUT CHUTNEY POWDER

This brown powder is made from dried, ground coconut, onions, ginger, tamarind, salt, chili, black pepper, cumin, fenugreek, and curry leaves. To use it, mix it with water and a squeeze of lime into a thin sauce or thick paste. It makes a delicious, tangy, hot dip or condiment. Look for the Palat brand in 7-ounce jars.

DRY GARLIC CHUTNEY

Thechaa. This is a brick-red, slightly moist, coarsely ground mixture of coconut, garlic, red chilies, coriander seeds, sesame seeds, and spices. Sprinkle it over dishes or place a pinch of it at the side of your plate to mix into foods. Use it in bread or vegetable stuffings, in yogurt dips, or with crispy snacks. Look for the Deep brand in 4-ounce plastic packets.

MINT CHUTNEY POWDER

Podina. This is a powdered blend of dried mint leaves, salt, green mango, pomegranate seeds, chilies, black pepper, melon seeds, citric acid, and nutmeg. It is mixed with water or yogurt to make a thick, tangy, spicy paste to accompany grilled meats, breads, or fried snacks. The paste can also be used as a marinade for kebabs or lamb, or it can be mixed with sour cream for a dip. It is sold in 3.5-ounce boxes. Look for the A-1A, Badshan, Eastern, MDH, National, and Shan brands.

SOUTH INDIAN SANDWICH SPREAD POWDER

sandwich spread powder

This light orange, lumpy chutney powder is made from coarsely ground Bengal gram, urad dal, red chilies, salt, mustard seeds, and asafoetida. To use it, mix it with a little water into a paste then serve it with idli, dosa, and dal dishes. It is also used as a sandwich spread mixed with ghee. Look for the Vasu brand in 3.5-ounce boxes.

Stocking Up

Once you have tasted hot, spicy Indian pickles, the standard dill pickle pales in comparison. Just keep in mind that the assertive flavors are best enjoyed in small doses. Ketchup will take a backseat once you discover the tang of fresh chutney. Pickle flavors are a personal taste. Some people adore the pucker of gunda while others prefer the bite of ginger pickle. Start by trying a mild mango pickle, then select a fresh coconut, coriander, or mint chutney. Add a fruity, jamlike cooked chutney.

13

Snacks

स्नेकस

Hindi word for "snack"

Indulge a craving for crunchy, salty, and spicy flavors with some Indian snacks. Snack nirvana may just be a mouthful of chewda, which is a jumbled melody of toasted nuts, puffed rice, fried lentils, raisins, chili powder, sugar, salt, and spices. Each bite teases the taste buds with hot, sweet, nutty, crispy, chewy, salty, sour, and spicy flavors. An integral part of these sassy snacks are chickpea-flour crisps. Dough is squeezed through holes of different sizes of a seviya press into hot oil, creating squiggles, swirls, sticks, ribbons, beads, and chips. They are dry, not greasy, and crumble in your mouth. Namkeen means extra spicy. You will also find such treats as salty crackers, sesame brittle, spice-stuffed pastries, and coconut cookies to crunch and munch your way through.

Nibblers

Mathari are crunchy nibblers. When Indians entertain, several types of mathari are offered to guests as they arrive. It is hard to resist these munchables anytime. The following companies carry most of the treats discussed here: Deep, Halidrams, Indore's Famous Rushi's Shahi Namkeen, Joy, Kashmir Crown Bakeries, Maya, Nirav, Surati Sweet Mart, Swad, and Vaishali. They are in colorful plastic bags in 8, 12, and 14 ounces.

BHADRAN MOONG

These are hot, spicy, salty, deep-fried, golden, split mung beans. Also good sprinkled over yogurt salads (raita), tossed greens, vegetable dishes, curries, rice, or cooked potatoes to add crunch and flavor.

BHUSU

This is a hot, crunchy mix of chickpea, flour puffs, peanuts, mung beans, puffed rice, cashews, raisins, split chickpeas, sugar, and spices. You can use this mix as a base for tossing together bhel puri with the addition of diced cooked potato, chopped onions and tomato with a sweet and tangy tamarind-coriander chutney sauce.

BHUJIA

These are very thin, squiggly, broken bits of chickpea-flour strands lightly salted and spiced. Aloo bhujia is the same thing, but it is made from a blend of chickpea and potato flour dough.

BOONDI

Krunchees. These are small, crunchy, fried or roasted, plain or spicy chickpea flour beads. Eat them out of the bag. Or mix them into a dish of yogurt and sprinkle them with chili powder, salt, and sugar.

CHANNA

Chickpree. These are crunchy, deep-fried whole chick-peas flavored with salt, chili powder, and spices. There is also mahabaleshwar channa, which are roasted, lightly salted, whole, small, dark-skinned chickpeas. When an unexpected guest or traveller shows up, Indian hosts offer a glass of water and roasted chickpeas as a welcome.

channa

CHANNA CHOR

Crunchy chore. These are small, dark brown, fried chips made from boiled, smashed, whole chickpeas flavored with salt, chili powder, black salt, and citric acid. They have a toasted, nutty, salty, spicy flavor. They are best served heated (1 minute in a microwave, 5 minutes in a hot oven), tossed with diced onion and a few squirts of lemon or lime juice, and garnished with chopped coriander leaves. Street vendors originally sold channa chor directly out of a hot clay pot with smoldering charcoal that was carried on a shoulder yoke. Look for the Deep and Surati brands. Refrigerate it to keep it crisp.

channa chor

CHAKALI

These crunchy, golden-ridged, deep-fried spirals are made from spicy rice flour and sesame seed dough that is flavored with chili powder, cumin, salt, and spices. They are light and crispy with a rich, spicy taste. They are delicious dunked in hot tea or munched with cold drinks. Look for the Vijaya Foods brand in 7-ounce bags.

chakali

CHAT PAPADI

These fried, white, crispy puffs are made from ground sesame seeds and white flour. Slightly sweet and light, they are good for crumbling over Chat salads for a crispy element. Look for the Deep brand in 10-ounce boxes with cellophane windows.

DAL MOOTH

These are dalmot or mung-bean munchies. They are salty, spicy, split, deep-fried mung beans. Kaju dal mooth has cashews added, while badam dal mooth has almonds.

FUL-VADI

Masala vadi. These are dark, orange-brown, sandy-looking, thick little logs of deep-fried, spicy chickpea flour dough. They are crunchy with a dense, hot, curry flavor.

GATHIYA

These are pale yellow, ridged, chickpea-flour sticks flavored with black pepper and spices. They have a light, crisp texture and a floury, nutty flavor. Goad gathiya (also called fafda) are fat, ridged sticks speckled with dark bits of caraway or ajowan seeds. Papdi gathiya or masala papdi are chickpea-flour chips flavored with chili powder or spices.

GREEN VANTANA

These are crunchy, deep-fried, bright green peas that are flavored with salt and spices. Veeteena are skinned, deep-fried, golden peas that are flavored with chili powder, salt, sugar, and turmeric. Protidal are skinned, split peas that are fried and seasoned with chili powder, salt, and spices.

PANI PURI

Gol gappa, puchka, or water puffs. These are a Gujarati specialty. The ping-pong-sized, light-golden, crisp puffs are sold in large, usually unlabeled bags. You poke a hole in the top of the treat, stuff it with boiled potato, chickpeas, tamarind chutney, cumin, and coriander-flavored water. Pop it in your mouth where it explodes in a burst of crispy shell, soft vegetables, and cool, spiced water. To make dahi puri, fill the treat with spiced yogurt.

PEANUT BHUJIA

These are battered, deep-fried peanuts. Roasted nuts are encased in a thick, dark orange, crunchy shell made of spicy chickpea flour.

RATLAMI SEV

These medium-thick, pale yellow chickpea-flour noodle bits are speckled with black pepper and seasoned with salt, chili powder, and spices. They have a light, crispy, melt-in-your-mouth texture and a spicy taste.

SEV

These are thin, crispy, chickpea noodle bits. Some are yellowish orange and the thickness of spaghetti. Others are very fine, pale yellow, and mild. Others are flavored with spinach or garlic. Fine sev is often labeled as sevian. The thicker, hotter types are flavored with chili powder, salt, and turmeric.

TUM-TUM

These thick, light, golden brown, ridged chickpea-flour ribbon bits are flavored with sesame seeds, chili powder, salt, black pepper, cumin, citric acid, and spices. They have a slightly sandy looking exterior, light texture, and are crunchy with a floury, nutty, spicy flavor.

tum-tum

Snack Mixes

BHEL MIX

This Bombay-style blend for making bhel-puri, a sweet- sour, crunchy snack, is tossed together by street vendors and scooped from mixing bowls with a flat puri. You can duplicate this by emptying the bag of bhel mix into a large bowl, adding chopped onions and diced potatoes, then drizzling tart, green coriander chutney and sweet, date-tamarind chutney over it. The mix contains chickpea noodle bits, puffed rice, wheat-flour chips, salt, sugar, and spices. It can also be nibbled from the bag.

CHEVDA MIX

chevda mix

This is a hot, spicy jumble of flattened, puffed rice (chivda), deep-fried chickpeas, split mung beans, roasted peanuts, raisins, sesame seeds, salt, chili powder, fennel seeds, sugar, citric acid, spices, and toasted bits of neem leaf. Poha chevda is made from deep-fried, crispy rice flakes with cashew bits added to the mix. Some brands add an extra ingredient or two to the blend.

CORNFLAKE MIXTURE

This is a crispy blend of cornflakes, potato straws, chickpea-flour noodle bits, cashews, green-tinted spinach, chickpea-flour pearls, raisins, sesame seeds, sugar, salt, and spices. It is not too hot. It is sold in 7-ounce foil bags by Haldriam's and by the Kashmir Crown Bakeries.

Snacks are an integral part of the Indian culture. From dawn to dusk the streets pulse with energy, a masala mix of colors, languages and smells. Food is cooked nonstop at curbside stalls or in mobile carts that line every busy intersection. Here will be the bhelwallahs with newspaper cones of the sticky snack mix. There are sev puri sellers piling a similar mix onto crunchy puri plates. Vendors selling pao bhaji (battered, spiced potato balls served on a roll), pakora, veggie sandwiches, and jalebi weave between traffic and pedestrians.

HOT MIX

This is a popular mix of chickpea-flour chips, fried lentils, mung beans, puffed rice, peanuts, cashews, black salt, chili powder, and spices. Hot, spicy, and so good that you won't believe you ate the whole bag.

KHASTA MIXTURE

This is a hot, tasty, crispy mix of chickpea-flour chips, deep-fried red lentils, peanuts, red chili flakes, citric acid, and spices. Look for Haldiram's in 6-ounce foil bags.

KHATTA MEETHA

This is a mildly spiced, slightly sweet, crunchy blend of chickpea-flour ribbons, blobs, and beads, thin and thick sev, green peas, peanuts, sugar, and salt. Look for the Haldiram's brand in 7-ounce foil packets.

KHAT MIX

This is a sweet-sour, spicy mix. A tongue-tingling blend of fried, split peas, chickpea-flour beads, potato straws, puffed rice, sesame seeds, and roasted fennel seeds, flavored with green-mango powder, ginger, chili powder, and citric acid.

PUNJABI MIX

A crunchy jumble of chickpea-flour noodle bits and ribbons, puffed rice, deep-fried rice flakes, fried mung beans, green peas, and lentils tossed in spices: chili powder, salt, sugar, citric acid, and toasted bits of neem leaf. This is hot and spicy.

punjabi mix

Biscuits, Pastries & Cookies

BHAKHARVADI

bhakharvadi

These fat, crispy, golden, deep-fried, savory pastries with a crumbly, dark brown, spicy, sweet filling are made of coarsely ground red chilies, salt, sugar, sesame seeds, and fennel seeds. They look like strudel rolls made from thick dough. They come four to a package. There are also mini bhakharvadi, which are small, crispy pinwheels of the pastry dough with a dark filling. They are sliced off a long roll and fried. The chickpea-flour pastry is hard and smooth. The Deep company makes both of them in 8- or 7-ounce packets.

JAGGERY GOLDEN PARA

This is a sweet, spicy, pale golden Indian shortbread made from chickpeas, wheat flour, butter, melted jaggery (cane sugar), and spices. It is a thick, hard, square cookie with a spicy, caramel flavor. It has a firm, yet soft and richly crumbling texture. The brand to look for is Karisons, in small packets.

kachori

KACHORI

These crispy, pale golden, golf-ball-sized, deep-fried pastry doughballs are stuffed with a spicy, sweet mixture. The filling is made of ground, grated coconut, sugar, nuts, sesame seeds, fennel seeds, garlic, spices, and salt. The pastry dough is made of chickpea, corn, and wheat flours. Look for the Deep brand in bags of six.

MATHRI

These tangy, deep-fried, small, yellow shortbread crisps are made from a flour dough that is flavored with ginger, lemon, salt, cumin, and other spices. It tastes like a savory cookie. Look for the Haldiram's brand in 7-ounce foil pouches, which comes with a packet of tomato ketchup for dipping.

mathri

NAN KHATAI

These sandy-looking, crispy, round cookies are made from wheat flour, vegetable ghee, sugar, and ground pistachio, all mixed into a dough. They have a crumbly texture and a nutty taste. Look for the TWI Foods brand with a dozen to a package.

As the world's largest delta, with over 5,000 miles of waterways, rivers, and canals, it is a must to float down a segment of the Ganges while in Bangladesh. I prepared to cross the Brahmaputra River. With the engine vibrating and moonlight streaming through the portholes, I ate salted biscuits with a cup of tea that was served in a battered tin cup. The old man next to me said that no one goes on a journey without these little comforting crackers. They are also considered lifesavers, replacing bodily salts lost due to the hot weather.

PUNJABI MATHI

These round, crispy, spicy shortbread biscuits are made from a blend of white flour and semolina. They are flavored with crushed black pepper and ajawon seeds. They are deep-fried until golden and have a tender, crumbly texture. Look for the Karison's brand in small packets.

SALTED BISCUITS

A salty, sweet, crispy butter cracker popular in Bangladesh. The dough is enriched with eggs, ground pistachios, and cumin. The tops are dusted in coarsely ground salt. They resemble small, thick saltines. Look for the Bangas Grand Choice brand in 3.5-ounce foil packets and the Peak Freans Salted biscuits in a 4-ounce red box.

salted biscuits

Candies

HAJMOLA CANDY

These are ayurvedic candy drops that contain herbs, cumin, black salt, pippali pepper, and tamarind or mango in a sugar base. They have a salty, spicy,

sweet-sour taste. They are good for sore throats, coughs, and nausea. Individually wrapped pieces are in small plastic bags. Look for the Darbur brand.

CHIKKI

chikki

This sesame or peanut brittle is made from boiled palm sugar, ghee, and nuts. It has a hard texture and a rich, toffee-nut taste. It is sold in large marble-size balls or thick, scored sheets of squares that are wrapped in cellophane. Look for the Gem brand in balls, and the Swad or Unique brands in bars, all in 7-ounce packets.

MAKHANA

These are small, round, white, lumpy textured balls that look like tiny popcorn puffs. They are made from malai, the thick layer of skin that forms on boiled cream. The candies are hard and crunchy, and they taste like sweet concentrated cream. They are put on hot bread, which melts the creamy balls so that they can be smeared like cream cheese. Makhana are also used as puja offerings because they are one of Krishna's favorite sweets. Look for the Swad brand in 7- and 14-ounce bags.

MISHRI & SAKAR

Mishri are little crystals of rock-sugar candy and sakar are big cubes, resembling lump sugar. Both can be used to sweeten hot drinks, make clear sugar syrups for sweets and glazes or small crushed bits that can be added to sweeten savory dishes and add sheen in marinades for grilled meats. Finely crushed bits are sprinkled over warm breads as a snack. Look for the Swad brand in 7- and 14-ounce bags.

SAKARIA

These tiny, knobby, white sweet balls are made from malai, the skin that forms on boiled cream. They are hard and crunchy. They have a sweet, creamy taste. A larger variety, which looks like it has been spackled, encases a roasted chickpea or peanut. They are also used as a puja offering. Look for the Swad brand in 7- and 14-ounce bags.

sakaria

SOAN PAPDI

These sweetened flour squares are made from roasted, lightly browned flour that is mixed with sugar, ghee, dried fruit, and pistachios. They are very sweet and crunchy. Look for the Haldiram's brand in boxes.

SWEET REWDI

sweet rewdi

These are sesame seed crunchies. They are crunchy, chewy, cream-colored, oval drops of boiled palm-sugar candy embedded with sesame seeds. They are eaten as a snack and exchanged at festivals. Look for Patel Brothers in 1-pound and 32-ounce bags and for the East End brand in 3.5-ounce bags.

OTHER

Other treats to discover include coconut-cream cookies, Cadbury chocolate fingers, cookie toast, fruit-cake
rusks, spicy cashews or peanuts, and mango-mood hard
candies. Biscuits range from boost bite, bourbon, and   *mango-mood*
glucose to Horlicks-cardamom, krackjack, Monaco, and orange cream.
There are coconut-curry puffs, raisin and cashew cookies, spicy potato
straws, and bags of papad crisps. New snacks show up on each visit to
the grocery store to keep you coming back in anticipation.

Stocking Up

Pick up a few bags of bhel mix, chewda, hot mix, and Punjabi mix for
your next party. Choose whichever snack looks best to you for munch-
ing. Try a new one each trip. Chikki always satisfies a sweet craving.

14

Sweets

Hindi word for "sweets"

Candy-colored diamonds, creamy balls, and Lego-like confections are arranged neatly in towering pyramids and concentric circles in the glass cases of large grocery stores. Smaller shops sell their sweets packed between waxed paper in plastic boxes in the refrigerator case. There are dozens of types on display: crunchy, chewy, creamy, crumbly, soft, syrupy, hard, grainy, striped, and speckled. They come in hot pink, lime green, lemon yellow, amber, and milky white. Some are studded with nuts or coated in gossamer thin sheets of beaten silver. Indian sweets made from thick, boiled milk, ghee, and cane or palm sugar are intensely sweet.

The fondness for meethi, or sweet things, is deeply ingrained in Indian customs. Newborn babies are given a taste of honey, elaborate gifts of sweets are exchanged at weddings, and every occasion from a birthday to passing an exam is celebrated with sweets. Friends dropping in are welcomed with the phrase "let us sweeten your mouth" along with a cup of tea and plate of sweets. Sweets are not just for dessert and are eaten throughout the day as snacks.

We will explore the whole sugary realm of sweets from creamy fudges, halwas, and sugared ladoo balls to chenna cheese and syrupy sweets. Most sweets are made by several esteemed, nationally distributed companies. These include Royal Sweets, Shaheen, Sharmiana, and Swad sweets. All are in hard, clear plastic boxes ranging from 1 to 5 pounds. You can buy boxes of one sweet or sampler boxes with five or six types.

Fudge & Milk Fudges

Indian milk fudges are delicious despite the unappetizing name: barfi, which comes from the Persian word for "snow". These fudgy confections are made by boiling milk until most of the moisture has evaporated, leaving a thick, doughy mass called khoa. The sugar in the milk begins to caramelize, adding a pale, tawny color and a caramel flavor. This is cooked with ghee and palm sugar into thick, soft, grainy-textured pastes, then cooled and cut into bars or rolled into balls or logs. Some are made with ground nuts, chickpea flour, or coconut. Others are delicately flavored with rose water, almond oil, cardamom, or saffron. Flecks of silver leaf adorn fancy ones. All are very sweet. Milk fudges keep for two to three weeks if refrigerated in a moisture-free container.

ALEPAK BARFI

alepak barfi

This is a ginger fudge. This tawny milk fudge is made with grated coconut and ginger paste. It is sold in square chunks. The coconut gives it a nubby texture, and the taste is gingery sweet.

BADAM BARFI

This is an almond fudge. This pale creamy milk fudge is made with almond paste, flavored with cardamom, and sold in small cubes that are decorated with sliced almonds. It tastes like rich, buttery marzipan.

badam barfi

BESAN BARFI

besan barfi

This is a chickpea-flour fudge. Creamy, butterscotch-colored cubes of milk fudge are made from besan flour. It has a sweet, nutty taste and a smooth, melting texture.

CHOCOLATE BARFI

One of the newest barfi flavors, this creamy delight is a milk fudge made with cocoa powder. It tastes like intense milk chocolate. It is sold in solid squares or in portions of half-white and half-chocolate milk fudge.

DHOODH BARFI

This is a milk fudge. This creamy, white fudge is flavored with lemon juice and cardamom. It has a sweet, slightly tangy, caramel flavor infused with spice.

DILPASAND

This triangle-shaped, triple-layered fudge is made from thin slabs of saffron and cashew barfi sandwiched between a fruity nut-gelatin layer. It is topped with silver leaf and pistachio nuts.

HUBSHIALWA

These pale brown slabs of fudge are made of cooked, pureed lentils, milk, sugar, and ground almonds. It looks like grainy milk chocolate and has a rich, nutty, marzipan flavor. It is sprinkled with sliced almonds.

KAJU BARFI

This is a cashew fudge. This parchment colored fudge is made from a paste of powdered raw cashews, sugar, water, and ghee. It is sold in thin diamond shapes. They are rich and dry textured, but they melt in your mouth. You may also find triple-layered kaju barfi. These thick diamonds feature a thin layer of pistachio barfi sandwiched between cashew fudge and a thick top layer of bright-yellow, saffron-flavored cashew fudge. They are decorated with bits of silver leaf.

KAJU KATLI

This is cashew milk fudge in a diamond shape. It is frosted with a thin, smooth layer of dark green, intensely bittersweet, pistachio paste. There are also yellow cashew milk-fudge logs made with a green, pistachio paste inside and a strip of silver leaf around the outside.

kaju katli

Babur, the first great moghul emperor, originally introduced sweets to Northern India. The Hindu tradition is even older. Hindu mythology is full of references to rich, sweet foods, from the tale of Krishna stealing butter from his mother to the story of goddess Sri, who was born from a sea of milk when it was churned to make ambrosia. Spiritual enlightenment is compared to the taste of nectar in one's mouth. Some sweets are even said to have medicinal qualities—as if you needed a reason to indulge!

KHARA BARFI

These pale, creamy, milk-fudge squares are made of melted palm sugar mixed with ghee, khoa, or milk powder. They are studded with toasted almonds and chopped, dried apricots or mango. They have a caramel, fruity, nutty, sweet flavor.

KULIYA

This milk-fudge cake is a special sweet that is made in large, fancy, round rosette or square molds. It looks like a tiny wedding cake and is garnished lavishly with slivered pistachios and strips of silver leaf. The fudge is made from milk, cream, and superfine white sugar. It is flavored with cardamom. The marble-white cake is sold whole or by the piece. It is only found in grocery stores with a sweets counter. It is very creamy and rich.

MESUBAKH

These crumbly, ochre-colored, spongy looking fudge squares are made of roasted chickpea flour, ghee, milk, and palm sugar. They have a rich, nutty, caramel flavor, They dissolve in your mouth.

NARIYAL BARFI

This is a coconut fudge. The pale, golden yellow milk-fudge squares or logs with grated coconut are flavored with cardamom and a pinch of saffron. Some have ground pistachios added and are pale green. They have a rough texture from the coconut shreds with a rich, toffee-coconut taste.

PENCIL ROLLS

These stubby rolls of pale yellow almond-paste sheets are rolled up with a sticky, brown, ground cashew, almond, and palm-sugar filling. They taste like marzipan and nutty brown sugar.

PERA

This is a powdered milk fudge. These fondant balls are made from creamed butter and confectioner's sugar kneaded with milk powder and cream. They are flavored with almond, orange, or rose essence. Some balls are stuffed with whole nuts.

PISTA BARFI

pista barfi

This is a pistachio nut fudge. These pale green, thick cubes are made from equal amounts of powdered pistachios and milk that are reduced to a soft, thick mass with sugar and ghee. The fudge is flavored with rose essence or almond oil and decorated with pistachio slivers and silver leaf. It has a rich, intense flavor and smells faintly like a perfumed face cream.

TARANGA BARFI

This triple-layer fudge is made from thick slabs of lemon-, strawberry-, and pineapple-flavored, pastel-tinted milk fudge. It is fruity and creamy sweet.

taranga barfi

TRICOLOR BARFI

tricolor barfi

This triple-decker milk fudge is made of three layers: a white layer of almond fudge, a pink cashew fudge, and a green layer of pistachio fudge. It is like eating marzipan and toffee with a touch of bittersweet.

OTHER

You might also find mango, pineapple, orange, or pumpkin barfis, depending on the season and size of the store.

triple layer kaju barfi

Halwas

The term "halwa" comes from the Arabic word, "halva," which means "sweets." Professional sweet makers are called Halwais. Indian halwas should not be confused with the Middle Eastern candy called halva, which is made from crushed sesame seeds and honey. Halwas are more like thick puddings. They are made from grains, vegetables, fruits, seeds, or legumes. The simplest is sooji halwa, which is made from toasted semolina flavored with sugar syrup. Some are reductions of chopped or shredded fruits or vegetables, which are slowly stirred with melted butter and sugar or cream until it is thick and fudgy. Others are dense and hard or translucent glaces. Most halwas will keep for about two weeks if refrigerated in airtight containers.

BADAM HALWA

Almond pak. This fudgy sweet is made from ground almonds cooked until thick with ghee, sugar, and milk powder. It is flavored with cardamom and rose water. It is sold in squares or flattened balls. It has a sweet, marzipan flavor and a creamy, dense texture.

BESAN HALWA

Mohan thal. This fudgy sweet is made from chickpea flour and chopped nuts toasted in ghee. It is cooked with sugar syrup into a thick paste. It is sold in thick, golden-brown slabs. It has a rich, toasted, sweet flavor and a moist texture.

CARROT HALWA

These are shredded carrots reduced with cream, butter, slivered almonds, sugar, honey, and spices into a thick, solid mass and cut into squares. It tastes like dense, moist, creamy, richly spiced carrot cake. To try making your own, see page 253 for a recipe.

carrot halwa

HABSHI HALWA

habshi halwa

These chewy, brown squares are made from whole-wheat flour, butter, sugar, ground pistachios, cashews, and almonds. They have a rich, nutty flavor and a dense, toothsome texture.

KADDU HALWA

This is a pumpkin pudding. It is a reduction of pumpkin with sugar, ghee, and milk, all flavored with saffron. The thick, deep orange, creamy paste is sold in small squares. It has a rich, buttery, pumpkin-pie flavor and a moist, dense texture.

KARACHI HALWA

karachi halwa

A sweet resembling stiff slabs or yellow or green Jell-O, this is made from cornstarch, ghee, sugar syrup, nuts, and food coloring. The yellow ones are embedded with sliced almonds, and the green ones have chopped pistachios. They have a gelatinous, chewy texture and a sweet, buttery, lemon flavor.

MOHAN BHOG

This is a ghee pudding. This thick, buttery, Bengali sweet is made from fine semolina and chickpea flour toasted in ghee. It is cooked into a thick, golden paste with milk, sugar, raisins, and spices, then it is cut into squares. It has a rich, sweet, buttery flavor with a hint of saffron and a moist, chewy texture.

MOONG DAL HALWA

This crumbly, yellowish sweet is made from pureed, skinless mung beans cooked with ghee, sugar syrup, and spices. It is made into a thick paste and cut into squares, and then decorated with raisins and chopped cashews. It has a dry texture and a rich, buttery flavor.

PETHA

These are pale, translucent slices of ash gourd (winter melon). They are simmered in sugar syrup for five days, then removed and drained to make this crystallized sweet. The pieces are firm on the outside and oozing soft when you bite them, dissolving in your mouth. They are so sugary sweet that you would never guess that it started off as a vegetable!

petha

SOHAN HALWA

sohan halwa

This is a hard, brittle, light, golden toffee. It is made of cream, butter, and palm sugar. It is sold either in large, plastic-wrapped slabs or in broken pieces in plastic boxes. Some have nuts.

SOOJI HALWA

The most popular halwa in India, this is often served in huge amounts at weddings and banquets or presented in small packets as puja offerings. It is a thick pudding made from fine-grain semolina that is fried in ghee until golden brown, combined with sugar syrup, and cooked until the liquid is absorbed and the texture is fluffy. Sooji is flavored with raisins, chopped nuts, cardamom, black pepper, fennel seeds, saffron, or orange zest. Sooji Besan halwa is made from a blend of chickpea flour and semolina. It is sold in solid masses or cut squares in boxes. It is a rich, golden color with a moist, grainy texture and a sweet, spicy flavor.

Ladoos & More

Ladoos are big, sweet, sugary balls made from fried dough crumbs, sugar, and ghee. Other batter or doughy sweets include deep-fried droplets, sweet vermicelli, and fudgelike, chickpea-flour sweets. Ladoos are associated with Ganesh, the plump elephant-headed god. Ganesh is much admired because he is a great lover of food. Ladoos are offered to him in prayer on his birthday each year. Ladoos are sturdy and will keep for two to three weeks if refrigerated in a well-sealed container, as will the dough beads and fudges.

BADANNA

Also called boondi or bundi, these are small, brightly colored, glassy-looking bead droplets. They are made from a flour-water batter poured through a strainer (or colander) over hot oil. Fine drops form and are skimmed out, drained, and soaked in warm, colored sugar syrups until they absorb the syrup and swell. They are lifted out

badanna

and left to dry. The crunchy drops are used in some ladoos, sprinkled over desserts as a garnish, or served in a bowl topped with slivered almonds. They are sold in small bags or boxes.

FENI

This is sweet vermicelli. Thin, round loops of unsweetened noodles are used to make feni, a specialty of Delhi. They look like spun sugar. The loops are dipped in a flavored sugar syrup until they soften, stuck together with a layer of sweet khoa, and sprinkled with nuts. Or you can just dip them in cordial syrup and serve with milk or thick cream.

LADOOS

These sweet balls are made from coarse wheat flour, chickpea flour, or a blend of flour and fine-grain semolina. The flour is kneaded with a

ladoo

little water and ghee into a stiff, dry dough and formed into patties. These are deep-fried until browned, drained, crumbled into the consistency of coarse breadcrumbs, mixed with sugar, ghee, nuts, and spices, then rolled into large balls. They are firm and shiny with a rough, granular texture. They taste like rich, crumbly sugar cookies. Some are rolled in poppy or sesame seeds. Choorma ladoos are made with wheat flour and nuts and are a specialty of Rajasthan. Kuruma ladoo is a variation made with puffed rice, melted palm sugar, and butter, shaped into balls. Moti chwoor ladoo is a lumpy, yellow or orange, golf-ball-sized sweet made from small, crunchy chickpea-flour pearls mixed

moti chwoor ladoo

with sugar syrup, crushed nuts, and colored beads of fried, sugar-soaked gram flour. They are crispy and crumbly. They are traditionally made for weddings and sent to friends and relatives.

MYSORE PAK

A famous South Indian sweet, this is a rich, melt-in-your-mouth, chickpea-flour shortbread. It is made by slowly adding roasted chickpea flour into a buttery, cardamom-infused sugar syrup, then stirring it constantly until it froths. The yellow-ochre mixture is cooled and cut into thick squares. It has a silky-smooth surface, a melting texture, and a rich, buttery, toffee flavor. It is usually garnished with sliced almonds.

mysore pak

PATISA

These flaky, yellow fudge squares are made from chickpea flour, ghee, and sugar. Inside is a crispy layer of crystallized, crispy bits of palm sugar, like a Butterfinger. The fudge is meltingly soft in contrast to the crunchy sugar layer. They are rich and delicious.

TONGRY

These deep-fried, sugary pastries, which are tinted green, pink, or pale yellow, are made from a chickpea flour batter. The fried balls are rolled in sugar and look like sugar plums. They are crunchy with a sweet, flaky, soft interior.

The festival of Ganesh, or Vinayak Chaturthi, begins on the 4th day of the Hindu month of Bhadon in June. Visitors are decked in flower garlands and anointed with a red rice paste. Lighted decorations of makeshift wood or tin stalls festooned with crepe paper line the streets. Piles of ladoos and coconut-filled dumplings called modak are sold on every street corner. Statues of Ganesh who sits cross-legged on lotus-petal cushions waving his multiple arms are everywhere. The festival ends when the statues are immersed in the river.

Chenna-Cheese Sweets

These creamy, cheese fudges and juicy, sweet cheeseballs, patties, and cheesecakes are all made from two basic ingredients: whole-milk chenna cheese and sugar. Chenna cheese is made from drained, kneaded curd cheese. It has a soft, light texture like whipped cream cheese. Commercially made chenna-cheese confections are bound with small amounts of flour, fine semolina, or arrowroot starch to help the sweets keep their shape when cooked. Most chenna sweets should be refrigerated and eaten within 2 to 3 days.

CHOM-CHOM

These spongy, white or pastel-tinted, squishy balls, patties, or logs are made from chenna cheese, which is blended with ground almonds and boiled in sugar syrup until it swells.

chom-chom

They can be flavored with rose essence, almond oil, or lemon. They are soaked in the syrup for up to 24 hours to produce a soft, spongy, sugar-saturated sweet. They are drained, and they may be rolled in grated coconut.

KALAKAND

This is Indian cheesecake. Creamy bars or diamond shapes are made from a condensed, boiled mixture of chenna cheese, ghee, milk, sugar, ground almonds, and pistachios flavored with cardamom. The cream-colored treat tastes like a cheesecake brownie with a dense, fudgy texture.

KHEERMOHAN

These deep-fried, golden brown, chenna-cheese dough-balls are sandwiched with condensed cream (malai). After the oval balls are fried, they are sliced lengthwise. One half is spread with the cream, and the other half is placed on top. The crisp, moist balls taste like a buttermilk doughnut that oozes sweet cream.

kheermohan

MALAI CHOP

This round, golden, syrupy sandwich is filled with cream and coated in silver leaf. The patties are made of chenna cheese and ground pistachios infused with cardamom. The cheese dough is rolled into balls and flattened. A spoonful of thick cream is placed in the center. The dough is pressed around the filling, forming a seamless ball, which is slightly flattened. The discs are then boiled and soaked in sugar syrup, drained, and decorated. They are sweet, spongy, and soft with a creamy center.

malai chop

Bengalis take to heart the Sanskrit recommendation of madhurena samapayet which holds that a meal should end with something sweet. Chenna-cheese sweets are Bengals contribution to the Indian world of sweets. Chenna sweets were invented by profesional sweetmakers, called moria, to supply wealthy landlords. Morias soon gained elevated status in Bengali society. These often rotund men can be seen in every town, sitting in front of a mountain of chenna balls and fanning away the inevitable flies that are drawn to the sweet syrup.

RAJBHOG

Giant Rosogolla. These large, creamy, white, chenna-cheese doughballs, about the size a jelly doughnut, are soaked in rose syrup and flavored with saffron. The name means "a sweet fit for a king" in Hindi, and this rich sweet lives up to its name. The squishy balls are garnished with chopped pistachios and silver leaf. They have a rich, creamy, sweet taste.

rajbhog

RASMALAI

This rich, luscious, creamy delight is considered the queen of all sweets. These are small, flattened, chenna-cheese patties boiled in sugar syrup and floated in a rich cream sauce. The sauce is made from Indian cream, or malai, infused with cardamom. Deluxe versions are stuffed with chopped pistachios and almonds, raisins, honey, and cream-soaked saffron. They are garnished with slivers of nuts and sprinkled with rose essence. Eat rasmalai as soon as possible or the cheese patties become soggy in the cream.

ROSOGOLLAS

These are Chenna-cheese balls boiled and soaked in flavored syrup. They have a juicy, spongy texture and a sweet, syrupy flavor. The longer they soak, the firmer and

rosogollas

more intensely flavored they become. Some are stuffed with nuts or frosted with milk paste and rolled in coconut. Flavors include rose, jasmine, orange blossom, pineapple, and mango.

SANDESH

Called sondesh in Bengali, this creamy cheese fudge is made from slowly cooked chenna cheese and superfine sugar or fresh jaggery. The thick, glossy mass is pressed into fancy molds, cut into squares and diamond shapes, or rolled into balls, patties, and logs. There are coconut, almond, lemon, saffron, and pistachio-rose flavors, all tinted different colors. There are tri-colored bars made from sandwiched layers of saffron, almond, and pistachio. Sandesh can be refrigerated for up to four to five days in a moisture-free container.

Syrupy Sweets

The common ingredient in these sweets is sugar syrup infused with aromatic scents. Syrup sweets are also cooked in ghee, adding a buttery, sweet richness. Most syrup sweets will keep for about four days if refrigerated in a sealed container, but they taste best when eaten at room temperature.

AMRATI

These deep-fried, shiny, orange dough loops resemble ornate, scalloped bracelets. The batter is made from urad-dal flour, sugar, and ghee. It is squeezed from a piping bag into hot oil. The loops are scooped out, then drained and dipped in a rose- or saffron-scented sugar syrup. They have a slightly crunchy texture and a melting, pure sugar flavor.

BALUSHAI

These fried flour fritters in syrup are also called Indian doughnuts. Dough enriched with ghee and yogurt is flavored with cinnamon and

aniseed. It is shaped into thick rounds, indented with a thumb print, and deep-fried in ghee until they are golden brown. It is then drained and soaked in heavy syrup. After draining they are dried on a rack, and pistachio slivers are sprinkled into the indent. Heavy but flaky, they taste like

balusha

a syrupy Danish.

GULAB JAMUN

This ubiquitous, round, doughnutlike, syrupy sweet is served in most Indian restaurants. They are deep-fried milk balls soaked and served in a warm, rose-scented syrup. The dough is made from milk powder, flour, baking powder, ghee, and milk. The large balls are carefully deep-fried in oil over low heat until they turn reddish brown, and are then dropped into a thin syrup flavored with rose water. The

spongy balls are sweet and juicy from absorbing the syrup. They taste like pancakes saturated in perfumed syrup. There is also a type that is fried longer, which is called kala or black jamun. It has a firmer texture. This is used to make cream cutlets, which are slices of the

cream cutlet   dark balls rolled in coconut shreds and sandwiched with a layer of thick malai cream. Alutua is gulab jamun that is made from a dough of mashed sweet potatoes and flour.

JALEBIS

These are deep-fried, pretzel-shaped loops. These shiny, sticky, orange spirals ooze syrup. They are made from a fermented batter that is squeezed through the nozzle of a piping bag into hot ghee to form double figure 8s. They are fried on both sides, scooped out, dipped in saffron-infused syrup, and drained. The hot syrup

jalebis

saturates the hollow insides of the loops, forming sugary strands. They melt in your mouth under a crispy shell. They are like eating pure melted sugar.

Stocking Up

Indulge your sweet tooth. Choose a mixed box that contains a bar of cashew fudge, a sugary ladoo, a cube of pistachio barfi, a slab of almond fudge, a piece of Mysore pak, and a gulab jamun. Chocolate barfi, kalakand, and jalebis are always popular. Or choose a box of whatever sweet morsel looks good to you.

· 15 ·

Tea

चाय

Hindi word for "tea"

Throughout the world today, 14,400 cups of tea are consumed per second. India not only drinks a fair share of the beverage, but it is by far the largest tea-growing country in the world. Commercial pressures led to the cultivating of tea in India. By 1833 the East India Company had lost its hold over the tea trade in China, and it decided that nearby Assam would be a good region to plant tea. Upon arriving, the British discovered that the Singhpo hilltribes had cultivated vast areas of a local tea, which was called viridis. This was cultivated commercially and it has flourished ever since. Assam tea plants were grown in the Darjeeling Highlands, in the Niligiri Hills in the southwest, and in Sri Lanka. The Sylhet region of Bangladesh, which borders Assam, is another major tea-growing area.

All tea comes from the same plant: camellia sinesis. This one species produces thousands of varieties. The distinct flavor of any tea is determined by where it is grown and how the leaves are treated once they are plucked. Like wine, tea has its vineyard. They are called gardens. Tea estates are called tea gardens. Thousands of acres of tea bushes are planted between shade trees to prevent the tender leaves from burning. In India, Bangladesh, and Sri Lanka tea buds and leaves are handpicked by saree-clad teams of women with nimble fingers.

184

Most Indian teas are fully-fermented blacks, except for the fragrant green tea that is relished in Kashmir. You will find boxes, bags, paper-wrapped blocks, and tins of teas on shelf 2 of the Rajas' grocery store. There are Assam blacks, Ceylons, Darjeelings, and many other blends, plus tea-masala powder. You can select from loose-leaf tea or tea bags. Most tea is a blend of different grades of tea leaves. To ensure uniform tastes in brands and grades, teas are blended by experienced tea tasters who rate and reblend each lot to keep the flavor consistent. Bulk tea blends are then sent to auction in the ports of Calcutta, Chittagong, and Colombo. From there they are exported around the world.

How Black Teas Are Made

Fully-fermented black teas start as freshly plucked leaves. They are brought to the withering rooms of tea-estate processing plants. They are dried on mats to soften for 8 to 10 hours, then rolled, crushed, and twisted by machines. After this they are sent to ferment, develop flavor, and darken. Pungent teas are the result of short fermentation. More flavorful teas take a longer time to ferment. Next, blasts of dry, hot air fire the leaves. Finally, they are sorted, cut, graded, and fired again.

Black tea is divvied into leaf sizes and broken grades, with about 80 percent broken. Orange pekoe is not a type of tea, but it refers to the leaf grade. Unbroken pekoe means closely twisted leaves, which may contain a tip or bud leaf and produce a pale liquor. Pekoe are small, tightly rolled leaves with a darker brew. Broken grades are broken orange pekoe, which are fannings and dust, the smallest grade produced. This is used in tea-bag blends. Leaf size affects brewing, but it is not an indication of quality. Most of India's teas are blends, except for some Assams and Darjeelings.

Choosing a Tea

Teas are sold under a variety of estate names from the garden where they were grown. Decide on a type, such as Darjeeling, then take a look at all of those available to make a selection. Buy only as much as you can use within a few months. Use it within six at the most. Tea won't spoil, but it does lose its sparkle. Store tea in an airtight jar or tin away from light, heat, and moisture. Never keep tea in the refrigerator. It will get damp and pick up odors.

Indian Teas

India produces 1 billion pounds of tea a year, with half available for export. There are over 4,000 tea gardens in India, and the teas from them are sorted by size into standard grades. Following is a list of types, where they are grown, and what to look for.

ASSAM BLACKS

Most of India's tea is grown at high altitudes in the far northeastern Assam Valley, which is nestled between Tibet and Myanmar. Assams brew into deep, reddish orange liquors and are full, thick, heavy teas with a rich smoky aroma and a lingering taste. The finest Assams are from Lakhimpur and Dum Duma. These are strong-bodied with a malty flavor. Medium-grade Assams are strong and pungent. These are mixed with plainer, lighter teas to make most of the black-tea blends from India. Bordering Assam is Srimangal in the Sylhet Valley, Bangladesh, which has three of the world's largest tea gardens in area and production. The Assam blacks from here go mainly into blends. Assam teas are also grown in the Duars, a region southeast of Darjeeling. Duar teas are dark and full-bodied with a soft, mellow liquor and a flowery flavor. South Indian Assams, grown in the Nilgiri Hills, are fine-flavored with a brisk, pungent taste and a lighter liquor. Anaimalai tea is an Assam that is grown in the Coimbatore district of Tamil Nadu. It is a strong, full-bodied tea.

An ancient Chinese legend has it that tea originated in India, where it grew wild in the hills of Assam or in the lower Tibetan mountains. During the Han Dynasty (25–221 A.D.), a Chinese scholar named Gan Lu went to India to study Buddhism. When he returned to China, he brought back not only his Buddhist beliefs, but some Assam tea seeds. With the planting of those seeds came the cultivation of tea in China.

Most Assam teas that you will find are a blend of fine and medium grades. They are sold in 1-pound bags or boxes. The word "mamri" on the label means "big leaf." For mamri loose-leaf teas,

assam blacks

look for the Indian CTC, B&A garden fresh, Swad, and Deep Tea of Assam brands. Look also for Taza India loose-leaf tea (an Assam blend) in boxes, Top Star Co. in 17-ounce red bags, and the Mumtaz brand in magenta-orange boxes and purple, paper-wrapped 1-pound blocks of pure Indian Barooti tea, which is packed in Calcutta. The Lasa brand has small boxes of Nilgiri-grown Assam. Look also for Assam Sonali in 15-ounce red-yellow boxes. For tea bags, look for Imperial Tea Assam in boxes of 50 bags.

CHAI MASALA

Next to water, chai is the most consumed beverage in India. Chai is tea brewed with water, milk, and sugar. Masala chai means that spices are added. You can grind whole spices or use handy commercial powders. These are a mix of dried ginger, black pepper, cardamom, cinnamon, and cloves. Look for the Swad brand's tea masala in 3.5-ounce shaker jars and for the Badshah, MDH, or Ramdev brands in small boxes. A recipe for chai masala is on page 253.

chai masala

DARJEELING TEA

One of the world's most prized teas, this is grown in the northeastern district of India along the slopes of the Himalayas. Darjeeeling tea is cultivated at altitudes from 1,000 to 6,500 feet, with the highest-grown tea the finest. The quality and flavor depends on weather conditions during growth and the garden that the tea came from. The blackish, dried leaves vary from small to "tippy," meaning that they contain a lot of young shoots or buds. Darjeeling teas have a rich, golden red liquor and a deep penetrating aroma.

darjeeling tea

Teas from the first picking in early spring (which are very rare), are light and slightly green with apricot overtones. Second-flush Darjeelings, picked later in the spring, are darker in flavor and deeper in body with a hint of muscatel. Third-flush Darjeelings, picked in the autumn, are deep and mellow flavored. Reputable single-estate gardens to look for include Makai Bari, Namring, Rungneet, Mim, and Castleton. Darjeelings are also added to Indian tea blends. It is sold loose-leaf style. Look for the Brooke Bond and Swad brand in tins, the Top Star Co. in 8.8- and 17-ounce dark green bags, and the Lopchu Tea Estate Darjeeling in pale blue paper blocks. Mango Republic has pure Darjeeling tea in foil pouches inside 1-pound burlap bags. Look also for Jahan's Darjeeling in round, blue and cream tins.

Thomas Lipton, a Scottish grocer from Glasglow, was in the market for a new enterprise just after a blight had devastated Sri Lanka's coffee crop. He sent an agent to scout for possibilities in Sri Lanka. It was the right place at the right time for the right price. He bought plantations for half of what he'd expected to pay, and he was in the tea business by 1891. Sir Tea, as Mr. Lipton was later called, still lends his name to the best-known tea brand in the world.

GREEN TEA

The small amount of green tea grown in India is produced in the northwest districts of Kangra and Dehra Dun. Kangra tea is grown in the hills south of Kashmir and west of Tibet. It has a delicate aroma, full body, and spicy flavor. Dehra Dun is a poorer grade. Kashmir tea is called kahva. It is made by boiling loose green tea in a charcoal-fired samovar. Sugar, crushed cardamom, and almonds or a pinch of saffron might also be added. This sweet, fragrant brew is sipped from breakfast to bedtime in well-worn, handleless, metal cups. Adding spices to the tea in cold weather maintains body heat. You might find Kangra tea, but more likely what is sold in Indian grocery stores is from the Middle East. Look for Dist. M. M.T. Corp loose-leaf tea in 16-ounce bags. It has Arabic lettering on the label. There is also Royal World Ceylon green tea in boxes of 50 bags.

CEYLON TEAS

Sri Lanka produces about half a billion pounds of tea a year, accounting for 30 percent of the world's supply. Tea is the island's primary export. A major blight on the coffee crop in 1869 actually proved to be quite fortuitous. Assam tea took hold and flourished in the central and south mountains, beginning a new industry.

Known as Ceylons, the teas are graded by leaf size under the name of the gardens where they were grown or in blends that are simply labeled "Ceylon tea." The best and lightest teas are grown at higher altitudes. The lower grown teas are stronger and less delicate. Teas from the Uva Highlands are full-bodied and fragrant. Dimbula Ceylons are flavorful with a fruity aroma, and Nuwara Eliya teas are delicate and lemony. Ceylon teas produce a reddish brown brew and, in general, are softer and less pungent than Assam blacks. A lot of Ceylon tea goes into blends and tea bags. Look for Alwazah pure Ceylon loose-leaf tea in 1-pound red boxes with a white-swan logo, Cross & Sword in 1-pound gold boxes, and Ceylon Special Opa Tea in a red box. For tea bags, look for Ahmad, Luck Leaf Ceylon breakfast tea, Goldup, and Royal World, all in boxes ranging from 25 to 100 bags.

ceylon tea

Dhabas originated in Punjab as cheap, storefront restaurants serving Punjabi fare. The concept evolved into 24-hour truck-stop cafes (some would say dives) along main roads throughout India. If you travel by bus or private coach, a stop at one is part of the trip. The food is hearty, if a bit greasy. Lots of long-simmered curries, fried rice, deep-fried doughnuts and oily paratha are served. The truckers order tea by traveling distance, such as 100-mile or 500-mile tea. The longer the trip, the stronger the brew. Even no-mile dhaba tea is potent, and a cup of chai will jolt you awake at whatever hour the bus pulls in.

Tea Blends

Most mass-market teas are blends. They are made from as few as four to as many as twenty teas. This is done to achieve consistency and to make sure that a brand is always available. Most teas you find on grocery shelves are blends that make wonderful cups of tea. Earl Grey, for example, is a pungent, flowery tea made from a blend of Ceylon and Assam black. It is scented with the oil of bergamont (a small citrus fruit). For Earl Grey, look for Royal World in small tins and for Top Star Co. in 8.8-ounce black bags. Some good brands of blended loose-leaf teas to look for are Connoissor, Danedar Tapal, Palak Finest, Swad India Tea, Lamsa, Nirav, Top Kalami, Tiger, CTC Mahesh Tea of Gujarat, and Wag Bakri. These are sold in

tea blend

14- to 16-ounce boxes or bags. Look also for Gulabi Barooti Calcutta loose-leaf tea in paper-wrapped, 1-pound blocks and for Shahrzad blended and scented tea, which has a logo of a princess playing a harp on the black bag. Taj Mahal Brooke Bond offers red-, green-, and yellow-label tea blends in loose-leaf form and tea bags. PC Tips and Imperial Tea offer boxes of tea bags.

FLAVORED TEAS

These are powdered, flavored, instant, black teas in small bags, boxes, or jars. Steep or mix them into hot water. Flavors include rose, chocolate, vanilla, and masala chai. Look for the Sapat Fantasy and Lamsa brands.

Stocking Up

Try several brands to find a black tea that you like, or mix them to create a custom blend. Wag Bakri is an excellent brand to start with. Assam teas are good morning brews. Add a Darjeeling for a superb hot or iced tea. Tea masala is a must for making quick, delicious, spicy chai.

16

Food for Thought:
The Ayurvedic Kitchen

Hindi word for "ayurvedic herbs"

Indian cooks fill edible prescriptions for both everyday meals and for those prepared to cure a specific ailment. The Indian kitchen doubles as a healing center, just as the Indian grocery store is also an Ayurvedic pharmacy. The word "Ayurveda" means "the science of life." It is an ancient medical system with a holistic approach. Ayurveda treats the whole person, not just the illness. The individual takes an active, responsible role in his or her own living and healing process. The concept of Ayurveda is to maintain a balance between body, mind, spirit, and environment, and by doing so, to prevent sickness. This involves a natural diet to suit your constitution, herbal cleansings, yoga, relaxation, and therapeutic massage. The purpose of Ayurvedic healing is to not just treat the cause, but to bring out-of-balance elements back into harmony. Treatments using foods are based on the six tastes, or rasas: sweet, sour, salty, pungent, bitter, and astringent. Each taste has therapeutic actions to adjust and keep the body's systems in balance. You don't have to become a yogi or ascetic to enjoy the benefits of Ayurveda. Food, as the ancients knew, is the best medicine for health.

Ayurvedic Basics

All foods are Ayurvedic. They are categorized by culinary and medicinal properties. Herbs and spices that harmonize with certain foods are cooked together to promote the body's own healing properties. Excessive warmth in the body is thought to be the cause of many illnesses, so "heating" and "cooling" foods are always balanced in Indian meals. Yogurt, ghee, honey, and rice are cooling to the body. Meat, mangoes, and cashews, to name a few, are heat-inducing foods that are eaten in moderation. Everyone needs a certain amount of each of the six rasas, but too much of one can be harmful, just as a lack of one can upset the body's balance (or doshas). With this in mind, it is easier to understand the complexity of Indian meals, which are designed to include all the rasas. There is always a spicy, sour dish, a cooling yogurt, a hot, bitter pickle, and a sweet. Indian cooks are aware of the healing properties of spices, herbs, and foods. The cooks fine-tune and adjust recipes accordingly.

Five Essential Ayurvedic Remedies

These are simple, easy to use, and effective. Most are probably in your kitchen right now, except for trifal. Trifal is a powdered blend of the three most used Ayurvedic herbs. It is sold in packets or jars. Keep in mind that Ayurvedic remedies have no harmful side effects, but they are not intended to replace seeing a licensed physician for the diagnosis or treatment of illness.

BLACK PEPPER

Pungent and bitter with hot energy, black pepper is a digestive and liver stimulant. It helps relieve bronchial asthma, colds, fevers, frostbite, fungal infections, poor circulation, toothaches, and upper-respiratory conditions. Take ¹/₂ to 1 teaspoon of pepper powder two to three times a day. Mix it with honey on a spoon, or sprinkle it on food. Whole peppercorns can be boiled and steeped.

black pepper

Pepper tea helps relieve the symptoms of the flu, colds, and painful menstruation. Rub crushed peppercorns on a throbbing tooth to ease a toothache.

GARLIC & ONION

Pungent, bitter, sour, and astringent with heating energy, both garlic and onions are antibacterial, antiviral, and anti-inflammatory. They aid digestion, lower cholesterol, and help flush toxins from the liver, promote high metabolism, and help relieve coughs, asthma, indigestion, acne, earaches and high blood pressure. Onions are high in iron and are prescribed for anemia. Rub the cut surface of a garlic clove and apply it to a sty—it will sting, but it will disappear in a few days. Garlic is more potent than onion is.

garlic

Both can be taken raw, juiced, or cooked. Chop a medium-sized onion and eat it as a salad with lemon juice. Mix a few ounces of onion juice with honey. For raw garlic, eat 1 to 2 cloves twice a day, whole, minced, or crushed with honey. Add liberal amounts of both in cooking.

GINGER

Pungent with hot energy, ginger is an anti-inflammatory and contains enzymes that encourage the body to digest fat, carbohydrates, and proteins. Ginger helps relieve fevers, colds, diarrhea, dizziness, motion sickness, nausea, stomachaches, and vomiting. Take $1/4$ teaspoon of ginger powder or $1/2$ teaspoon of freshly grated ginger in warm water, or steep several slices of

ginger root

ginger in a cup of boiled water and honey and take it 3 times a day. Use ginger in cooking, and sprinkle grated ginger over foods. Ginger powder mixed into a paste can be used as a poultice to ease muscle and joint aches, chest pains, and headaches. It also stimulates circulation.

TRIFAL

trifal

This is a powdered compound of three Ayurvedic herbs: amalaki, bibbitaki, and haritaki. It has a sour, astringent, bitter, pungent taste and warm energy. Trifal is antibacterial, antiviral, antiyeast, anti-inflammatory, and antitumor. It lowers blood pressure and cholesterol. It is also a digestive, a diuretic, and a laxative. It is revered as a rasayamma, or balancing and rejuvenating formula. Trifal also helps relieve anemia, constipation, lung ailments, hypertension, indigestion, skin blemishes, and yeast infections. It is used as an intestinal cleanser because it helps digest food, then aids in its elimination. As a powder, take 1 to 2 teaspoons three times a day washed down with water, or steep it in a cup of boiled water and drink it. It is very bitter, so add honey.

TURMERIC

Bitter and astringent with hot energy, turmeric is antibacterial, antiviral, anti-inflammatory, antioxidant, antiparasitic, and a diuretic. It helps cleanse the liver, purifies the blood, and promotes digestion. It helps relieve acne, allergies, burns, indigestion, gall-bladder problems, liver damage, skin rashes, and ulcers. Recent studies have shown it to be effective against cancerous tumors and HIV. You can apply turmeric to stop cuts from bleeding. Pat the powder on your skin to treat pimples and rashes, or mix it with a little coconut oil and apply it. Be aware that it leaves a yellow stain for several days. Take $1/2$ to $1 1/2$ teaspoons two to three times a day with honey washed down with water. Also use it in cooking.

Ayurvedic Herbs & Natural Products

Herbs are used as special foods to eliminate excesses and strengthen deficiencies. They stimulate functions such as digestion, detoxification, metabolism, waste elimination, and heating or cooling of the body. Foods are the main nutritional source, while herbs provide subtle nutrition and therapeutic properties. Herbs are sold whole or as powders (churan). Whole herbs are steeped as teas or soaked and chewed. Powders are mixed with ghee, honey, rice, or milk, or they are washed down with water. Following are herbs that you will find in Indian grocery stores and what they are used for. Swad carries many. Some are in packets with the store's name and the herbs name on a sticker. A few are sold in tablets.

AMALAKI

Dried amla, or Indian gooseberry. Amalaki is sour, sweet, and has cooling energy. It is good for the eyes, liver, and stomach. It rebuilds and maintains tissue, increases red blood cells, cleanses the mouth, strengthens teeth, nourishes bones, and is the highest natural source of vitamin C. Amalaki is a blood purifier, and it relieves symptoms of bleeding disorders, anemia, gastritis, hepatitis, osteoporosis, constipation, spleen and liver weakness, hair loss, and general debility. It is believed to also strengthen the pancreas of diabetics. It is sold dried in small packets of black, wrinkled chips. To use it, boil and steep it as tea, soak it, and chew or grind it into powder to take it with honey. Look for the Eastern brand in 12-ounce bags.

AMLA POWDER

amla powder

This finely ground, olive green powder is made from dried amla (Indian gooseberry) and sold in small boxes. Mix it with water into a paste and rub it into the scalp and hair. Leave it on for 1 hour and rinse it off. Amla powder is used to prevent hair loss, strengthen the roots, and promote luxurious, healthy hair. It can also be used as a tea for cold and fevers. Look for the Hesh brand in 3.5-ounce boxes.

ARITHA

These large, round, sour, dried berries are from a tamarind-like Indian tree. They are used as a soap and shampoo. Soak until soft and rub into the scalp and hair. Stimulates the scalp, promotes healthy hair, and adds glossy shine. Acts as a deep-cleansing natural soap, good for the skin.

aritha

ALUKA

Wild yam. This dried, chalky, white tuberous root is sold powdered. It is sweet, bitter, and cooling. It is good for the nervous, reproductive, digestive, and urinary systems. It improves digestion and is considered a nutritive and rejuvenative tonic. Aluka helps with impotency, senility, hormonal deficiency, and abdominal pains and cramps. Steep it in boiling water as tea or take the powder with milk. For a daily restorative drink, simmer 5 grams in a cup of milk with ghee and honey.

ASHWAGANDHA

Withania. Winter cherry root, also known as "Indian ginseng." This herb is bitter, astringent, sweet, and has heating energy. It smells like a horse and is said to give the vitality and energy of that animal. It is good for the muscles, bones, marrow, nerves, and the reproductive system (especially males). It is used for general and sexual debility, nerve exhaustion, insomnia, loss of memory, weak eyes, fatigue, and anemia. Considered the best rejuvenative herb, it promotes healing from stress, overwork, and lack of sleep. It is calming and promotes sleep. Ashwagandha powder is best taken with milk, or as a paste mixed with medicated ghee (tikta ghrita) or with rice, milk, and pippali pepper.

BALA

Indian mallow root. In Sanskrit "bala" means "what gives strength." This has strong tonic properties. It is sweet and has cooling energy. Bala is a heart stimulant and helps relieve inflammation of nerve tissue, exhaustion, chronic fevers, and asthma. It is considered the best heart herb and a rejuvenative tonic. It strengthens cancer patients before and after chemotherapy. The root can be steeped as a tea or boiled with milk. For fevers crush it into a powder and take it with ginger or black pepper.

BAWAL GUNDAR

These are small, clear, light-amber resin crystals with a bland flavor. They are chewed in the winter for a warm feeling. They are also ground and made into milk and sugar sweets that are eaten to relieve back pain after pregnancy. They are sold in small plastic bags.

BHRINGARAJ

Eclipta Prostrata. The whole, dried plant is used. It is bitter, astringent, sweet, and has cooling energy. It is thought to help maintain and rejuvenate bones, teeth, hair, eye sight, hearing, and memory. Considered to be the best herb for the liver, it is used to treat cirrhosis, chronic hepatitis, bleeding, and anemia. It helps calm the mind and promotes sound sleep. Take it as an infusion of the dried herb or powdered with medicated ghee. Applied externally as a paste, it helps draw out poisons and reduces swollen glands. The plant grows wild in the southwestern United States. It has reddish brown stalks, pointy, jagged-edged leaves, and small, white flowers.

BIBHITAKI

Beleric Myrobalan. A tiny, dried, berrylike fruit from one of the varieties of tropical Myrobalan trees, this is used medicinally in India. It is astringent, and has sweet heating energy. It is good for plasma, muscle, and the bones. A powerful rejuvenative herb and lung tonic, improves vision, promotes hair growth, aids digestion, is a strong laxative, and tones the stomach. It is one of the 3 herbs in the compound trifal. Take it as an infusion, powder, or paste. Mixed with honey, it is good for a sore throat and hoarse voice. Used externally, it is an antiseptic.

BRAHMI

Water hyssop. In Hindi the name means "divine creative energy." A creeping succulent with fleshy, spatula-shaped leaves, it grows in marshes. The dried aerial parts are used. It is bitter, sweet, and has cooling energy. Taken for nervous-system disorders, including epilepsy and mental illness, it is also taken for indigestion, ulcers, constipation, asthma, bronchitis, and infertility. Brahmi is also believed to improve mental function, memory, and reduce learning time. Brahmi tea is taken with honey before meditating. Take the powder as an infusion in hot water or with ghee or honey.

CHYAVAN-PRASH

This is a thick, sticky, brown paste made from boiled amla (Indian gooseberry) blended with over forty herbs and spices. According to legend, it was first made by a forest sage named Chyavan, and it was thought to have magical powers. The paste available today is a general tonic and restorative medicine. It can be taken daily if followed by milk that helps absorb it. It has a sweet-sour, bitter, spicy flavor. Also sold as a powder, it is taken mixed in warm water. It has antioxidant, antistress, liver-

chyavan-prash

protecting, digestive-aiding, and anti-inflammatory properties. It fights infection and improves resistance against colds and coughs. Look for the Darbur brand in 1- or 2-pound plastic jars.

DRIED GINGER

dried ginger

These hard, frosty, beige knobs of salted, sun-dried gingerroot are steeped as a tea for coughs. Ginger tea is also believed to settle the stomach.

DUSHANDA

dushanda

An herbal blend of leaves, twigs, roots, seeds, and banafsha, this type of herbal flower is good for fevers. Use it boiled in water and steeped as tea. It is considered to be the best relief for colds, flu, and fevers. Look for the Eastern brand in 1.75-ounce boxes. A similar blend is labeled Joshanda, which is sold under the Hamdard brand in small, white, plastic packets.

GANTHODA

Small bits of dried, brown, muddy-looking roots are boiled with jaggery (cane sugar) and taken after a pregnancy and in the winter to feel warm. Look for the Swad brand in half-ounce packets.

GOKSHURA

Caltrop. The small, dried fruit of a common weed, called goats head or puncture vine, is used as an herb in India. It is sweet, bitter, and has cooling energy. It helps with difficult or painful urination, water retention, kidney stones, bladder stones, cystitis, impotence, and rheumatism. It is considered the best herb for urinary tract disorders because it is thought to promote the flow of urine to nourish and strengthen the kidneys, and to calm the nervous system. Boil it in water and milk and drink it. Or take it as a powder mixed with honey. Mixed with ginger powder, it relieves back pain.

In June, when monsoon season starts, thousands of asthmatics visit the Battina Gowd brothers on the fringes of Hyderabad for a rather unique Ayurvedic cure. A small, live fish is wrapped in herbs and stuffed down their throats. According to ancient Vedic texts, the fish wriggles around inside the body, clearing the breathing passages and generating body heat to help combat the chills and coughs of the rainy season. Extra trains run to Hyderabad this time of year to handle the masses arriving for this free service.

GOTU KOLA

Indian Pennywort. This is an herb with small, fan-shaped, scalloped leaves that grows in swampy areas, including the southern United States. It is bittersweet, sour, and has cooling energy. The dried aerial parts are used. In India the fresh leaves are added to salads. It is a rejuvenating tonic and cleansing herb taken for skin problems, digestive disorders, and fevers. It strengthens nervous function and memory and is believed to help mental concentration. It acts as a mild diuretic and sedative. It has an anti-inflammatory effect and is used to treat eczema, rheumatism, and arthritis. Steeped in milk it makes a good nerve tonic. Mixed with basil and black pepper, it is good for fevers. As a daily revitalizer, mix the powder with ghee and wash it down with water.

GUGGUL

Loban. Closely related to myrrh, these brown crystals of resin from a small, thorny tree are used in many Ayurvedic blends. It is bitter, pungent, sweet, and has heating energy. It has strong purifying and rejuvenating powers, and it increases white blood cells. It also increases appetite, clears the lungs, and helps heal skin and mucous membranes. It is considered the best herb for arthritic conditions. It contains phytosterols, which have a hormonal action, and it is used to treat menstrual problems. Grind it into a powder and take it as a paste mixed with water. The lumps are also burned to make smoke for puja.

HARITAKI

Chebulic Myrobalan. Also called harden, hurda, or Indian gall nut, this is the shriveled, dried, brown, oval fruit of a type of the Myrobalan tree. In Tibet it is known as the king of medicines. It is astringent, bitter, and has heating energy. It is one of the three herbs in the compound trifal. It helps coughs, asthma, hiccups, vomiting, heart diseases, skin diseases, itching, and nervous disorders. It regulates the colon, improves digestion and nutrient absorption, and promotes vision. Considered a rejuvenative herb, it is believed to aid longevity and increase wisdom. Boil it in water and drink it. Or grind it into a powder or mix it into a paste to wash it down with water. It can also be soaked and chewed with honey to sweeten the bitterness. It is also sold preserved in syrup (see page 159).

haritaki

HIMAJ

These are small, unripe haritaki fruit. It is mainly chewed for stomach problems, indigestion, sore throats, or a hoarse voice.

KACHRI

These are dried baby papayas. They look like small, light-brown, leathery, wrinkled plums.

Soak and mash them to use them as a meat tenderizer, or add several of them to meat stews to soften tough cuts. Look for the Swad brand in 3.5-ounce bags.

kachri

KAMAR KAKADI

These are lotus seeds. They are called padma, pushkara, and kamala in Sanskrit. Sold whole, the dried, black seeds are sweet, astringent, and have cooling energy. The lotus is sacred to Laxmi, the goddess of wealth and prosperity, and brings material and spiritual abundance. The lotus is believed to calm the mind and subdue restless thoughts and dreams. The seeds are thought to improve aspiration, devotion, and concentration. They are made into prayer beads. Lotus seeds are also said to improve speech and stop stuttering. They help with bleeding disorders, diarrhea, impotence, and heart weakness.

They are good for the uterus. They are considered a rejuvenating food, when soaked and ground into a paste or crushed. They are taken three times a day with spiced, sweetened rice. Look for the Nirav brand in 4-ounce bags.

kamar kakadi

KUTKI

Katuka. This is a bitter, dried rhizome of a small, leafy plant that is used as an herbal remedy for stomach ailments, liver dysfunction, and as a laxative. For liver toxicity, take the powder mixed with aloe vera juice. For stomach problems and constipation, take it with honey or wash it down with water. It is also sold in pills.

LICORICE ROOT

Yashti Madhu (also spelled jethi madh), mulethi, or honey stick. These are the dried roots and underground stems of the licorice plant. They are sold as fibrous, woody, blackish brown, ridged sticks, as a powder, and in solid sticks of concentrated essence, which are black, glossy, taste bittersweet and are

licorice root

used partially dissolved in water. Licorice tastes sweet with a bitter aftertaste and has cooling energy. It helps relieve coughs, colds, bronchitis, sore throats, laryngitis, ulcers, painful urination, stomach aches, and general debility. Chew on licorice sticks to relieve a sore throat. Gargle with an infusion of it to relive a dry cough. Drink it as a tea with ginger, sugar, and milk to sooth an upset stomach or gastric ulcers. Licorice is believed to calm the mind and nurture the spirit, promoting concentration, and harmony. Look for the Swad brand in 3.5-ounce bags and the Swastik brand's concentrated essence, which is sold in orange boxes or by the stick. In India the swastika is a symbol of peace, and it is often seen above temple gates.

MALATANI MATTI

These are flat shards and small chips of reddish clay. To use them, grind them into a powder and mix them with water to form a paste. Apply the paste to the face as a cleansing mask. It helps the skin feel cool in the summer, and it clears pimples. It is sold in small, plastic bags.

malatani matti

MANJISTHA

Indian Madder. These are the dried roots of a plant with four-lobed leaves and tiny red flowers. It is considered the best blood-purifying herb. It is a bittersweet herb that is believed to cool, detoxify the blood, stop cuts from bleeding, arrest hemorrhages, and promote blood circulation. It is also good for the female reproductive system, increases blood flow, and promotes the healing of tissue that is damaged by injury or infection. It helps broken bones heal and cleanses the liver, spleen, and kidneys. Take it steeped as tea, as a powder with ghee, or in a paste. Mixed with honey, it can be used externally for skin inflammations. Mixed with licorice, it can be applied to sunburns.

MUSTA

Nutgrass. The dried rhizomes of this grassy plant grow in marshy areas and rivers. It is one of the most important herbs for women. It relieves menstrual pain and eases the bloating and tension of PMS. It also acts as a digestive and liver stimulant, and it is commonly used for intestinal disorders like gastritis. Musta is pungent, bitter, astringent and has cooling energy. Take it simmered in water or as a powder. Mixed with ginger and honey, it is a good, all-purpose digestive aid.

PADMAKA

This is a wild cherry bark. The inner bark is used to cleanse and decongest the lungs and lymphatic system. It is bitter, astringent, and has cooling energy. It is thought to help coughs, bronchial spasms, palpitations, skin problems, and eye inflammations. Steep the bark in hot water or take it as a powder. It is also available as a cough syrup.

PIPPALI

pippali

Indian long pepper. The dried fruit pods of this close relative to black pepper are ground into powder and used to help digestion and respiratory problems. It is pungent and has heating energy. It removes congestion. It is considered a rejuvenative tonic for the lungs and liver. It helps relieve coughs, colds, asthma, laryngitis, and arthritis. It is also considered an aphrodisiac and strengthens the reproductive functions. Take it as an infusion in water or milk, or as a powder with honey.

SAFETA MUSALI

White Musali. These are tuberous, off-white roots of a type of wild asparagus that is closely related to shatavari. They look like long, dried jasmine petals. It is bitter, cold, and sweet. It is good for the reproductive and respiratory systems. Many take it for general or sexual debility, diarrhea, and low appetite. It also helps nourish the fetus during pregnancy and increases milk flow afterward. Grind it into a powder and steep it in warm milk, or make it into a sweet.

safeta musali

SHATAVARI

Hundred Husbands. This is the main Ayurvedic tonic for women. Its rejuvenative action on the female organs is said to give a woman the ability to have a hundred husbands. This sexy herb comes from the dried roots of an Asian asparagus plant. It is sweet, bitter, and has cooling energy. Some think it helps with sexual debility in general, infertility, libido, menopause, stomach ulcers, diarrhea, dehydration, herpes, coughs, and chronic fevers. It is good to take after menopause as it supplies female hormones. Take it steeped in water, simmered in milk, or as a powder or paste mixed with honey. Mixed in warm milk with honey, it is believed to increase fertility and aid love and devotion. Western asparagus root has many similarities, but it is more diuretic.

TAGARA

Indian Valerian. This rhizome is one of the best herbs for nervous disorders. It is bitter, pungent, sweet, and has heating energy. It is said to help insomnia, convulsions, vertigo, nervous coughs, palpitations, migraines, and skin diseases. It cleanses toxins from the colon, blood, joints, and nerves. It calms muscle spasms and relieves menstrual cramps. Steep the root in hot water as tea. To induce sleep, take 1 or 2 teaspoons of powder in warm water.

TIKTA GHEE

This is a bitter ghee. This Ayurvedic compound made of ghee and various bitter herbs is used to make herbal powders.

TRIATU

This stimulative compound, also called "the three spices," made of ground ginger, black pepper, and pippali (Indian long pepper). It detoxifies the body and improves digestion, absorption, and assimilation of medicines and foods.

TULSI

This is also called holy basil. This pungent herb with heating energy helps coughs, colds, sinus congestion, headaches, arthritis, and fevers. The dried leaves are taken as an infusion, powdered, or in medicated ghee. For sore throats and colds, take it as a tea steeped with crushed cardamom, cloves, cumin, fennel seeds, and honey. Holy basil is said to open the heart and mind and to strengthen faith, clarity, and compassion.

> Here are some Ayurvedic tips for stress avoidance and relief:
> - eat at routine times every day
> - sip hot water all day (lukewarm water in summer)
> - make lunch your main meal
> - eat dinner by 8:00 P.M.
> - go to bed by 10:00 P.M.
> - sleep without an alarm clock
> - meditate
> - use a tongue scraper (or the back of a spoon) to remove plaque every morning

OTHER

The Ayurvedic system of healing seems simple. The basic concept is to treat the whole body—the interconnectedness of mind, body, diet, and nature. Yet it is much too complex to cover in this brief introduction. Hopefully you have realized the importance of treating both the illness and the cause. It appears that the ancient wisdom of Ayurveda is just as relevant today as it was 3,000 years ago.

Stocking Up

Make sure that you have black pepper, onions, garlic, ginger, and turmeric for all-around health and home remedies. Helpful herbs are Trifal, Ashwagandha (for men), Amla (for the hair) Manjistha (for the blood), Brahmi or Gotu Kola (for the brain), Musta and Shatavari (for women), Bala (for the heart), Bhringaraj (for the liver), Chayavan-prash (for a general tonic), and licorice.

17

Bombay Bazaar: The Rest of the Indian Market

Hindi word for "bazaar"

Here we will discover miscellaneous items throughout the grocery store, reflecting the great bazaars of India, Bangladesh, and Pakistan. We'll check on types of sweeteners, nuts, seeds, and dried fruit. We'll examine exotic essences, cordial syrups, food-coloring powders, silver leaf, fried onion crisps, vinegars, and convenient snack mixes. We will check out dried and frozen foods. Lastly, our spicy journey will end with a look at breath-freshener blends and paan-leaf fillings.

Sweeteners

Sugars are used sparingly in Indian meals but lavishly in sweets. In savory dishes, sugar is an important balancing element to other flavors. A little sugar tones down acidic, salty, or bitter flavors in sauces, marinades, soups, and curries. Sugar mellows spices in dals and adds flavor to baked goods, roasted cereals, grains, and snack mixes. Sugar is used in fudgy sweets, boiled candies, brittles, glazes, and syrups. Sugar acts as a preservative in chutneys and jams, and it sweetens hot or cold drinks and yogurt. While granulated white sugar is used, most Indian sugar is thick and brown, made from sweet saps, and sold in firm forms.

GUR

This is palm sugar. It is a creamy, tan sugar made from the sap of the coconut, date, and sugar (palmyra) palms. The sap is boiled into a semisoft mixture and poured into coconut half-shells, bamboo sections, palm-leaf baskets, or clay vessels called sharas to solidify. Unmolded gur is hard, grainy looking, and has a delicate coconut-caramel flavor. Gur is sold in jute-cloth-wrapped loaves, smaller half rounds, cylinders, cakes, or in tubs. To use the chunks, pry off a piece and use a small garlic or cheese grater to shave bits off. To get at the type in tubs, dip a sturdy spoon in hot water and scoop the sugar out. Palm sugar is used extensively in sweets—but not in milky puddings as unrefined sugar can curdle milk. Small amounts are added to split peas, dals, and vegetable dishes to balance spicy flavors. Refrigerate it in a dry container or tightly wrapped in plastic to prevent mold. It is best used within six months. Look for the Bansai Deep brand in 2.2-pound cakes, and for the Swad brand in 17- and 32-ounce loaves and various-sized plastic tubs. It is often sold in plain jute or plastic bags with no label.

> *Bengal in winter is when khejur gur is made from the sap of date palms. The cool air is scented with the smoky sweetness of sap boiling in huge pans set over burning wood. The sap is made into a thin liquid, a thick paste, or solid chunks called patali. Halen gurer sandesh, made from chenna and fresh gur, is also made at this time of year. Markets sell the thin liquid, known as jhola gur, in clay pots. It can also be fermented into a type of cheap liquor.*

JAGGERY

Also called gool, this is thick, boiled, golden sugar cane juice. The word comes from the Indo-Portuguese word "jagara." Cut stalks are crushed in a press to extract the juice, and the clear liquid is boiled until it becomes thick and fudgy. The pale golden liquid is poured into trays or molds to cool and solidify. Jaggery has a sweet, musky caramel flavor, and it is semisoft. It is sold in huge jute-cloth-wrapped loaves tied in thick cord that look like they were unmolded from giant flowerpots. You will also find jaggery in smaller cakes, half rounds, cylinders, and dark-blonde blobs in sealed plastic bags. Varieties range from golden yellow to deep amber, depending on the quality of sugar cane. It is sticky but can be easily crumbled, unless it is very old and has petrified into a rock-hard lump. Chip off a piece and grate it. When melted it becomes soft and gooey, and it smells like sweet sherry.

jaggery

Jaggery is used in sweet making (except in milk puddings as it curdles milk) and to balance tangy or hot, spicy flavors in curries, dals, and vegetable dishes. The thick sugar makes a delicious spread for breads. Grated coconut and melted jaggery stuff karanji, which are deep-fried pastry puffs. Ras Amrit is jaggery milk made from coconut milk blended with grated sugar and flavored with cardamom powder.

Store jaggery in a clean, dry container in a cool place, or refrigerate it to prevent mold. Use it within six months. The best quality comes from Kolhapur, a town in Maharashtra. This will be stated on the label. Look for the Laxmi brand's Kolhapur in 2.2-pound tubs and small blocks wrapped in plastic, the Swad brand in 17-ounce loaves and plastic tubs, the Deep brand in 2.2-pound loaves, and M/S Shah Amrathalal Hiralalco in large, melted-looking blobs in plastic bags in the refrigerator case. Gur and jaggery can be used interchangeably.

Sugar cane, a giant grass native to India, was first discovered in the Ganges Delta. According to legend the ancestors of Buddha came from the land of sugar, or Gur, the name then given to Bengal. The word "saccharin" is derived from the Sanskrit word for sugar, "sakara." Originally, sugar was used as a medicine called Indian salt, which was worth its weight in silver. For centuries sugar was associated with India. Indians were called "they who drink the sweet juice from a weak reed," by the Greeks and Romans.

KHANDSARI

This lumpy rock sugar is made from boiled, crystallized sugar cane juice. The large crystals are clear and have a richer, more subtle flavor than refined sugar. It is used as a sweetener in hot drinks and creates the luster in glazed dishes. Rock sugar is reduced with water to make sugar syrups for sweets or sugar-coated nuts. This gives boiled and crystallized sweets their glassy look. If the lumps are very large, break them into smaller pieces with a hammer or rolling pin. It is sold in plastic bags, often with no label.

KITUL TREACLE

kitul treacle

This is palm honey. It is a thick syrup made from the sap of kitul palms. The sap is boiled until thick, then smoked. This gives it an unusual, delicious flavor like smoky honey and molasses. The dark brown syrup is used in sweets and brittles. It is poured over ice cream, custard, yogurt, or pancakes. It is mainly made in Sri Lanka. It is sold in large bottles, jars, or tins. Look for the MD and Larich brands in 24-ounce bottles and 16-ounce tins.

HONEY

Called madhur or nectar, this golden liquid has been collected since ancient times in India. Cave paintings over 20,000 years old show men taking honey from beehives and being stung for their efforts. Today honey is produced in artificial hives with movable inner frames, then removed by centrifugal force. Honey is not used in cooking, as heating makes it slightly toxic. It is used to sweeten drinks, yogurt, and custards. It is drizzled over fruits, nuts, or sweets. Honey is also the base from which many medicines are made. Honey can be dabbed on cuts and wounds, as it is a disinfectant that contains one of the elements also found in hydrogen peroxide. You will find many types of honey, from runny, clear, and golden to thick and almost black. Some have a mushy layer of crystals on the bottom and clear, amber syrup on top. Look for the Darbar brand in 7-ounce jars and the Ziyad brand in 1-pound jars with a green-yellow label.

honey

N u t s , S e e d s & D r i e d F r u i t

Here you will find a selection of dried fruits, seeds, and whole, chopped, and sliced nuts. There are creamy cashews from Goa, pistachios from Turkey, almonds from Kashmir, apricots from Pakistan, and several forms of coconut to choose from. Nuts contain oils and become rancid unless refrigerated and stored in airtight containers. They are best used within six months. For this reason some stores keep bags of nuts in the refrigerator cases. Larger stores stock nuts on the shelf. Store dried fruit in dry, airtight containers, and use it within six months.

ALMONDS

Badam. Almonds have long been a symbol of romance and luxury in India. They were first introduced to Indian cookery by the moghuls, who made lavish use of the nut in their rich, Persian-influenced court dishes. Almonds are grown in Kashmir, but it is more likely that the golden brown nuts come from the orchards of California. Almonds have a delicate sweet taste and add a nutty milkiness to dishes. They are sold whole, skinned, slivered, blanched, thinly sliced, ground, chopped, or powdered. Ground almonds thicken curries or are fried as a garnish. Slivers are used in sweets, snack mixes, and biryanis. Rice, sweets, and curries are dusted with chopped almonds. Powdered almonds flavor kulfi (Indian ice cream) and milk fudge.

Almonds are high in protein and calcium and are considered nourishing. In hot weather when appetites flag, thandai, a cool almond drink, is made from blanched almonds creamed with black pepper, cardamom, milk, and sugar in a blender. Almonds are credited with the power to sharpen concentration, improve eyesight, and provide energy. Almond paste makes a good face wash. Almonds are good for the skin. Buy large, plump nuts and avoid old ones with a rancid film of white dust. They are sold in plastic bags that are often unlabeled or just have the store's name on a sticker. Look for the Swad and Patel Brothers brands in all forms in 14-ounce or 2-pound bags. Also look for the Nirav and Ziyad brands in 1- or 2-pound bags.

APRICOTS

Khubani. Dried Indian apricots come from Kashmir. They are pale, tan, shriveled, hard, and about the size of a big cherry. They have a fruity aroma, are sweet and chewy, and contain pits. Hunza apricots are similar and come from Pakistan. Both types are leathery and have to be soaked until soft to use them. You may also find bright orange, soft, pitted California apricots. Dried apricots are used in rich lamb, chicken, and vegetable curries, biryanis, and pulaos. They absorb the cooking juices and plump up. Apricot delight is a sweet made of the dried fruit stewed with cream and sprinkled with chopped almonds. Poached apricots are used as a garnish for meat dishes. Any recipe with the word "jardaloo" in the name means that dried apricots are included. Look for the Standard Foods Rasoi brand in 7-ounce bags. Swad has the softer type in 14-ounce bags. Apricots are used in the chicken curry recipe on page 249.

apricots

BETEL NUTS

Areca nut or pak-ku. These are the small, coconutlike fruits of a tall palm. They grow in clusters and turn bright orange when ripe. After sun-drying until hard and brown, they are split open and the small nuts are removed. Betel nuts are round, about $1/2$ inch in diameter, and tawny brown. The insides are striated with creamy, white-brown markings. The name refers to the chips and curls that are shaved off the nut and used in betel-leaf chews. Colored betel-nut shreds are added to breath-freshening mixes. The chips are also chewed plain. Betel nuts are sold whole or as chips in small, unlabeled plastic bags. Whole nuts are used as puja offerings. Betel slices steeped in boiling water aid digestion and a sluggish liver.

Betel nuts are considered sacred. They are placed in front of puja kumbhas (pots filled with water, covered with leaves, and crowned with a broken coconut and flowers) on fresh betel leaves. Either five, seven, or eleven betel nuts must be offered. In the past, kings placed a betel nut in the open court and asked anyone willing to take on a difficult task to pick it up. Even today, giving a betel nut to someone means that you authorize them to act on your behalf. The nuts are also offered to temple priests who carry out puja rituals.

CASHEWS

Kaju. Native to Brazil, the cashew was brought to Goa by the Portuguese. It now thrives along the southwestern coast of India. The name is derived from the Portuguese word "acaju." In the regions where cashews grow in India, the fruit symbolizes prosperity and

cashews

plenty. Brides are given a gold necklace called a jod pod. Tiny, golden cashews, rice grains, coconuts, pineapples, and mangoes are strung on a chain to bring good luck and plenty to the bride's new home. Cashew trees bear fleshy, red, astringent fruits called cashew apples. A large, kidney-shaped seed grows outside the fruit and hangs from the bottom end. Cashew nuts grow inside the hard shell, which is cracked open to extract them. They are creamy, white, and soft when fresh, but they turn pale beige and hard when dried. Cashews have a sweet, creamy, nutty taste and are available whole, broken, chopped, roasted, fried, salted, and spiced. The best, large nuts come from Goa and Kerala.

Cashews complement both savory and sweet dishes. They are used whole in stir-fries and in meat or vegetable curries. They are ground into a creamy paste to thicken curries and sauces or to make milk fudge. Golden, fried cashews garnish rice dishes, puddings, and sweets. They are added to snack mixes and made into nut brittle. Street vendors in India peddle mango-leaf-wrapped cashews boiled in turmeric and salt. In Goa no feast is complete without feni, a potent liquor made from fermented cashew apples. Look for the Nirav brand's whole and broken pieces in 1- and 2-pound bags. Look also for the Swad brand's whole and broken cashews in 14-ounce or 2-pound bags, and for their roasted, salted, and spiced cashews in 3.5-ounce packets.

CHAAR MAGAZ

In Hindi, "chaar" means "4." Chaar magaz is a mixture of four types of dried white seeds: melon, watermelon, pumpkin, and squash. The seeds are ground with a little water, and the paste is used to thicken and flavor sauces and curries. Safed murgh korma, or white chicken, is a classic, moghul court dish. Chicken breasts are cooked in a white sauce made of ground, blanched almonds, chaar magaz, sweet spices, and yogurt. It was served at banquets under a full moon on a white, marble terrace to white-clad guests seated on white pillows on white carpets. The seeds are also added to chutneys, snack mixes, and breath-freshening mixes. It is sold in small packets. The seeds can easily be ground in a blender. Look for the Eastern, Nirav, and Swad brands in 3.5-ounce packets.

chaar magaz

CHIRONGI NUTS

Charoli or chirolo nuts. These are small, lentil-shaped kernels of an Indian fruit. When the fruit's seed dries to a brittle hardness, they are cracked open and the nuts extracted. They are pale brown and speckled with darker patches. They have a musky aroma. They taste like a cross between almonds and hazelnuts. Chirongi nuts are used to garnish desserts. They are ground and added to minced-meat kebabs and kormas for a nutty flavor and texture. They are also toasted and sprinkled over meat curries, rice, salads, and sweet yogurt. They are sold in jars or bags. Look for the Swad brand in 3.5-ounce jars or packets and in 7-ounce bags.

chirongi nuts

COCONUT

Nariyal. Coconuts are the interior nut of the large fruit of the coconut palm tree. They have a hairy, brown, hard, woody shell. They have a firm, white, interior meat and produce clear water that makes a refreshing drink. The grated, pressed flesh produces coconut milk. You will find whole coconuts, dried flakes, finely powdered coconut, and hard, dried, halved kernels in the half-shell called copra. There is also dark brown, roasted, and ground coconut powder that is used to thicken curries. Creamed coconut is sold in boxes or jars in the refrigerator case. It is used like coconut milk, but it is oilier. When buying a fresh coconut, shake it to see if there is water sloshing around inside; if not, it's dry and tough. Coconuts will keep for about one week. To crack one open, place it on newspaper on

coconut

the floor and bang the shell or pierce one of the black "eye" indentations with a skewer. Drain the water out, then tap firmly around the middle of the nut with a hammer. When a crack appears, insert the point of a sturdy knife and pull the crack apart. Use a small knife to pry out large pieces of the meat, and peel the brownish skin with a vegetable peeler.

Coconut flesh has a sweet, nutty flavor with a crisp texture. The flesh can be grated or scraped off into thick curls and roasted. Dried, grated coconut shreds are used in salads, chutneys, and sweets. They are fried until golden brown and blended into a spice paste to thicken curries and thorens, which are chopped vegetable stir-fries. Rice-flour pancakes are rolled up with a grated coconut-sugar filling. Creamed coconut is used as a base for rich curries and soups. To use copra, shave off curls from the hard, waxy coconut meat in the shell. This is used for its high oil content as a cooking medium or to enrich curries. Coconuts feature in Hindu religious ceremonies. They are often used to represent deities, with three black spots symbolizing the eyes and sacred tikka dot on the forehead. Whole coconuts and creamed coconut are in the refrigerator case. Desiccated flakes, chips, shreds, or powder are in the aisle with nuts in various-sized plastic bags. Look for Swad creamed, shreds, powdered, and copra halves. Patel Brothers have 1- and 2-pound bags of shreds and powder. The KTC brand has pure, creamed coconut in 7-ounce green boxes. Flakes, chips, and powder are also found in unlabeled plastic bags that are sold by weight.

DATES

Khajur or khajoor. Dates grow on palms in the desert regions of the Punjab and Rajasthan. They grow in hanging bunches of over 200

dates

dates, with each bunch weighing close to 40 pounds. Dates also are imported from the Middle East. You will find semi-moist, dark brown, oval dates and rock-hard, dried, whole, or diced dates called chhuara or kharek. The most common soft dates are the Deglet Noor, or "date of light," Medjool, Zahidi, Halway and Bardhi, with or without a stone. Large stores may sell them loose, and they may be sold by the pound at the front counter, especially during the month of Ramadan, as a date often breaks the fast at sundown. Dates are dark to golden brown with a sugary, rich flavor and a sticky texture. They are eaten as a snack, chopped and added to bread fillings and chutneys, or stuffed with almond paste. Hard, shriveled, dry dates have a white film. They are grated into date sugar or soaked until soft and added to meat stews, curries, and biryanis. They are also ground with tamarind and spices as chutney. Soft ones should be plump and even-colored. Look for the Swad brand's soft, dry, whole or pitted dates. Look also for the Nirav brand's dry dates in bags and the Sunglow brand's pitted, soft dates in 10-ounce tubs.

PEANUTS

Moongphali or ground nut. In India, peanuts are grown in Gujarat and Maharashtra. They are an important part of religious feasts and the worship of Ganesh. You will find them sold in the shell, shelled, spiced, salted, battered, or fried. Peanuts are used powdered, crushed, or whole in vegetable and dal dishes, curries, salads, chutneys, snack mixes, candies, and sweets. Khamang kakdi is a salad made from finely chopped cucumbers, roasted peanuts, grated coconut, salt, sugar, and spices. An unusual fruit curry is made by simmering chopped pineapple, stirring in ground coconut, peanuts, and chilies, then pouring it over ghee seasoned with cumin seeds. Ground peanuts are added to bread and pastry stuffings. Whole peanuts are candy coated or roasted with salt and spices as snacks. They are best used within three months as older peanuts can turn rancid. Look for the Nirav brand's raw peanuts in 1- and 2-pound bags and for the Swad brand in 14-ounce and 2-pound bags.

PINE NUTS

Chilgoza. These are teardrop-shaped, cream-colored seeds of pine cones from the Neosia pine that grows in Kashmir. The pine cones ripen in October, are picked just before they open, and are heated to expand the scales so that the nutshells can be easily shaken out. They have a delicate, sweet flavor with a slightly resinous aftertaste and a creamy texture. In Kashmir they are a staple, that

pine nuts

is used whole, crushed, or ground. They flavor rice, meat, and vegetable dishes, while slivers garnish sweets. Pine nuts are added to snack mixes, made into candy brittle, and during holidays are exchanged as gifts. They are added to a side dish made of whole cashews, almonds, and dried apricots fried in ghee with honey, lemon juice, and grated ginger. They are sold in slightly charred shells (crack them open to extract the smoke-tinged nuts) or shelled. Buy pale, creamy nuts; yellowish ones are old and may be rancid. Refrigerate them in an airtight container for up to six months. Sold in small, unlabeled bags, they are often found in the refrigerator case.

PISTACHIO NUTS

Pista. These bright green nuts are native to Afghanistan, Iran, and Turkey. They are also grown in California. The small, oval nuts have a sweet, rich taste and a smooth texture. They are covered in brittle, dark, purplish brown skins. They are encased in hard, pale, cream-colored shells that split open lengthwise when the nuts are ripe. They are sold in the shell, shelled, dried, roasted, salted, or chopped. Pistachios are essential to Indian cooking and are used in savory and sweet dishes. Powdered pistachios are made into milk fudges and are used to flavor kulfi (Indian ice cream). Chopped pistachios garnish sweets and are added to dumpling and pastry stuffings. Sliced nuts are added to biryanis and sprinkled over meat curries and rice puddings. The greener and larger the kernel, the better the quality. They can be refrigerated for up to 8 months. Look for the Nirav brand's whole, shelled nuts in 1- and 2-pound bags and for the Swad brand's whole, shelled, and chopped nuts in 14-ounce and 2-pound bags. Look also for Patel Brothers' whole or shelled nuts in 1- and 2-pound bags.

pistachio nuts

PUFFED LOTUS SEEDS

Makhanna. These speckled, off-white puffs resemble smooth, hull-less popcorn and are often eaten in the same fashion. They are made from lotus seeds that are dropped into woks filled with hot sand. They swell and burst into 1-inch, round puffs. They are light, airy, and chewy with a bland, toasty flavor. They are eaten like a breakfast cereal with milk and honey, or they are fried in butter as a snack. They are also boiled in sweetened, thick milk until they dissolve to make a thick, earthy milk pudding. They are sold in plain plastic bags with the store's name on a sticker.

puffed lotus seeds

RAISINS

raisin concentrate

Kish mish or manuka. These sweet, plump, dark or golden raisins are made from the grapes grown in the orchards of Maharashtra and Karnataka. Raisins go into rich meat or vegetable curries, biryanis, pulaos, yogurt salads, sweet pickles, chutneys, and puddings. They are added to sweet or savory stuffings and snack mixes. They add sweetness to spinach dishes and leafy green salads. You may also find Drakshasava, an Ayurvedic tonic made from raisin concentrate. It is taken for heat exhaustion and weakness. Look for the Baidyanath brand in small glass bottles. For raisins, look for the Nirav, Swad, and Ziyad brands in 1- and 2-pound bags.

WALNUTS

Akhrot. Walnuts grow in Kashmir and are dried in the sun on colorful cloth sheets. Vendors in gondolas on the lakes sell walnuts. You will find the shelled nuts in whole or broken pieces in plastic bags in the grocery store. Walnuts are rich and have a slightly bittersweet aftertaste. Walnuts are ground and used in rich meat and vegetable curries or desserts. They also garnish pulaos and biryanis. The nuts are also used as a meat substitute by vegetarians or made into kofta balls cooked in a spicy sauce. Walnuts have a high fat content and should be stored in the refrigerator. Look for Patel Brothers in 1- and 2-pound bags.

Cordial Syrups

These are bottles of concentrated, sweet syrups diluted with water or ice to make flavored drinks. Fruit squash is made from strained fruit pulp that is heated with sugar syrup and bottled. Some dark purple, currant-based concentrates are fortified with vitamins, minerals, and glucose to combat fluids lost through sweating. They have names like Vimto, Lucozade, and Ribena. Brands that make most of the following syrups are Ahmed, Hamdrad, and Kalverts in 26-ounce bottles.

ROOH ALFA

Gulab sharbart. This rose-flavored syrup is often labeled "the summer drink of the East." This dark pink, sweet syrup is extremely popular when thinned with water and served at Muslim weddings or feasts, as alcohol is taboo. It is refreshing any time over crushed ice.

SANDAL SYRUP

This pale-golden syrup is flavored and scented with distilled sandalwood essence. Sandalwood is cooling to the body, so this is a good hot-weather drink over ice. It has a sweet, exotic taste.

KHUS SYRUP

This pale green syrup is flavored and scented with khus essence, which is an extract from the roots of an aromatic tropical grass. It has a sweet, woodsy flavor.

FRUIT SYRUPS

These include mango squash, orange, pineapple, pomegranate, soapberry (lychee), lime cordial, mixed fruit, raspberry, quince, and passion fruit. These are also good poured over ice cream.

Essences

Known as ruh or ittars, some of these concentrated flavorings have been used since ancient times. The moghul emperors had royal greenhouses where rare blossoms were grown to make perfumes, essential oils, and essences. Essences are still used in cooking and religious ceremonies. They are made by a water-distillation process that doesn't use alcohol. Most are based on natural aromatics. Some are mixed with water to make less concentrated forms. They are sold in small bottles and will keep for two to three years if stored in a dark place with the cap tightly screwed on. Only a few drops, added near the end of cooking or after cooking is completed are used. They mainly scent and flavor sweets and drinks.

ROSE ESSENCE, ROSE WATER

Ruh gulab or gulab jal. These are diluted forms of pure rose oil made from the petals of damask roses. They have a sweet, floral scent and are used in milky desserts, sweets, and drinks. They are added to rose-petal jam. Rose water and rose petals are sprinkled over wedding guests. Diluted rose water is sprinkled about homes and temples as a room freshener. Look for the Ahmed, Areoplane, Key, and Hesh brands'

rose water

rose water in 7-ounce bottles and for the Cortas brand in 10-ounce bottles. Look also for the Swad brand's rose essence in 1-ounce bottles.

KEWRA ESSENCE, KEWRA WATER

Ruh kewra or ruh kevda. This essential flavoring is extracted from the fragrant flowers and petal-like leaves of the tropical screwpine shrub. The flower petals, called tayai, are floated in silver dishes at special occasions. Both the essence and the more delicate water have a flowery, vanilla flavor. They are used in sweet dishes, or a few drops may garnish a rice pulao. Syrups are scented with kewra and used in

kewra water

cold drinks. Look for the Ahmed, Areoplane, Key, and Laxmi brands in 7-ounce bottles and for the Swad brand in 1-ounce bottles.

ELACHI ESSENCE

This aromatic essence is extracted from cardamom seeds. It is used to impart the flavor of cardamom in drinks, desserts, and rice dishes without leaving the black specks from ground seeds. Look for the Swad and Viola brands in small bottles.

ORANGE BLOSSOM WATER

This sweet, floral fragrance is extracted from orange blossoms and diluted with water. It is used in drinks, slushes, and sweets. Look for the Cortas and Ziyad brands in 10-ounce bottles.

FRUIT ESSENCES

These natural or artificial, concentrated extracts are used in drinks, candies, sweets, and ice cream. Flavors include banana (imitation and very strong), orange, lime, chickoo, mango, and pineapple. Look for Swad, SMC, and Viola in small bottles.

FOOD FLAVORS

These artificial extracts are used to scent rice (biryani) or sweets (ice cream and vanilla). Look for Swad, SMC, and Viola in small bottles.

Food Colors

Small mounds of magenta, scarlet, saffron, and cobalt blue powders, called abeer, fill the markets in India. Made from rice powder, they are used in cosmetics, as forehead dots, and for kolam floor decorations. Equally brilliant food powders are found in Indian grocery stores in small glass jars. They are used to color tandoori pastes, curries,

food coloring powder

and sweets. Pistachio fudge is tinted with green powder, and the red glow of tandoor-seared meats is enhanced with vermilion powder. They are made from finely ground salt mixed with edible dyes. A little goes a long way—use just a pinch. Orange, green, red, and yellow food colors are made by the Swad and Preema brands in 1-ounce bottles—except for the tandoori orange, which is in 16-ounce jars. Minar has jars of orange, and the 999 brand offers saffron yellow.

Odds & Ends

AGAR-AGAR

China grass. This processed-seaweed jelling agent is used as a quick-setting base for sweets and desserts. Its advantage is that it sets without refrigeration in the tropical heat. It is sold in dried sheets, flakes, instant powder, and in crinkly, white, red, or green strands in long, cellophane packages. To use it as a gelatin, soak the strands until they dissolve and strain out any lumps. It has almost no smell or flavor. It is halal, meaning that it contains no pork products (which gelatin does), so it is acceptable to Muslims. Treats such as almond-milk jelly flavored with cardamom are popular, as are pink, rose-scented cream-jelly diamonds. They are made from agar dissolved in sweet milk with flavorings, then set and cut into fancy shapes. Agar-agar will keep indefinitely. Look for the Swad brand in 2-ounce packets of strips, for Golden Banyan white strands, and for the Kings brand's instant, sweet powder in mango, cardamom, and vanilla in small boxes.

agar-agar

SUBJA SEEDS

Takmaria. These tiny teardrop-shaped, black seeds are collected from the flowers of a type of wild Indian basil. When soaked the seeds swell and turn pale grayish then become encased in a translucent jelly. They add texture, having no aroma or taste. The outer jelly is soft, and the seed center is crunchy. Subja seeds are added to the popular rose-milk drink, falooda, and to raat ki rani, or "night cooler," a soothing, sleep-inducing, after-dinner drink made from the soaked seeds mixed into milk with honey and cardamom. Look for the Mr. Manish brand in 7-ounce packets.

subja seeds

VARAK

This is thin, edible silver or gold leaf. Small balls of silver or gold dust are pounded between sheets of parchment to produce tissue-paper-thin sheets. The small, square sheets are sold by the dozen. They are layered between sheets of tissue paper and newspaper. They are sold in packets behind the front counter of the grocery store. They are about 50 cents a sheet. It is used purely as an opulent garnish to embellish rich sweets and special-occasion saffron rice. In India about 13 tons of pure silver is made into varak each year! Varak is extremely fragile and has to be carefully used. Lift off a sheet along with its tissue, turn it over on top of the finished dish, and press it lightly down. It is almost impossible to stick it on uniformly. There will be rumples and tears. The Kailash brand is commonly found.

MASTIC

mastic

Sakiz or gum Arabic crystal. This is the resin from a small acacia tree in the cashew family. It is used in chewing gum and to flavor sweetbreads, ice cream, and puddings. Mastic has a slightly sweet, resinous taste and is found in various-sized crystal chunks in small plastic packets or boxes. Crush it with a teaspoon of granulated sugar just before using.

VINEGAR

Sirka. Vinegar is mainly used in the regional cuisines influenced by the Portuguese: Goa, Kerala, Mangalore, Anglo-Indian, and Parsi. The vinegar used on the western coast is made from fermented, distilled coconut-palm sap that is clearish and has a sour, acidic taste. Parsis use molasses vinegar made from the by-product of processed sugar cane. It is dark brown with a heavier flavor. Vinegar adds tang to soups, sauces, and curries. It is mixed with ground spices into a paste as a marinade, or it is fried in oil before adding meat or fish. Spicy Goan vindaloos are based on vinegar-spice pastes. Parsi Dhansak (lamb with lentils) is finished by stirring in vinegar and seasoned oil. It is also used in pick-les and chutneys. Vinegar is considered cleansing to the system, and it is also used as a hair rinse. It is sold in glass bottles. Look for the MD brand's coconut vinegar in 25-ounce bottles. Balsamic vinegar can substitute for the molasses type, which is harder to find.

CRISPY FRIED ONIONS

These crunchy bits of dark golden, deep-fried onion are used as a garnish. They are sprinkled over soups, curries, vegetables, rice, salads, and eggs. They are rolled up in soft chapatis. They are also added to savory snack fillings and crunchy snack mixes. They are sold in tubs, cans, and bags. Look for the A-1A, Ahmed, Chirag, Moon, or Sultan brands.

MALDIVE FISH

Umbalakada. This dried, salted, flaked tuna or bonito from the Maldive Islands, is used in vegetable curries. The fish is cured by a lengthy process of boiling, smoking, and sun-drying until it resembles hard slabs of mahogany. This preserves the fish indefinitely without refrigeration. The reddish lavender flakes or powder are sold in plastic bags, cans, or jars. It has a subtle, smoky flavor. Small amounts are used in soups, curries, and spicy sauces as a thickening and flavoring agent. Most brands are from Sri Lanka. Look for the Larich and MD Lanka Canneries brands in 7-ounce cans or jars.

maldive fish

BOMBAY DUCK

Loitta, bombil, or bummalo. This is a type of small, translucent flying fish that is caught off the west coast of India. It is sun-dried whole. To use it, wash and cut the stiff, skinny, twisted specimens into pieces (remove the head with its large ring of teeth), soak it in cold water for 1 hour, wash it again with lemon juice and salt, then fry it in oil. They brown very quickly. After draining, mix it into rice and curry, or crumble and cook it to make a chili sauce with onions, dried red chilies, garlic, salt, and lime juice. It can also be cooked in a curry sauce with chopped onions and vegetables until it is tender, which takes about 30 minutes. It is sold in plastic bags or glass jars, by weight. It is also sold fresh or frozen.

bombay duck

Convenience Mixes

Snacks, known as farasan in India, can be a crispy fritter or a light meal—tasty but oftentimes consuming to make. This is where instant powdered mixes come in handy, sold in 7-ounce boxes and pouches to make a variety of fried and steamed snacks and spicy sauces for rice. A few require special equipment—steaming racks, molds, or a tava pan. These are sold in the cookware section and are worth getting if you plan to do a lot of Indian cooking. Directions and recipes are on back panels or on papers inside the boxes.

BISIBLEBATH

This South Indian mix for rice is made from ground yellow lentils, rice flakes, roasted coconut, tamarind, garam masala, salt, sugar, and spices. Mix it with water and simmer it until thick (about 15 minutes), then mix it into cooked rice. You can also add soaked, split peas and vegetables. Garnish it with chopped cashews, mustard seeds, and curry leaves fried in ghee. Serve it with pappadams. It has a hot, tart taste and is a specialty of Karnataka. Look for the MTR brand.

DAHI WADA MIX

This is a powder for making deep-fried fritters. The wada balls are made from a blend of mung-bean and urad-dal flours, baking soda, and spices. After frying, they are served in a dish of spiced yogurt (dahi). Look for the Ramdev brand in boxes.

DHOKLA

This popular snack from Gujarat is made from a fermented batter. The mix is a blend of cream of rice, ground urad dal, chickpea flour,

salt, spices, and baking soda. The batter is steamed in molds or in a pie plate, then cut into diamond shapes. Dhokla are like spongy, spicy cornbread. They are served with chutney or stir-fried in ghee and garnished with grated coconut and chopped coriander leaves. Khaman dhokla are the same thing, but they are made from just chickpea flour. There is also a variety made from a blend of green-pea and chickpea flours, which yields pale green cakes. Look for

dhokla

Tarla Dalal Instant khaman or green-pea mix in pouches. Gits and Ramdev have plain and khaman in 7-ounce boxes.

DOSA

Also spelled dosai, these thin, crisp, crepe-like pancakes are served with coconut chutney or hot, sour rasam. Masala dosa are stuffed with a spicy, mashed potato filling. They are eaten for breakfast or as a light snack.

Dosa mixes save soaking and grinding time. They are a blend of rice flour, ground urad dal, salt, and spices. To use them, mix them with water into a thin batter and cook them on a tava or iron pan. Rava dosa are the same, but they are made from a blend of fine semolina and rice flour. The same mix can also be used to make thicker pancakes called uttappam, which are sprinkled with chopped onions and chilies as they cook. Look for the Gits and Ramdev brands in 7-ounce boxes and for MTR in pouches.

dosa

GOTA

This is a snack ball mix made from a blend of chickpea flour, sugar, chili powder, and spices. The doughballs are deep-fried and served hot with chutney. Look for the Ramdev brand in boxes.

IDLI

These are South Indian, steamed rice cakes that are eaten for breakfast or as a snack with rasam and coconut chutney. The mix is a blend of rice flour and ground urad dal. To use it, mix it with water into a thick batter, fill the depressions of a tiered, aluminum idli or small, oiled, metal bowl, and steam it in an inch of water in a large covered pot. Rava idli are the same, but they are made with fine semolina and ground urad dal. Vermicelli idli is a variation with bits of broken noodles in the spicy chickpea-rice flour. The MTR brand has all three types in pouches. The Gits and Ramdev brands have idli and rava idli in boxes.

idli

KHARABHATH

Also called upma, this mix is for making a South Indian, sweet, spicy cream-of-wheat breakfast or a snack dish of fluffy porridge. It is a blend of semolina, ground lentils, powdered cashews, spices, and tamarind. Mix it with boiling water and melted butter, stir it until thick, and serve it garnished with chopped coriander leaves. You can also add peas or chopped vegetables for a heartier dish. Look for the MTR brand.

kharabhath

South Indian street snacks are among the spiciest and hottest in India. Vendors offer leaf-wrapped peanut-chili salads, flying-saucer-shaped idli with seasoned oil poured over them, and appams, which are rice-coconut batter pancakes cooked in small, deep woks so that the center is thick and chewy and the edges are crisp. Men sweat over huge vats of bubbling oil, lifting out their batter-dipped wares. Beachside stalls sell kabob jhinga, which are spicy skewers of shrimp.

MURUKU POWDER

This orange powdered mix for making deep-fried crispy rings is made from a blend of rice flour, ground urad dal, and spices. The soft dough is pressed through a muruku mold into hot oil and fried until crisp and golden. You can pipe the dough through a pastry bag. Look for the MTR brand.

PAKORA MIX

A spicy chickpea flour is mixed with water to make a batter for tempura-like, deep-fried fritters. Dip sliced vegetables in the batter and drop them into hot oil. Serve them with chutney or chili sauce. Look for the Gits brand in boxes.

PAV BHAJI MASALA

A specialty of Gujarat, this is a mix of spices and flour that makes a thick curry sauce. It is mixed with mashed vegetables and eaten with bread or chapatis. Look for MTR in pouches and for the Ramdev brand in boxes.

POTATO SUGU MASALA

This is a South Indian spice mix for boiled potatoes. To use it, heat some oil in a pan, add mustard seeds, a little Bengal gram, chopped green chilies, ginger, and onions. Add a cup of this masala with a squirt of lime juice and some water. Bring it to a boil. Add smashed, boiled potatoes and simmer them until thickened. Garnish it with fresh coriander leaves. The mix contains chili powder, salt, sugar, ground coriander, turmeric, and asafoetida. Look for the MTR brand.

PULIYOGARE POWDER

This is a South Indian mix for preparing tamarind rice. It is a blend of powdered coriander, cumin, fenugreek, mustard seeds, chili, tamarind, black pepper, cinnamon, turmeric, and curry leaves. To use it, fry the mixture in oil, add water, and stir it. Add cooked rice and stir it until the rice absorbs the sauce. Garnish it with fried, chopped peanuts and grated coconut. It has a tart, spicy taste. Look for the MTR brand in pouches.

After a visit to the famous Buddhist caves of Ajanta, heavy rain began and soon washed out the bridges. With travel impossible, I was taken in by a family who ran a small hotel which was filled with other stranded travelers. We shared platters of vegetable pakoras, fried in great, golden heaps by the owner's wife and washed down with glasses of "Knock-Out" beer. The next morning I woke up in the cow shed—the driest place in the damp, leaking hotel.

VADAI

Also called medu vada, this mix for deep-fried fritters is made from a blend of ground urad dal, wheat flour, spices, and a rising agent. Onion vadai are flavored with onion powder. Mix it with water into a thick batter. Roll it into balls (grease your fingers first), flatten the balls, poke a hole in the center of each with your finger, and slide them into hot oil. The batter produces crisp, reddish brown patties with a rough surface. Serve them with hot and sour sambhar, chutney, and yogurt. Look for the Gits brand in boxes and the MTR brand in pouches. Look also for the Vasu brand in 8-ounce pouches.

vadai

VANGHIBHATH POWDER

This South Indian mix for cooking rice is made from a blend of ground lentils, chilies, coriander, cumin, fenugreek seeds, cinnamon, and cloves. Yellow-lentil (toovar) dal is partially cooked, soaked raw rice is stirred in with tamarind-lime juice, coconut oil, chopped eggplant and a few teaspoons of the spice powder. Then it is cooked until the rice is tender. Garnish it with ghee seasoned with mustard seeds and chopped cashews. Look for the MTR brand.

Frozen Foods

The freezers of most Indian grocery stores hold boxes of heat-and-serve entrees, dals, soups, vegetables, and snacks. Pakistani grocery stores have plastic- and paper-wrapped halal meats. Bangladeshi markets will have large freezers crammed with sweet-water (freshwater) fish. We will take a peek at popular frozen meals, snacks, and the selection of fish that you will find.

Frozen Entrees & Snacks

All of the following meals are offered by the Deep brand's "Gourmet Indian Cuisine" in 7-, 10-, and 11-ounce boxes. Choose what sounds good. Heat and serve them with rice or bread for meals in a jiffy. Many of these are the same as those described in more detail in the chapter on canned goods.

Aloo Began is a spicy potato-eggplant stew.

Aloo Mater is a spicy potato-pea stew.

Chole are whole chickpeas seasoned with green peppers and onions in a spicy gravy. (See the recipe on page 245.)

dal makhani

Dal Gujarati style is a yellow-lentil (toovar) soup with sautéed spices.

Dal Makhani are black chickpeas in a cream gravy with tomatoes, onions, and spices.

Kashmiri Dum Aloo are boiled, stuffed, and deep-fried potatoes. The filling is a mixture of spiced, crumbled paneer cheese, peas, and ground cashews.

Khaman Chickpea Squares are dhokla. They are lightly spiced, steamed, chickpea-flour cakes.

Kofta Curry are vegetable dumplings in a spicy sauce.

Navrutha Korma is a mixed vegetable dish with a mildly spiced, creamy sauce.

Palak Paneer are curd-cheese cubes in spicy, creamed spinach.

Paneer Masala are curd-cheese cubes mixed with green peppers and onions in a spicy sauce.

Pav-Bhaji is a thick, spicy, mixed mashed vegetable stew that is eaten with rolls or chapati.

Ragdo is a mixture of whole yellow peas, cubes of potato, and tomatoes that are sautéed with spices in a thick sauce.

ragdo

Sambhar is a stew in a 12-ounce box that is hot, sour, and spicy. It is made of yellow lentils, vegetables, and tamarind.

Undhiv is a mixed-vegetable stew that comes in a creamy, spicy grated-coconut sauce.

The Curry Classics brand offers chicken biryani, chicken curry, tandoori chicken, lamb curry, and chicken Moghali, which is a creamy, rich, North Indian-style dish. There is also chicken tikka makhanwala, which is boneless chicken pieces seasoned with yogurt, broiled, and simmered in a spicy cream sauce. All are in 10-ounce boxes. The Jaipur brand has vegan chili, kidney bean stew in a spicy tomato sauce, and lima beans and veggies in a sweet-and-sour sauce. They come with basmati rice in 11-ounce boxes.

chicken biryani

Vegetables

Most Indian grocery stores have jumbo 5- to 10-pound unlabeled plastic bags of frozen peas and mixed vegetables, which are mainly purchased by restaurants. There is also a small selection of Indian vegetables. Use these as an alternative to canned vegetables or if you can't find fresh ones. The Swad brand has 1-pound packages of drumsticks, kantola (spiny bitter gourd), parval (cucumber gourd), Punjabi tinda (melon squash), and suran (yam).

Snacks

Try the small, frozen, cocktail samosas or vegetarian spring rolls at your next party or as appetizers to a meal. Most are prefried. Some have to be dropped into hot oil to cook.

SAMOSAS

samosas

These are spicy, potato-pea stuffed, deep-fried pastry turnovers. Just heat and serve them with a tangy chutney. Look for the Deep brand with 9 to a box or 40 tiny cocktail samosas to a package. The Ravi Snacks brand has cocktail samosas stuffed with potatoes and peas, or spicy chickpeas with 50 to a box. The Swad brand offers packages of 10 potato-cheese or vegetable samosas or 32 cocktail samosas.

VEGETARIAN SPRING ROLLS

These Indian-style egg rolls are stuffed with a spicy, shredded vegetable mixture. Look for the Deep brand with 35 small rolls to a box and for the Ravi Snacks brand with 30 to a package.

DAHI VADA

These are ready-to-deep-fry dal-batter fritters. After frying the frozen balls, serve them in spiced yogurt. Look for the Ravi Snacks brand with 12 fritters to a box.

MASALA DOSA

These are thin rice-lentil crepes that have a spicy potato filling. They come with chutney for serving. Look for the Deep brand with 4 to a box.

VADA

These deep-fried, spicy patties are made from black-eyed peas and ground lentils. Heat and serve them with chutney or chili sauce. Look for the Deep brand with 10 pieces to a box.

VEGETABLE CUTLETS

These spicy mixed-veggie patties are made from mashed potatoes, peas, cubed carrots, onions, and green peppers. They are coated in breadcrumbs and deep-fried. Bake, pan-fry, or microwave them. Look for the Deep brand with 4 to a box.

Frozen Fish

Fish is a staple of West Bengal and Bangladesh, where it is abundant in numerous waterways and estuaries or in tanks. The water that the fish lives in affects its taste. Most are from freshwater rivers. These have mild, delicious white flesh, if unfamiliar names. Besides fish, you may find Bengal bagda chingri (striped tiger prawns) and galda chingri (king prawns, which are similar to crayfish). Small shrimp are called kuncho chingri.

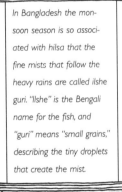

In Bangladesh the monsoon season is so associated with hilsa that the fine mists that follow the heavy rains are called ilshe guri. "Ilshe" is the Bengali name for the fish, and "guri" means "small grains," describing the tiny droplets that create the mist.

Two of the biggest exporters of frozen, cleaned fish are the Chandpur Sea Corporation LTD and Legal and Marque, both from Bangladesh. The fish is specially packed for export and distributed nationwide. Large, whole fish are plastic wrapped, while steaks and smaller fish are frozen in blocks. All have a label stating type, weight, date of packing, and expiration-of-freshness date. In Bengal, recipes are selected by which part of the fish is to be used: the daga, or back portion, or the peti, the stomach portion. Backs are usually more bony. The stomach is softer and more succulent. All of the following are processed by these reputable brands. They are listed from the tastiest and most popular to the lesser used. After selecting a fish, you can have them trimmed of heads, fins, and tails while you wait.

HILSA

Also called Elish, this is considered the tastiest of all large freshwater fish. It ranges from 10 to 15 pounds. Hilsa is a type of shad in the herring family. It has tiny bones and sweet-tasting

hilsa

flesh. The silvery fish spends the winter months in the deep waters of the open sea. Then in early March it leaves the Bay of Bengal. In large shoals it swims its way up the Ganges and other rivers of the Ganges Delta to spawn—and to be caught by fishermen. Bengalis are passionate about this fish that is also a symbol of fertility. On their wedding day, grooms send brides a hilsa fish to touch—and then release it into the family fish pond to breed and multiply.

A bonus in whole, frozen hilsa is the masses of tiny, brown eggs in two kidney-shaped membrane sacs of the female fish. They are sliced into thin pieces and lightly fried or mashed with spices as a delicacy. The oil released from hilsa when it cooks is also relished. It is poured over rice or used for cooking greens.

Hilsa is good broiled, steamed, baked, curried, fried, or added to fish soups. The traditional cooking method is to rub cut pieces of the fish with a thick paste of ground mustard seeds, chilies, turmeric, salt, and mustard oil. The fish is then wrapped in banana leaves and steamed with a pot of rice. The fish comes out tender, moist, and infused with the spices.

Cox's Bazaar is wedged between the Bay of Bengal and the Arakan mountains on a spur of Bangladesh that runs into Myanmar. Named after Captain Cox, a British man who settled the area in 1798, it has one of the longest stretches of natural beach in the world. Warm, safe waters entice you to swim. You can laze in a hammock under coconut palms, hunt for rare conch shells, surf the waves, or eat well. Fresh seafood is featured in small cafes right on the seafront.

TAPSHE

This is also called tapaswi and Bengal mango fish, as it is caught during mango season when they are plump with roe. Considered one of the best fish by Bengalis, it is a small 7- to 8-inch-long type of river catfish. The word "tapshe" means "one who meditates." The fish gets this name due to its long, trailing whiskers that resemble a holy man's beard. It has a delicious, mild catfish taste. To cook it, marinate the whole fish in an onion-ginger paste, dip it in beaten egg, and breadcrumbs, then deep-fry it.

RUPCHANDA

rupchanda

Chamna or Silver Pomfret. This is a popular, firm-fleshed, flat, silvery, white fish with a snubbed head, long fins, and a graceful, flowing, split tail. It has a central bone that is easily removed. The flesh is delicate, sweet, and firm. It is good rubbed with spices and fried, grilled, broiled, or cooked in spicy coconut milk. It is also good steamed with garlic, ginger, and fresh coriander leaves, then served with coconut chutney and a squeeze of lime.

SURMAI

Kingfish or King mackerel. This large ocean fish averages 10 pounds. It has a streamlined, spindle-shaped body, crescent fins, and bluish silvery skin with no scales. Its good tasting, slightly oily dark meat surrounds one central bone. Cut it into steaks and grill or pan-fry it in spices. It can also be cooked in coconut milk.

surmai

RUHU

Labeo Rohita or Buffalo fish. This large, black, silvery-scaled fish in the carp family has one central bone. It is sold whole or cut into steaks. Fry it in a small amount of oil. Sprinkle it with turmeric, salt, spices, and fried onions. Add some water and cook it until tender. You can also cook it with spices, potatoes, and chopped vegetables.

ruhu

My rickshaw, painted with livid Bengali-cinema scenes, swerves and pirouettes in and out of traffic like an experienced surfer. Moments later I'm delivered to the morning market of Cox's Bazaar, a seaside town in southern Bangladesh. Wooden fishing boats are moored in a shallow cove of the river near the town center. Sellers and buyers squat over piles of fish and shellfish. Fisherman walk back and forth with loaded baskets on poles that are slung across bronzed shoulders. Nearby, salted fish dry on mesh screens, others dangle like monstrous laundry clipped to wire lines.

KOI

This is climbing perch, not the ornamental Japanese carp. This mild, white-fleshed, medium-sized fish becomes fat and oily in the winter. It has a rich taste, but it must be eaten carefully due to its potentially lethal curved bones. It is usually sold whole. To cook it, cut off its head and tail, chop it into pieces, and dust it with chili powder, turmeric, and salt. Cook it in the juice of a grated onion with ginger and some chopped green chilies. Serve it with plain rice to soak up the sauce. Kamala koi is a Bengali-Muslim dish of lightly fried koi that is cooked in the juice and pulp of oranges with spices.

BOAL

Wallago attu. This very big, grayish 4- to 5-foot-long, 30-pound river fish has one central bone and tasty, mild white flesh. It is sold whole and cut into steaks. Pan-fry, grill, or cook it in curry.

AIRE

Similar to ruhu and boal, this 30-pound river fish with mild, sweet flesh is sold in thick slices. Rub it with spices and pan-fry it with onions, chopped chilies, and garlic, or simmer it in coconut milk.

MAGUR

Similar to catfish, this river fish with a dark, slender body is about a foot long. It has sweet flesh that is very high in iron. Cut it into steaks and pan-fry it with spices. Or fillet it, dip it in batter, and deep-fry it. Or add it to curries. Pooti maach are baby catfish with a delicate flavor, like smelt. They are fried whole and served in a spicy sauce with rice.

PABDHA

Ompok pabda. These 6- to 7-inch river and canal fish are found throughout India, Pakistan, Myanmar, and Bangladesh. They have a mild, sweet flesh with one middle bone. They are very tasty when cut into steaks, rubbed with spices, and cooked in a curry sauce or pan-fried. Silong is a smaller type of pabdha. Bacha is a white variety, but it is not as tasty and has a lot of tiny bones.

PANGASH

This 60- to 70-pound fish is sold whole or cut into steaks. It is fatty and oily with a good taste that suitable for spicy curries. To cut the oiliness, sprinkle it with lemon or cook it with a tart seasoning like kokum or tamarind.

CHITAL

Chitol, humpback, featherback or banded knifefish. These large, dark gray, elongated river fish have a feathery lower fin that extends from the head to the tail, small scales, a curved back, a pointy head and many tiny bones. It has a very soft, oily stomach and front portion and a bony back portion. It is prized

chital

by Bangladeshis for making chitol koptas, which are fishballs served in a spicy sauce. In another preparation the skin is pulled off, the bones picked out, and the flesh ground up and cooked with spices into a sort of sticky paste. This is wrapped in the fish skin, deep-fried, and sliced into delicious morsels. Folichanda is a smaller, gray featherback.

CHOIL

Shol or maral. This foot-long, dark, slender fish has one middle bone and small side bones. It is sold in 2-pound blocks of steaks. Rub it with spices and fry or cook it in a curry sauce.

It is mid-day and Cochin market is at its peak. Dark, wiry men load brightly painted trucks decorated with Jesus, Krishna, and wild floral motifs with goods from rice barges afloat in the canals. A fierce sun blazes down on their bare shoulders and muscular arms hefting baskets of bananas, mangoes, lemons, papayas, and pineapples. The Muezzin's call wafts on a current of salty air infused with the fragrance of ripe fruit. Women leave the market with bunches of bananas or pineapple crowns on their heads.

In Bengal, choil is always bought live and kept in a bucket of water until it is ready to cook. This fish is reputed to be very hard to kill, thus a dead one is assumed to be very diseased. There is even a story of a choil that lived after being roasted! According to the legend, a king who had incurred the wrath of a god lost his fortune and ended up a forest hermit. Just as he was about to eat the choil he had caught and roasted over a fire, the fish slipped away and swam off.

POA

This small, 6-inch-long freshwater fish has soft, edible bones. Rub it with salt, pepper, and spices. Fry, grill, or cook it in a spicy sauce.

KAZALE

Ailia Coila. This is a very small, smelt-like, silvery river fish. It is delicious deep-fried or added to curries.

KESKI

Cornica Soborna, chiring white, or kachki. These are frozen blocks of tiny freshwater fish that look like whitebait. They are a popular everyday fish in Bangladesh, as they are rich in vitamins and good for the eyes. To use them, make a sauce by frying onions, garlic, turmeric and spices, add a little water or coconut milk, add the fish, and cook it until tender, which takes about 10 minutes.

MOLA

This small type of anchovy is sold in frozen blocks. To cook it, chop an onion, mix it with the fish, fry it in oil with green chili and turmeric, add a little water, cover the pan, and cook it for about 30 minutes.

OTHERS

Other frozen seafoods that you may find include bata, a 4-inch fish, bailla, an 8-inch fish with lots of bones, kajoli, a 2- to 3-inch-long fish with one central bone, sharpuntai (olive barb), and several types of eel called baim.

Supari Mixes & Paan Fillings

Betel-leaf paan is the traditional grand finale to Indian meals. It is considered a symbol of hospitality that is always offered to guests. What goes into these leaf envelopes of chew can range from the simple to the extravagant. For those not inclined to chew betel, there are breath fresheners, known as supari that are offered after a meal. They can be plain, silver-leaf, or candy-coated fennel seeds, or they can be mixes of roasted spice seeds, bits of betel nut, toasted melon seeds, pine nuts, colored sugarballs, spices, and salt. You will recognize this section of the grocery store by the strong, perfumed aroma.

Paan Fillings

MEETHA PAN MASALA

Spiced chuna-dani, or slaked lime (calcium oxide). This white paste is spread over paan leaves before the other fillings are added. It is very corrosive to teeth and gums. It is sold in small plastic or glass containers.

KATTHA

This astringent extract of the heartwood of Acacia trees is sold in small, red slabs. The slabs are ground into a powder, mixed into a thin paste, and smeared over slaked, lime-spread paan leaves before the other fillings are added. It stains teeth, gums, and lips orange. It is sold in small plastic bags.

ANGUR VATI

These dried raisins are flavored with cumin, black pepper, ginger, sugar, ground cassia, and lime juice. They are intensely tart and slightly sweet. They are also chewed as a breath freshener. Look for the Chandan brand in small jars.

ORANGE VATI

These are small bits of dried orange flavored with lemon juice, cumin, black pepper, and rock salt. They are sour and salty. They are also chewed as a breath freshener. Look for the Chandan brand.

CATECHU

These slightly sticky, sour, dark brown bits of tamarind seeds are flavored with cardamom and lime juice. They are also taken as a breath freshener. Look for the Tulsi brand's pan masala in small tins.

CHHUHARA SPECIAL

chhuhara special

These are small jars of rounded bits of tart, spicy dates with a crumbly, dry texture. They are flavored with sour pomegranate-seed powder, sugar, and spices. They are also chewed as a breath freshener. Look for the Chandan and Ritu Mukhwas brands in small jars.

SAFFRON PAN CHATNI

This honey-colored, highly aromatic saffron jelly is made from thick, scented sugar syrup suspended in flecks of edible gold leaf. This is used mainly for special-occasion paan. Look for the Meenakshi Store brand in 1-ounce jars with an orange-black wrapper and orange lid.

saffron pan chatni

CHAALIYA

These flavored chips of betel nut are used in paan or chewed as a breath freshener. They are sold in small packets or tins. Look for the Tulsi brand's pan masala in silver-striped, small tins with blue lids.

ROSE PETAL JELLY

This dark red, sweet, perfumed jam is made with rose petals. Look for the Ahmed brand in 14-ounce jars.

Supari Mixes

These are small packets and jars of pastel-colored, candy-coated fennel seeds, roasted spice seeds, or blends of aromatic spices and tinted sugar balls. Called jintan, they are chewed to freshen the breath and aid digestion after eating. Many are in unlabeled, small plastic baggies or have just the store's name on a sticker. Supari blends are usually in a little dish by the cash register of Indian grocery stores and restaurants. Take a pinch as you leave. It is an appropriate ending to a hot, spicy Indian meal and to our ramble through the Bombay bazaar.

DHANA DAL

These split, flat, roasted coriander seeds resemble ochre-colored, small, oval lentils. They are chewed on their own or added to blends. Look for the Swad brand in 7- and 14-ounce bags.

FOUR FLAVOR MUKHWAS

four flavor mukhwas

The word "mukhwas" means "after-dinner mint." These round, plastic containers have a rotating cap for dispensing the contents of four compartments, each filled with a different supari mix. There is Jamnagari mukhwas, which is a mix of dhana dal, red sugarballs, perfumed-sugar sesame seeds, and candy-coated fennel seeds. Garden court mukhwas is a mix of candy-coated fennel seeds, dhana dal, roasted melon seeds, perfumed-sugar sesame seeds, dried fenugreek leaves, and red sugarballs. Black beauty mukhwas is a dark brown mix of mint-coated fennel seeds and dried fenugreek leaves. Special mukhwas is a blend of dried rose petals, silver jintan, plain and multicolored fennel seeds, and a bit of all the other mixes. All are highly aromatic, smelling of rose, spices, and perfume. Look for the Ashoka brand in a 7-ounce clear jar with a pink lid.

GREEN OR RED MUKHWAS

These supari mixes are made of a blend of green- or red-colored sugarballs, candy-coated fennel seeds, dhana dal, roasted melon seeds, fenugreek leaves, aniseed, and scented, colored bits of betel nut. Look for the Swad and Kishan brands in 14-ounce bags and small shaker jars.

LAKHNAW FENNEL

These fennel seeds are from Lucknow in Uttar Pradesh. They are reputed to be the best in India. They are sold in small, round plastic containers. There are also madhur (sweet), silver foil-coated fennel seeds. Look for the Ashoka brand for both.

ANARDANA CHURAN

This is pomegranate powder mixed with cumin seeds, ground turmeric, and spices. Look for the Ritu Mukhwas brand in 4.8-ounce plastic jars.

SOFTY SILVER DATES

These scented, flavored bits of date are covered in silver foil. They look like small silver nuggets. They are sold in round plastic containers. Look for the Ashoka brand.

PAN MASALA

This is a mouth-freshener mix of red coconut shreds, sugar, bits of Brazil nut, fennel, poppy, sesame, and coriander seeds flavored with cardamom and saffron. Look for the Hira Moti brand in small plastic jars with a paan-leaf logo. Look also for small, silver-foil, individual

pan masala

packets of Shalimar brand's tulsi meetha pan masala. They contain sweet betel-nut shreds, dry date bits, and aniseeds. They are sold at the front counter for 10 cents.

Stocking Up

You will want palm sugar or jaggery, almonds, cashews or pistachios, dried apricots, grated coconut, raisins, rose water, crispy onions, instant pakora mix, frozen samosas, a favorite frozen entree or fish, and a packet of candy-coated fennel seeds.

Conclusion

I hope that you've become much more familiar with the contents of Indian grocery stores with the help of this guide—and by actually walking through a store. If you love the spicy bite and complex flavors of Indian foods, but have been too intimidated to attempt cooking them in your own kitchen, now there is no excuse! Head for the nearest Indian grocery store with this guide, and begin putting together your own pantry of basics.

While no two Indian grocery stores are exactly the same—that's the beauty of discovering each one and the specialties within—they all follow the logic of the Rajas' little store. Your best bet is to find an Indian grocery store near you and learn its layout by repeated visits. After frequent visits you will be as familiar with the aisles as you are with your local supermarket. You will also make friends with the owners, who will be more than glad to assist a loyal customer. And like Mr. and Mrs. Raja, they will give you advice and recipe suggestions.

While I could not possibly cover every single of the thousands of products stocked in the many Indian grocery stores that I explored for this book, I hope that most of your questions have been answered. When in doubt you can slip this book out of your pocket or purse and look up what you don't recognize. Certainly, I hope that I have inspired you to enter an Indian grocery store and shop with enthusiasm and confidence!

· Appendix 1 ·

Kitchen Equipment

In India kitchens are simple and sacred places that are kept spotlessly clean. Women clad in clean sarees cook while perched on small wood stools hovered over the chula, a charcoal stove set in the center of the floor. You can duplicate the cooking of India at your stove, using the pots and pans that you already have. There is no need to buy a lot of special cookware. However, a few basic items that you may want to try are listed below.

SPICE GRINDER

grinding stone

In India grinding stones are used to hand-grind spices. It is much easier to invest in an electric spice grinder or coffee grinder and use it just for spices. You could also purchase a stone or brass mortar and pestle for crushing seeds and spices into powder.

ELECTRIC BLENDER

A powerful blender is useful for grinding many spices, nuts, and coarsely pulsing ingredients into fresh chutneys or for pureeing cooked dals into creamy soups. It is also good for whirling yogurt with flavorings to make lassi and other creamy drinks.

KADHAI

Almost the same as a wok, this is a frying pan with a curved bottom that helps distribute the heat and oil quickly and evenly as you cook. A kadhai is a little taller and more rounded, but a wok will work just as well if you have one. If not, you can use any shallow pot for frying. If you get a kadhai, the stainless-steel or carbon-steel types are best for stir-frying and sautéing, while cast iron ones are best for deep-frying.

kadhai

TAVA

tava

This is a slightly concave or completely flat, lightweight, iron or steel skillet with a wooden handle for ease in lifting. It is used for cooking chapatis, other flatbreads, and dosas (crepes). There are nonstick tavas that are especially good for dosa. You can use a nonstick frying pan, cast-iron skillet, or griddle instead.

PATLI

This round, wooden rolling board is used to roll flatbread dough. Any flat, smooth surface will work, but the round shape of a patli helps form perfectly round breads.

VELAN

This Indian rolling pin is made from a solid, smooth piece of wood. It is wider in the middle and gradually tapers at the ends. The wideness at the center helps iron out any uneven dough thickness, but any rolling pin will work.

patli & velan

TONGS

These are helpful for turning pappadam wafers as they crisp over a burner or for removing them from hot oil.

MESH OR NYLON SIEVE

This is useful for draining rice and other small grains that slip through the holes of a colander. It is also good for draining yogurt to make curd cheese, sprouting beans, or peas. It is also good for pressing tamarind pulp to extract the juice.

IDLI STEAMER

idli steamer

This is a round, stainless-steel, tiered stand of three or four trays that screw together to a central rod. Each rack has four shallow, round depressions with small holes in them. Larger holes are around the tray's edges to circulate steam. The greased depressions are filled three-fourths full with idli batter. Each rack is set one on top of the other, screwed tight at the top, and set in shallow water in a large pot with a tight-fitting lid. Idli take about 15 to 20 minutes to steam. Be careful removing the rack from the pan. Let the first wave of steam escape and use hot gloves to reach in and lift the rack out. Set it aside to cool for several minutes, and remove the idli with a rubber spatula.

· Appendix 2 ·

Indian Cooking Methods

Most Indian cooking is done on the stove, using direct heat. Clay tandoor ovens are used for baking and some cooking, but a gas or electric stove can be used with good results. Indian food is a blend of spices, seasonings, and flavorings combined to bring out the unique taste and aroma of each ingredient. What can make recipes seem intimidating is the often long lists of spices, but once those are ground and assembled, the rest is easy. Foods can be roasted, sautéed, simmered, cooked in sauces, or fried. Following are basic spice preparations and Indian cooking techniques.

DRY ROASTED SPICES

Roasting or browning spices brings out their taste and aroma. Whole spices are heated in a heavy pan over low heat and constantly stirred to prevent burning, which makes them bitter. When they smell fragrant and are toasty brown, remove and grind them. Use them in cooking or as a seasoning in uncooked foods like salads and yogurt.

BHUNA

Whole spice seeds and ground spices are added to hot oil or ghee and browned. Keep the temperature low and stir constantly to make sure that the spices don't stick to the bottom of the pan or scorch. Add more oil if they stick and scrape. Other ingredients can be sautéed with the spices or added after the spices are browned and aromatic.

MAKING A RASA (CURRY)

A rasa is a cooking sauce or curry gravy. In India curry means a spicy gravy—but not the kind of liquid sauce that is made from meat juices and thickened with flour. A rasa, or curry, is a dish made by cooking meats, fish, or vegetables in a combination of spices and thickening agents—but not flour. The simplest rasa starts by sautéing spices in oil, adding water, putting in the main ingredients, and simmering them in a covered pot to make sure that the aromas don't escape. If you are using coconut milk in a curry, don't cover the pan. Coconut milk tends to break apart and curdle, so it should always be brought to a boil slowly with frequent stirring. Once it comes to a boil, lower the heat and simmer it uncovered. Curries can be either dry with all the liquid absorbed or soupy. Wet, soupy curries go with rice, while dry ones are eaten with bread.

THICKENING A RASA

If the sauce is too thin, remove the lid of the pan, increase the heat, and boil it to the desired consistency. The liquid will evaporate, leaving a thicker sauce. Rasas are also thickened with ground seeds, nuts, chopped onions, garlic, or tomatoes. Yogurt is another thickening ingredient that adds creamy texture and tang. Yogurt curdles when heated. To avoid this, lightly whip the yogurt with a whisk to break up the lumps. Add one tablespoon at a time into a browning sauce or while sautéing spices in oil. Fry until the yogurt is fully absorbed before adding the next tablespoon. Continue adding yogurt until the sauce is as thick as you want. Keep the temperature low, and simmer yogurt sauces uncovered.

TEMPERING

Also called chounk, baghar, or vaghar, this is the most common and simplest way to season food. Oil or ghee is heated until it is very hot and almost smoking. Spices such as mustard seeds, cumin seeds, or curry leaves are dropped in the hot oil and sizzled for a few seconds until the seeds begin to brown, pop, or change color. The seasoned oil enlivens basic ingredients and enhances the flavors of the spices and the food. Seasoned oil can be poured over a dish to finish it, or foods can be added to the oil to continue cooking.

DEEP-FRYING

This method produces a moist interior and a crisp crust. Foods prepared this way should be drained and served hot. For perfect results, use pure, clean oil or ghee. It should be several inches deep and very hot. To test whether or not it is hot enough, drop a small bit of uncooked food in the oil. If it the oil is at the correct temperature, it will immediately sizzle and bubble. Frying in small batches allows for even cooking and keeps the oil temperature constant. When deep-frying puri, fry one bread at a time. Crowding causes the temperature to drop and produces the dreaded greasy result. Remove cooked foods with a wire strainer or slotted spoon, and drain them well on paper towels.

TANDOOR-STYLE COOKING

To duplicate the smoky flavor of breads and roasted meats in a baked clay oven, you can use a regular oven. Bake breads in a hot oven on a pizza griddle, greased baking sheet, unglazed pizza stone, or tile. A pizza stone or tile produces a light crust, similar to tandoor-cooked naan. After baking, toast the bread under a broiler. For meats, marinate pieces in yogurt and spices then bake them uncovered in a hot, preheated oven for about 30 minutes. Turn them over, brush them with marinade, and bake them until tender. Then broil them to get an even color and blistered surface.

SERVING INDIAN FOOD

A typical vegetarian menu for an Indian family includes rices or bread (or both), dal or beans, two or more vegetable dishes, a yogurt raita, pickles, chutney, and fresh fruit. A nonvegetarian menu substitutes one vegetable dish with a meat, chicken, or seafood dish and includes a rice dish. There is no set rule, so this is just an example. Each person at an Indian meal is served on a round, metal tray called a thali, on which is placed metal bowls, called katori, that contain the various dishes for a meal. Rice or bread, which is the main part of the meal, is placed in the center of the tray with the bowls around it. Fried or toasted pappadam wafers are served on top of the rice. The dishes may also be served on

a banana leaf, which is also referred to as a thali. The foods are placed directly on the leaf instead of in little bowls. Food is eaten with the fingers of the right hand—the left is considered unclean. Of course, you can serve an Indian meal on plates and eat with forks and spoons. You would still serve several dishes with everyone at the table helping themselves.

serving indian food

· Appendix 3 ·

Recipes

Ground Spice Mixtures (Masalas)

The term masala is believed to have evolved from the Arabic word "necessities," now meaning necessary or essential seasoning. Spice blends are the vital, vibrant core of Indian cuisine and there are countless types and combinations of spices used to season certain dishes, regional specialties, and personal tastes. Following are several of the best known and most used classic masalas.

Roasting spices before grinding enhances their flavor. While commercial garam masala can be used to save time, it is not as aromatic and flavorful as the freshly ground spices. Chaat masala is a tangy blend used to flavor salads made of chopped, boiled potatoes, vegetables, and fruits. South Indian curry powder is also best made from dry-roasted, freshly ground spices—the yellow store bought powder cannot compare.

GARAM MASALA

Garam is derived from the Persian word garm, meaning "warming."

- 2 tablespoons coriander seeds
- 2 tablespoons whole cloves
- 4 tablespoons cardamom pods (remove seeds from pods after roasting)
- 4 tablespoons cumin seeds
- 2 3-inch cinnamon sticks
- 2 tablespoons black peppercorns
- 1 whole nutmeg

Preheat the oven to 200 degrees. Roast all the spices except nutmeg in a small, flat pan for 20 to 30 minutes, stirring frequently. Remove and discard cardamom pods, saving seeds. Grind the spices in a blender, pepper mill, spice grinder, or by hand with a mortar and pestle. Finely grate the nutmeg with a garlic grater and mix in. Store in a glass jar for up to four months.

Makes a little over $^1/_2$ cup

CHAAT MASALA

This blend can also be used to jazz up coleslaw and creamy salad dressings.

- 1 $^1/_2$ tablespoons cumin seeds
- $^1/_4$ teaspoon black peppercorns
- 2 tablespoons dried mint, crushed
- $^1/_8$ teaspoon asafoetida
- $^1/_4$ teaspoon nutmeg
- 2 tablespoons amchoor (green-mango powder)
- $^1/_4$ teaspoon cayenne pepper
- 1 tablespoon kala namak (black salt)
- $^1/_4$ teaspoon salt

Roast cumin seeds and peppercorns in a small, heavy frying pan over high heat until fragrant, about 4 minutes. Reduce to low heat, add mint, asafoetida, and nutmeg. Toast another 2 minutes. Remove from heat and cool slightly. Grind into a fine powder in a spice grinder, coffee mill, or with a mortar and pestle. Transfer to a small bowl and stir in amchoor, cayenne, kala namak, and salt, mixing well. Store in a glass jar in a cool place for up to six months.

Makes about $^1/_2$ cup

SOUTH INDIAN CURRY POWDER

This is the spice blend from Tamil Nadu on which commercial curry powder is based.

2 tablespoons cumin seeds

2 tablespoons black mustard seeds

1/2 tablespoon fenugreek seeds

1/2 tablespoon split yellow lentils (toovar dal) or split yellow peas

5 to 6 whole, dried red chilies

20 to 25 curry leaves, fresh or dried (preferably fresh)

1 teaspoon black peppercorns

1/3 cup ground coriander

2 tablespoons ground turmeric

Combine the cumin, mustard, and fenugreek seeds, yellow lentils or peas, chilies, and curry leaves in a large, heavy frying pan. Roast over very low heat, stirring constantly for about 10 minutes or until the seeds and lentils or peas turn golden brown. If you use dried curry leaves, add at the end and heat 1 or 2 minutes. Remove pan from heat and add peppercorns.

In small batches, grind the roasted spices in a coffee mill or spice grinder until they become a fine powder. Add the coriander and turmeric and mix well. Store in a glass jar for up to four months

Makes almost 1 cup

Appetizers & Snacks
ALOO CHAAT

This is a tongue-tingling snack that is seasoned with chaat masala, which is a special salty, tangy powder that you can make yourself (see page 237), or use a store-bought blend. Just one taste and you will see why this is such a popular snack in India.

2 medium potatoes, boiled, peeled, and cut into small cubes

1 small onion, chopped

1 green chili, seeded and minced

1 1/2 tablespoons fresh coriander leaves, chopped

2 plum tomatoes, chopped

2 teaspoons chaat masala, or to taste

Place all ingredients in a medium-size bowl and toss lightly until mixed well. Taste and add more chaat masala if desired. Serve plain or with tamarind or green-chili chutney. Serve at once.

Variations: You can add any number of ingredients for texture and crunch. Try roasted, chopped cashews or peanuts, puffed rice, chickpea-flour crisps, crushed potato chips, chunks of mango, or a handful of pomegranate seeds.

Serves 4 as an appetizer or makes 2 snack-sized portions

ONION BHAJIS

These are delicious, crispy, batter-fried onion snacks. These are a staple of roadside cafes and food stalls throughout India and are popular appetizers in restaurants.

3/4 cup chickpea flour, sifted

1 tablespoon oil

1 teaspoon ground coriander

1 teaspoon ground cumin

salt to taste

2 green chilies, seeded and minced

1/2 cup warm water

2 onions, finely sliced and cut into 1/8-inch cross-sections

fresh coriander leaves, chopped to garnish

Blend flour, oil, coriander, cumin, salt, chilies, and warm water into a smooth batter. Use a blender or whisk by hand. Pour batter into a bowl, cover, and let stand about 30 minutes.

Stir onions into batter. Fill a deep pan or deep-fryer with oil until half full. Heat over medium heat or until a bread cube browns in 50 seconds. Add 2 tablespoons of batter to oil in small batches. Fry 5 to 6 minutes until golden.

Do not cook too quickly, or more than three or four at a time, or the centers will not cook completely. Drain on paper towels and continue frying until all the batter is used. Serve hot, sprinkled with chopped coriander leaves and a chutney or chili sauce for dipping.

Serves 4

DOSA

My all-time favorite Indian snack. Dosa are South Indian, paper-thin, platter-sized crepes. Homemade dosa are delicious once you master the basic cooking technique. In my first attempt, I wasn't counting on the mess that I had to scrape off the pan and toss. Be prepared to do the same until the pan is seasoned and hot enough. You can also adjust the batter thickness. Just don't try to make a dosa larger than 6 inches or it will break. Dosa take advance preparation. Start the night before for best results.

   ¹/₂ cup split urad (black-lentil) dal, with or without skins (the skins
      come off after soaking)
   1 cup long-grain rice
      salt to taste
   1 green chili, seeded and minced (optional)
   1 onion, cut in half
      coconut chutney (see recipe on page 251)
      rasam (see recipe on page 252)

Put the rice and urad dal into separate bowls, cover each with water and soak for 6 hours. Drain well. Place the urad dal in a blender on high and process with water until thick and smooth. Pour into a large bowl. Puree the soaked rice in the same way and pour into the dal puree and mix together with salt. Cover the bowl with a damp cloth and set aside at room temperature for 12 hours or overnight. The longer the batter sits, the better.

Stir in green chili, if using, and add enough water to make a thin batter, about the consistency of thick cream. Heat a skillet, flat pan, tava, or nonstick frying pan over high heat. Rub pan with half an onion (this cools the surface slightly). Brush pan with oil and pour in a ladle (about ¼ cup) of the batter, smearing it quickly with the back of the ladle to form a thin pancake, about 5 to 6 inches in diameter. Cook 2 to 3 minutes until the bottom is golden and the top is starting to set. For extra thin dosa, scrape off a layer of the setting batter with a spatula and discard. Do this carefully so as not to destroy the whole pancake. Turn it over and cook on the other side another few minutes. Continue until batter is used up, keeping dosa warm in a preheated oven. Serve with coconut chutney and rasam.

Makes about 8 to 10 pancakes

CHAPATI

This whole-wheat flatbread is easy to prepare, contains no added fat, and has a delicious flavor and a chewy texture. Serve it with butter, melted ghee, or plain to scoop up thick curries.

> 1 cup whole-wheat chapati (atta) flour, or 1/2 cup whole-wheat flour
> mixed with 1/2 cup all-purpose white flour
> 1/4 to 1/2 cup lukewarm water

Place flour (or flours) in a large bowl and make a well in the center. Add up to 1/2 cup water into the well, a little at a time. Begin mixing by hand and use only enough water to form a dough that can be gathered into a compact ball.

On a well-floured board or clean, hard surface, knead at least 10 minutes or until dough is smooth and elastic. Keep dusting with flour to keep dough from sticking. The more you knead, the lighter the bread will be. Cover with a damp towel and let dough rest for about 1 hour. Divide dough into 8 small balls. With a rolling pin, roll each ball to the thickness of a thin pancake. Be sure the board or work surface is well-floured to prevent sticking.

Heat a heavy griddle, tava, or nonstick frying pan until a drop of water sizzles on contact. Without adding any oil or grease, cook each chapati 1 minute or less on each side, or until lightly browned. Transfer to a serving plate and keep warm while you cook remaining breads.

Serves 4

Rice
BOILED WATER METHOD
(OBLA CHAWAL)

In much of South India, rice is boiled like pasta in lots of salted water. Use enough water so that the rice rolls freely in the boiling water. Test a grain before draining. It should be cooked through and be tender but firm, not mushy.

    2 cups basmati rice
   12 cups water
    1 teaspoon salt
    4 to 5 tablespoons melted ghee or butter

Wash rice until the water runs clear to remove starch. Place it in a bowl and add cold water to cover by about 2 inches. Let soak 25 to 30 minutes and drain. Fill a large pot with the 12 cups of water, bring to a boil, and add salt, 2 to 3 tablespoons ghee or butter, and rice. Bring back to boil and cook 9 to 10 minutes, uncovered, until rice is just tender.

Drain thoroughly using a mesh sieve. Serve fluffed with a fork and drizzled with remaining ghee or butter.

Serves 4

ABSORPTION METHOD
(BHAPA CHAWAL)

This is the method preferred in North India. Though boiling does cook the rice faster, it all comes down to personal preference. In this method all the cooking water is soaked up by the rice, expanding the grains.

     2 cups basmati rice
    2½ cups water
       pinch of salt
     2 tablespoons ghee or melted butter

Wash the rice until the water runs clear to remove starch. Place it in a bowl and add 2½ cups cold water. Let soak for 25 to 30 minutes. Drain in a mesh sieve, reserving soaking water.

Place rice in a heavy pot with the reserved water and salt. Bring it to a rolling boil. Stir gently, cover tightly, and put the heat on low. Cook 15 minutes, turn off heat, and let stand, covered, for 10 minutes. Try not to lift cover and peek. Serve fluffed with a fork and drizzled with ghee or butter.

Serves 4

Dal Dishes
MASOOR DAL

This is the quickest-cooking dal. It takes only 20 minutes. It is a basic dal that can be part of any Indian meal, or it can be thinned with broth to make soup. You can also add chopped, cooked vegetables. The dal is finished with seasoned oil and garnished with crispy onions.

Dal Mixture

- 1 cup whole red lentils (masoor dal)
- 3 cups water
- 1 teaspoon turmeric powder
- 1 teaspoon salt
- 1 tablespoon lemon or lime juice
- 1 teaspoon garam masala (see page 237)

Seasoning Oil

- 1 tablespoon oil or ghee
- 1 teaspoon cumin seeds
- 1 teaspoon cayenne-pepper powder
- 1 teaspoon coriander-seed powder

Garnish

- 1 onion, sliced and fried until golden brown in oil, or use store-bought onion crisps
- fresh coriander leaves, chopped

Pick over lentils to remove any foreign particles or small stones. Wash in a sieve under running water.

In a heavy 3-quart saucepan, bring water and lentils to a boil with turmeric. Cover, turn the heat to low, and simmer for about 20 minutes. Turn off heat, add salt, lemon juice, and garam masala.

Heat oil or ghee in a small, heavy skillet over medium heat, add cumin seeds, and fry for 1 or 2 minutes. Turn off heat. Add cayenne and coriander powder. Stir and pour over the cooked lentils. Mix well and serve garnished with fried onions and chopped coriander leaves.

Serves 4

CHOLE, PUNJABI CHANNA DAL

This is a thick, Punjabi-style, chickpea-tomato curry. Serve it with chapati for a light meal or as a side dish as part of an Indian meal. Using canned chickpeas makes this a time-saving recipe.

Chickpea Mixture

- 3 tablespoons oil
- 1/4 teaspoon mustard seeds
- 1/4 teaspoon cumin seeds
- 1 cup sliced onions
- 2 cloves garlic, peeled and chopped
- 1 1-inch piece of gingerroot, grated
- 2 cups tomatoes, chopped
- 2 teaspoons coriander powder
- 1 teaspoon turmeric powder
- 1/4 teaspoon cayenne or chili powder
- 1/8 teaspoon black pepper
  - salt to taste
- 1 1/2 cups water
- 2 cans (15 1/2 ounces each) chickpeas, rinsed and drained

Garnish

- 1 lemon, quartered
  - fresh coriander leaves, chopped

Heat oil over medium-high heat in a large, deep pan. Add mustard and cumin seeds. Fry until they pop, then add onions, garlic, ginger-root, and tomatoes. Fry them, stirring frequently until the onion is soft and the edges browned. Add the coriander, turmeric, cayenne or chili powder, pepper, salt, and 1/2 cup water. Continue frying and stirring until the tomatoes break apart, about 3 to 5 minutes. Add chickpeas and remaining cup of water. Bring to a boil, turn heat to medium-low, and simmer for about 5 minutes. The mixture should be fairly thick. If dry, add more water. Salt to taste.

Remove from heat. With a potato masher or back of a large spoon, mash about half of the chickpeas. It should only take 3 or 4 passes. Garnish with chopped coriander. Serve with lemon wedges on the side.

Serves 6 to 8

Vegetables
VEGETABLE BIRYANI

This is a layered casserole of mixed vegetables and fragrant, spiced rice. It makes a main dish with bread, yogurt salad, and chutney. Or it is a side dish to accompany meat curry, grilled meat, or fish

Layer 1

- 4 tablespoons oil
- 1 teaspoon cumin seeds
- 2 medium onions, thinly sliced
- 1/2 head cauliflower, chopped
- 4 small potatoes, peeled and diced
- 1/2 cup fresh or frozen green peas
- 1 cup green beans, chopped
- 1 teaspoon turmeric powder
  salt to taste
- 3 tablespoons garam masala (see recipe on page 237)
- 1 cup yogurt

Layer 2

- 3 cups raw long-grain rice
- 6 cups water

Layer 3

- 1 cup ghee
  juice of 4 lemons
- 1/4 teaspoon saffron, soaked in 2 teaspoons warm milk
- 1 cup fresh mint leaves, chopped
- 1 cup fresh coriander leaves, chopped

Begin with layer 2. Rinse rice and place in a 3-quart saucepan with 6 cups of water, bring to boil, turn heat to medium-low, and simmer covered for 15 to 20 minutes. Set aside with the lid on to keep the rice warm with a towel under the lid to keep it from getting mushy.

Mix together ingredients of layer 3. Set aside.

Prepare layer 1. In a wok or wide, shallow pan, heat the oil over a medium-high flame and add cumin seeds and fry until golden, about 1 to 2 minutes. Add the onions, cauliflower, potatoes, peas, and green beans and fry 3 minutes, stirring. Cover and simmer on low for 5 minutes. Add turmeric, salt, garam masala, and yogurt and stir gently. Remove from heat.

Grease the inside of a heavy pot. Put the layers into the pot in order: a half-inch layer of vegetables, a one-inch layer of rice and 1 or 2 tablespoons of the lemon-ghee mixture. Repeat, layering until all the ingredients are used up, ending with a rice layer. Cover the pot and simmer on a low heat for about 5 minutes. Serve garnished with additional chopped coriander leaves.

Serves 8 to 10

MASHED CURRIED EGGPLANT
(BAIGAN BHARTA)

This thick, spicy eggplant dish is good with bread as part of a meal. Blended with yogurt or sour cream, it makes a delicious dip.

- 6 slender Asian eggplants, or 2 large Western eggplants
- 4 large onions, finely chopped
- 1 tablespoon oil
- 1 teaspoon cumin seeds
- 1 teaspoon curry powder (see page 238)
- salt to taste
- 1 teaspoon lemon juice
- 1 teaspoon garam masala (see page 237)

Preheat oven to 400 degrees. Prick the eggplants once or twice with a fork to prevent them from exploding. Bake the eggplants and whole onions on a cookie sheet or similar size pan for 25 minutes or until tender. Peel the eggplants when cool enough to handle and coarsely mash the pulp.

Heat oil in a on high in a large frying pan. Add cumin seeds and chopped onions. Fry for 2 minutes. Add eggplant, curry powder, and salt. Cook for 5 minutes over medium heat, stirring to keep eggplant from sticking. Remove from heat, add lemon juice and garam masala and blend.

Serves 6

GREEN BEAN THOREN

This is a quick-cooking dry curry from Kerala in South India. It is made with chopped green beans and grated coconut. Any green bean can be used, but snake beans (yard-long beans) are the bean of choice in Kerala. Serve it with any meal as a side dish.

2 tablespoons oil

1 teaspoon mustard seeds

1 to 2 green chilies, finely chopped

1/2 onion, finely chopped

1/2 cup dehydrated, unsweetened grated coconut

1/4 teaspoon cumin powder

1/2 teaspoon turmeric powder

1/4 teaspoon cayenne powder

6 to 8 curry leaves, fresh or dried

  salt to taste

1 pound green beans, cut into small pieces

6 to 8 tablespoons water

Heat oil over medium-high heat in a large frying pan. Add mustard seeds. When they pop, add the chili and onion. Reduce heat to medium-high and stir-fry until softened. Stir in the coconut, cumin, turmeric, cayenne, curry leaves, and salt. Then add the green beans and water. Cover pan and simmer a few minutes. Then remove lid and cook, stirring over low heat until the liquid has evaporated.

Serves 6

Main Courses
JARDALOO MURGHI
(APRICOT CHICKEN CURRY)

This is a popular Parsi dish. Cooking with dried fruit dates back to the Parsi's Persian ancestry. The dish is traditionally served with potato straws, which are deep-fried potato shreds. It is good with plain rice.

2¹/₂ pounds of chicken pieces, such as legs and thighs

¹/₂ teaspoon paprika or chili powder

1 tablespoon garam masala (see recipe on page 237)

1 1-inch piece of gingerroot, grated

2 garlic cloves, peeled and crushed

1 cup dried apricots

²/₃ cup warm water

2 tablespoons oil

2 onions, finely sliced

4 tomatoes, chopped, or 1 14-ounce can of chopped tomatoes
salt to taste

1 tablespoon sugar

2 tablespoons vinegar

Rinse chicken. Pat dry with paper towels and put into a large bowl. Add paprika, garam masala, gingerroot, and garlic. Toss well to coat chicken. Cover and refrigerate for 2 to 3 hours to allow chicken to absorb flavors. Place apricots in a separate bowl and soak in warm water. Californian apricots only need about 30 minutes to soak. Indian apricots require 2 or 3 hours.

When ready to cook, heat oil in a heavy 3-quart saucepan over high heat. Add chicken pieces and cook over high heat for about 5 minutes, or until browned. Remove chicken from pan and set aside. Add onions to pan and cook, stirring, about 5 minutes, until soft. Return chicken to pan with tomatoes. Cover and cook over low heat for 20 minutes. Drain apricots. Add to pan with salt, sugar, and vinegar. Simmer covered for 10 to 15 minutes, until tender. Serve hot with rice.

Serves 4

MEEN MOLE
(FISH IN COCONUT SAUCE)

I learned to make this fish dish from Shawon Ahmed and his wife, Taslima, at the Fish Corner in Chicago. Serve it with rice, crisped pappadams, and mango pickle. Any firm, white fish can be used: sea bass, cod, snapper, monk fish, halibut, or pomfret.

    2 tablespoons oil
    1 onion, finely sliced
    1 1-inch piece of gingerroot, grated
    4 garlic cloves, peeled and crushed
    1 green chili, seeded and finely chopped
    1/2 teaspoon ground turmeric
    1/4 teaspoon cayenne pepper
    1 14-ounce can of coconut milk
      salt to taste
    6 to 8 curry leaves, fresh or dried
    2 tablespoons fresh coriander leaves, chopped
    4 large fish steaks

Heat oil in a large frying pan over high heat. Add onion and sauté for a few minutes, until translucent. Add gingerroot, garlic, and green chili and cook for another few minutes. Stir in the turmeric and cayenne. Cook for a few seconds, then pour in the coconut milk. Bring slowly to a boil, stirring and decreasing the heat. Add some salt, then the curry leaves. Simmer for 2 to 3 minutes on medium-low heat until the mixture thickens slightly, then add the coriander leaves. Cook another minute. Add the fish and cook for 2 to 4 minutes, depending on the thickness of the steaks. Then cover pan, remove from heat, and set aside for about 5 minutes. The fish will continue cooking in the heat of the coconut sauce.

Serves 4

Sauces & Soups
CUCUMBER RAITA

Raita, which is a chilled blend of yogurt and chopped vegetables or fruit, is served as an accompaniment to every Indian meal. It provides a refreshing, cool contrast to hot, spicy dishes.

- 1 medium cucumber
- 1 teaspoon cumin seeds
- 2 cups plain, whole-milk yogurt
- 1 clove garlic, peeled and minced
- 2 tablespoons fresh coriander or mint leaves, chopped
  cayenne or paprika to garnish

Peel cucumber. Cut lengthwise into ¼-inch strips, then into thin slices crosswise. Blot off moisture with paper towels. Toast cumin seeds for a few seconds in a small, heavy frying pan over high heat. In a bowl, stir yogurt until it is smooth. Mix it with the cumin, garlic, and coriander or mint leaves. Combine mixture with cucumber slivers, sprinkle with cayenne or paprika, and chill before serving.

Serves 4 to 6

COCONUT CHUTNEY

This is delicious with dosa and fried snacks or as an accompaniment to any Indian meal. It is also good as a spread for chapati or blended with sour cream as a dip.

- 1 cup dehydrated, unsweetened, grated coconut, soaked in ½ cup water for 1 to 2 minutes
  juice of 1 lemon or lime
- 1 tablespoon sugar
- 1 to 2 green chilies, deseeded
- 1 teaspoon salt
- 1 cup fresh coriander leaves, thick stems removed

Put all ingredients in a blender and blend into a coarse puree, adding a little water if necessary.

Makes about 1 cup

RASAM

This is a hot and tangy South Indian soup to accompany rice, steamed cakes, and dosa crepes. You can serve this as a first course or as part of a meal.

1 tablespoon tamarind pulp (seeded) or concentrate (seedless)

1 cup water, for soaking

1/4 cup split yellow lentils (toovar dal) or split yellow peas

2 cups water

4 cloves garlic, peeled

2 teaspoons peppercorns

1 teaspoon cumin seeds

2 dried red chilies, broken into pieces

salt to taste

2 medium tomatoes, chopped

2 teaspoons seasoning oil (baghar)

1/2 teaspoon mustard seeds

8 to 10 curry leaves, fresh or dried (preferably fresh)

Soak tamarind pulp in 1 cup water for 1 hour. Strain and discard the pulp and seeds. Set the liquid aside in a small bowl. If using tamarind concentrate, simply mix it with a little water to make a thin pasty liquid and set aside in a small bowl.

Wash yellow lentils or split peas and boil in 2 cups water in a heavy 2-quart saucepan. Lower the flame and simmer covered for about 25 minutes or until tender. Set aside.

Crush the garlic and peppercorns coarsely with a mortar and pestle (or use a heavy can). Add this to the tamarind water along with cumin seeds, broken chilies, and salt. Simmer for 10 minutes in a 2-quart saucepan. Add the chopped tomatoes and cooked lentils or peas. Blend together and boil about 5 more minutes. Pour into serving dish.

Heat the oil in a small skillet over high heat, drop in the mustard seeds and curry leaves. When the seeds pop, remove from heat and pour over the soup. Stir and serve.

Serves 6

Sweets & Tea
CARROT HALWA

This is one of the simplest Indian sweets, although it does require constant stirring to keep the sweet mass from scorching. It has a course, lumpy texture.

- 4 carrots, coarsely grated
- 4 cups whole milk
- 1 cup sugar
- pinch of cardamom powder

Put grated carrot and milk in a heavy saucepan. Bring to a boil over high heat. Reduce to medium heat and cook, uncovered (keeps milk from curdling), for about 25 minutes. Add sugar and cardamom. Boil for another 10 to 20 minutes, stirring constantly, until the mixture thickens and turns deep red. Remove from heat and serve in bowls, warm or chilled. Garnish with chopped pistachios or cashews and a dollop of yogurt, if desired.

Serves 6 to 8

CHAI MASALA

This sweet, spicy tea is a cinch to make using commercial chai-masala powder.

- 2 cups water
- 1 cup milk, or more for a richer tea
- 1 teaspoon chai-masala powder, or to taste
- 1 to 2 heaping teaspoons loose-leaf black Indian tea
- sugar to taste

Heat the water and milk together with the chai powder in a heavy saucepan on high until the mixture just starts to foam and boil. Turn off heat and add tea leaves, or pour mixture into a tea pot with leaves in the bottom. Cover pan or pot and steep for 5 minutes. Strain tea leaves out and serve with sugar.

Serves 4

· Appendix 4 ·

Mail-Order Sources

BAZAAR OF INDIA IMPORTS
1810 University Ave.
Berkeley, CA 94703
TEL: 800–261–7662
Ayurvedic herbs, books, and herbal beauty products

MAHARISHI AYER-VED PRODUCTS, INC.
P.O. Box 49667
Colorado Springs, CO 80949–9667
TEL: 719–260–5500
Ayurvedic herbs and beauty products

KALUSTYAN'S
123 Lexington Ave.
New York, NY 10016
TEL: 212–683–8458
rices, bengali bash ful, spices, nuts, pickles, chutney, and some Ayurvedic herbs

LITTLE INDIA STORES
128 East 28th St.
New York, NY 10016
TEL: 212–683–1691
rices and spices

SPICE CORNER
135 Lexington Ave.
New York, NY 10016
TEL: 212–689–5182
red rice and spices

LOTUS FOODS
921 Richmond St.
El Cerrito, CA 94530
TEL/FAX: 510–525–3137
WEB: www.worldofrice.com
Bhutanese red rice, gobindavog baby basmati, and other
exotic rices

FISH CORNER
6408 N. Campbell Ave.
Chicago, IL 60645
TEL: 773–262–7173
all varieties of frozen Indian and Bangladeshi fish

Glossary

Ayurveda—"Science of life." Holistic Indian healing system using natural herbs and a dietary approach to health.

Bengal—A former province in northeastern India, now divided between India and Bangladesh. East Bengal is in Bangladesh, and West Bengal is in India

Bhel puri—Bombay-style, sweet-sour, crunchy snack mixed with salad.

Bindi—Stick-on forehead decoration, originally representing the "third eye."

Bollywood—Indian movie industry, based in Bombay.

Brahmin—Hindu of the highest caste. Often a priest.

Calyx—The outermost group of floral parts on a flower. Green, cuplike, leafy petals.

Chai—Tea brewed with water and milk.

Chittagong—A port in southeastern Bangladesh on the Bay of Bengal.

Cru—Vineyard where wine grapes are grown.

Dhaka—Capital of Bangladesh.

Gujarat—Northwest Indian state on the Arabian sea. Gujaratis are natives of this state.

Gulal—Red powder that symbolizes joy and happiness. Tossed at weddings and festivals.

Halal—Meat blessed before slaughtering. Important to Muslims.

Henna—A reddish orange dye made from the leaves of an Asian shrub. Used in coloring hair or hands.

Hilsa—Large, silvery fish. A type of shad in the herring family.

Jain—An adherent of Jainism, an Indian religion emphasizing asceticism and nonviolence toward all living creatures.

Karachi—A seaport in southern Pakistan, near the Indus delta.

Kathakali—Pantomime dance popular in Kerala in South India.

Khus—Extract of the roots of an aromatic tropical grass.

Kolam—Colored rice-powder painting. Floor decoration.

Krishna—The incarnation of Vishnu. One of the most popular Indian deities. Usually depicted with blue skin.

Kulfi—Frozen dessert made by freezing a mixture of boiled milk, sugar, ground nuts, and flavorings in a conical, metal mold.

Lassi—Frothy, whipped yogurt beverage. Either salted and spiced (namkeen) or sweet.

Liquor—Brewed, poured tea.

Malai—Condensed cream made by skimming off the skin of boiled cream.

Masala—Powdered blend of ground spices.

Mehndi / Mindi—Stencil and henna dye for applying decorative patterns on womens hands. Often used by brides.

Monsoon—Season of very heavy, southwestern rains falling between June and September in India.

Parsis—Zoroastrians. Followers of a religion based on the cosmic struggle between spirits of good and evil. Fled from Iran to India in the eighth century A.D. to avoid religious persecution.

Pulao—Seasoned, steamed rice pilaf.

Puja—Offerings to deities in worship.

Quinine—Bitter, antimalarial alkaloid.

Raga—Melodic pattern or mode in classical Indian music.

Raita—Yogurt salad made of yogurt, finely chopped or shredded vegetables, fruits or nuts, spices, and seasonings.

Ramadan—The ninth month of the Muslim year. Observed as sacred, with fasting practiced from sunup to sundown.

Ramayana—Ancient Sanskrit poem telling the life and adventures of Ramachandra and his wife, Sita.

Rhizome—Underground root.

Samovar—Metal urn for heating water to make tea.

Sedge—Tufted marsh plants with thick stems and dry, flattened, convex fruit.

Seviya Press—Mold with various-sized holes for shaping dough, which is pressed through it into hot oil.

Tikka—Small cubes of meat, fish, or vegetables grilled on skewers. Also means a decorative, stick-on forehead pendant worn by Indian ladies.

Vishnu—"The preserver." The second member of the Hindu trinity of deities. Believed to have descended from heaven to earth in several incarnations, most importantly as Krishna.

Wallah—A suffix placed at the end of a name or commodity. It means the seller or producer of that product. For example, a teawallah is a vendor of tea.

Zest—Small strip of grated citrus peel used for flavoring.

Index

· Notes ·

· Notes ·

· Notes ·

· Notes ·

About the Author

Linda Bladholm is a regular contributor to the *Miami Herald*. She is the author of *The Asian Grocery Store Demystified* (Renaissance Books). She is also a designer, illustrator, and photographer who has contributed to *Singapore and Asia Pacific Magazine* and *Big O Magazine*. A graduate of the University of San Francisco, she has designed books for Noto Publishing and designed and illustrated for FEP/McGraw-Hill, Gunze Company, and World Books International. She has appeared on the National Television Network (NHT) of Japan in conjunction with a series on Japanese art and culture. She has published two books, *Kanzawa, the Heart of Japan* (Noto Printing Co.) and *Singapore Memento* (FEP International). For ten years she lived in and traveled throughout Asia as a teacher, photographer, and representative of the Japan National Tourist Office. She traveled extensively throughout India and Bangladesh to research this book. She resides in Miami Beach Florida, where she and her husband are directors of World Island Design.